Professional Studies
Primary and Early Years

Achieving

QTS

Professional Studies
Primary and Early Years

Third edition

Edited by Kate Jacques and Rob Hyland

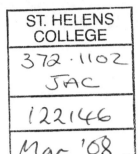
First published in 2000 by Learning Matters Ltd.
Reprinted in 2001.
Reprinted in 2002.
Second edition published in 2003.
Reprinted in 2003.
Reprinted in 2004 (three times).
Reprinted in 2005.
Third edition published in 2007.

British Library Cataloguing in Publication Data
A CIP record for this book is available from the British Library.

ISBN 978 1 84445 095 4

Cover design by Topics – the Creative Partnership and text design by Code 5 Design Associates Ltd
Project management by Deer Park Productions
Typeset by PDQ Typesetting Ltd
Printed and bound in Great Britain by Bell & Bain Ltd, Glasgow

Learning Matters
33 Southernhay East
Exeter EX1 1NX
Tel: 01392 215560
info@learningmatters.co.uk
www.learningmatters.co.uk

Contents

Contributors

Rob Hyland teaches in the Education Department at Durham University where he is responsible for Primary Partnership arrangements for the BA(QTS) at Queen's Campus, Stockton. He is also involved in research projects with the Human Nutrition Research Centre at the University of Newcastle.

Professor Kate Jacques is Pro Vice Chancellor and Dean of the Faculty of Education and Sport at the University of Bedfordshire.

Both Kate and Rob have extensive experience of working in the field of education and teacher training.

Pam Banks is a Languages graduate and currently works for Luton LA as an MFL Advisor. She has been a primary head teacher and Primary Tutor at the University of Bedfordshire.

Uli Dunne is Senior Lecturer in Primary Education at the University of Bedfordshire.

Tony Ewens was Head of Division of Education Studies at the University of Cumbria and Principal Lecturer in Religious Education.

Paul Frecknall is an experienced Primary Tutor at the University of Bedfordshire. Currently he is leading the four-year Undergraduate BEd Degree.

Lisa Genesis teaches Professional Studies at the University of Bedfordshire and is currently working on research around the Achievement of Minority Ethnic Groups in Bedford Schools.

Nicola Ivett worked at the University of Bedfordshire as a Primary Humanities Teacher. She has wide experience of working in primary schools and SEN settings.

Kath Langley-Hamel is an experienced primary tutor at the University of Cumbria. Her expertise is in literature and special needs.

Barbara Leedham is a Senior Lecturer at the University of Bedfordshire. She is the science strand teacher and part of the Primary Education Team. Before this she worked as a science advisory teacher and has worked in primary schools in both Gloucestershire and Buckinghamshire.

Jenny Lovesey teaches Education Studies at the University of Bedfordshire. She has a range of teaching experience in lower schools and has expertise in Early Years and Foundation Stage education.

Pat Macpherson is Head of the Division of Childhood, Adolescent & Creative Studies at the University of Cumbria and her expertise is in Early Years education.

Ray Potter is a Senior Lecturer at the University of Cumbria where he leads ICT and has extensive experience of primary education.

Andrea Raiker is a Fellow of the Centre of Excellence in Teaching and Learning at the University of Bedfordshire. Andrea's interests include E-learning and the Language of Assessment. Andrea is currently Course Leader for the Foundation Degree in Professional Practice.

Cathy Thornhill is a Principal Lecturer in charge of the Primary PGCE at the University of Bedfordshire. She was previously a head teacher on two occasions in Bedford schools.

1
The complete teacher
Rob Hyland and Kate Jacques

This introductory chapter sets out the context for those which follow and explains how to use the book. It also seeks to place the objective of meeting national requirements for attaining the award of Qualified Teacher Status (QTS) in a broader framework.

By the end of the chapter you should:

- **understand the overall objectives of the book;**
- **have considered some of the general requirements of becoming a teacher;**
- **understand the significance of the Professional Standards for the award of Qualified Teacher Status;**
- **be aware how the chapter relates to meeting the Standards for QTS.**

Becoming a primary school teacher and making a difference

If it is your intention to become a primary school teacher then you should need no convincing that this is an important, challenging and rewarding undertaking. Primary teachers have a vital position in the education system: they play a key role in the learning of nearly all children between the ages of five and eleven. Collectively and cumulatively teachers in primary schools have a significant influence over a long and important period in their pupils' development. Though they are by no means the only influence, primary schools and those who work in them can make a difference in the lives of their pupils; they lay the foundations for so much which follows. To embark upon the process of becoming a primary teacher is to undertake a serious preparation for a valuable social role.

For children, however, the felt experience of primary teachers is not one of valuable social roles or collective or cumulative influences; it is so much more immediate. For children at any given moment that experience is very much of Miss Oliver, Mr Abbas, Ms Jones, Mrs Rodrigues, Mr Hamilton... And when you are that person, then the quality of their experience – at least for the time they are with you – is very much in your hands. The majority of primary teachers have extensive responsibility for a class of children for an academic year and therefore your knowledge, skills and commitment can have a considerable effect. Individual teachers do make a difference. That is a large part of what makes teaching challenging and worthwhile.

The aims of this book

The purposes of this book are both general and specific. The overall aim is to encourage and assist you to consider a range of professional issues related to qualifying as a primary school teacher. The more specific objectives of this book are to assist you in understanding and meeting the broad professional requirements of the Professional Standards for Qualified Teacher Status for Primary and Early Years.

Meeting the Professional Standards for QTS

The current formal requirements for you to achieve QTS are set out on the Training Development Agency for Schools website at **www.tda.gov.uk**. The Standards have been revised to take account of the stages available to all teachers. These are:

- **those recommended for the award of QTS (Q);**
- **induction/main scale teachers (I);**
- **post-threshold teachers (P);**
- **excellent teachers (E);**
- **advanced skills teachers (a).**

The Standards relating to the award of QTS are set out in the Appendix at the back of the book. Only those trainee teachers who meet all of the Standards will be awarded QTS. The meaning is unambiguous. The Standards are requirements and not simply desirable attributes or ideal goals. Curiously these Standards do not apply to the whole of the United Kingdom; different regulations apply in Northern Ireland, Wales and Scotland.

At this stage it is important to recognise that qualifying as a primary school teacher is a demanding process, but you should not get the formal requirements out of perspective. One of the key purposes of this book, along with its companion volumes in the series, is to show you how these requirements can be met. It aims to demystify and make plain some of these demands in such a way that you recognise how they relate to effective teaching, how you might meet them and in due course demonstrate that you can do so.

The knowledge and understanding and Teaching Standards for specific subjects are covered by other books in this series. For a full list of those publications, visit the Learning Matters website at **www.learningmatters.co.uk**. It should also not be forgotten that primary teachers may teach the whole range of subjects in the primary curriculum and need to be well informed in all areas they teach. The importance of the primary teacher's subject knowledge, and the need for the would-be teacher to develop a sound grasp of how to teach children the particular skills and concepts of the various curriculum areas, are taken as fundamental by the authors of this book. This volume, however, is concerned with professional issues which run across all subjects and indeed beyond the formal subject curriculum.

QTS and the complete teacher

At the outset it was important to make clear that meeting the government's Standards is central to qualification as a teacher: these Standards are not optional – at least not if you wish to qualify! But it is also important to recognise the limitations of these formal statements of the knowledge and skills required for QTS. Underpinned as they are by statutory powers and backed by all the apparatus of official authority, they tend to give an appearance of universal agreement on what is required of teachers.

You will soon learn that there is always some disagreement among teachers and those who train them over just what knowledge, skills and attitudes are essential for the Newly Qualified Teacher (NQT), or indeed the experienced teacher. The requirements of the TDA Standards are by no means the only 'standards' which we might wish to consider, nor the only version of what it might mean to be an effective beginning teacher. There has been considerable argument about the requirements for QTS; the debate is ongoing. Nevertheless, despite all the debate about the details and how they are expressed and assessed, there is broad consensus about the general requirements for beginning teachers. It is not merely to meet the Standards that teachers need to be able to plan appropriate work for children, to take account of aptitudes and needs, to assess children's work, to report progress, to manage the classroom, to build positive relationships with children and so forth: these are the core aspects of teaching. It is difficult to think of an effective teacher unable to do these things. These days head teachers claim that NQTs are better prepared than ever before because they do demonstrate competence and an ability to meet the Standards.

It is also important to recognise that the Standards are those for the award of QTS. They are not the last word on what a skilled teacher can achieve. The new Professional Standards are designed to bring coherence and occupational standards for the whole school workforce including teaching/classroom assistants (TAs) and higher level teaching assistants (HLTAs) as well as the range of teachers from NQTs to Advanced Skills Teachers (ASTs). While you will bring your own distinctive style to your teaching, the Standards provide a valuable framework for you to track your own progress and regularly self-assess your own performance.

The range of professional issues covered by this book

There is no limit to the range of professional issues which might be relevant to the teacher in training. This book concentrates on the key areas which the beginning teacher needs to understand. For convenience it is divided into sections of related chapters but it is important to recognise the links between different aspects of professional knowledge and skill. The first section, Planning and Assessment, focuses on the planning, assessment and reporting of children's work; the second section, Management, Organisation and Delivery, looks at managing for learning; the third section, Children and Individual Needs, includes chapters on SEN, individual differences and equal opportunities; and the final section,

Becoming a Professional, gives an overview of professional responsibilities outside of teaching.

Section 1 looks at the related requirements for effective planning, assessment and reporting of children's work. Chapter 2 explains the fundamental skills of planning lessons; this is not simply a matter of formulaic presentation but of grasping the underlying principles of organising for teaching. Chapter 3 discusses 'differentiation' in some detail because it is fundamental to effective planning for learning when children are so different in their prior knowledge, experience and capabilities. Chapter 4 discusses 'assessment for learning' and how important it is to chart children's progress to encourage them, to inform their parents, and to guide your subsequent teaching.

Section 2 focuses on learning. Chapter 5 establishes the importance of the foundation stage. Chapter 6 outlines some of the major theories of learning. Chapter 7 examines many of the practical issues of organising the classroom for learning. Chapter 8 considers the climate of the classroom and the importance of promoting self-esteem in children to create a positive climate for learning in which all children are valued and are encouraged to value others. Chapter 9 raises issues of self-presentation and engagement with other adults in the classroom. Chapter 10 examines some possible responses to children's more challenging behaviour.

Section 3 looks at some broad issues which are important in all schools. Chapter 11 examines some ways in which teachers may encourage the development of spiritual, moral, social and cultural values within the classroom. Chapter 12 discusses issues of inclusion and the legislative position with regard to equal opportunities. Children with special educational needs (SEN) are such a central concern to all primary schools today that two chapters are devoted to this topic. Chapter 13 outlines some of the requirements relating to the implementation of national policy while Chapter 14 considers some of the more general principles of personalising learning to respond to the range of individual differences which may be encountered in a modern primary classroom.

The final section examines some of the implications of becoming a teacher. The broader professional issues here are crucial. There is a legal aspect to joining a profession and Chapter 15 sets out some of the statutory and contractual obligations you take on as a teacher. There are broader issues involved in becoming a member of the teaching profession and Chapter 16 examines the level of commitment to professionalism which teachers should demonstrate in their work.

The chapters can be read sequentially, but individual chapters can be referred to as necessary. In any case it is important to return to some of the guidance of earlier chapters in the light of issues discussed in subsequent ones. Many issues run throughout the book and there are repeated references to Every Child Matters (ECM) and its core principles.

Though the knowledge and skills of the competent teacher may be identified and classified as in the Standards, effective performance requires a constant synthesising of insights into different aspects of the teaching experience. Lesson planning, for example, is not just the mastery of formal organisational and presentational skills; to maximise the positive effects upon children's learning a lesson plan may have to take into account so many factors from SEN to health and safety. You may quickly grasp the formal essentials of planning, how to set your desired learning outcomes for children, your content and resources, but the insight you bring to the task will develop with experience. Learning to teach is itself a good illustration of the 'spiral curriculum' . You will find yourself revisiting the issues discussed in this book with progressively more understanding as you spend time in classrooms and reflect on all you see and do. We include Early Years and those of you who wish to focus on this age range will need to look at the Foundation Stage. We have a new Chapter 5 which takes you through foundations for learning.

Survival, qualification and beyond

Almost inevitably, as you train to be a teacher the immediacy of so many of the demands upon you can induce an understandable preoccupation with survival! This book will help you towards meeting the Standards for attaining QTS. The team of authors intends that it should illuminate many of the requirements for doing so and give you some practical guidance upon which you can act. But the book is more than a survival aid: the authors also hope that you will see these national requirements in a broader perspective, that you will be enquiring, reflective and critical. Becoming a teacher is partly about acquiring fundamental skills and knowledge but also involves taking on professional values and standards. Not the least important aspect of a teacher's commitment is the acceptance of the need to continually develop and upgrade skills, to remain informed and keep the ideals of professional service and its broad responsibilities for children's' education in mind. If the immediate aim must necessarily be to achieve qualification – to 'meet the Standards' set down for QTS – the longer-term aim must be to work towards developing the skills, knowledge and personal attributes of 'the compete teacher'.

FURTHER READING FURTHER READING FURTHER READING

Browne, A. and Haylock, D. (2004) *Professional Issues for Primary Teachers*. London: Paul Chapman.

Cooper, H. and Hyland, R. (eds) (2000) *Children's Perceptions of Learning with Trainee Teachers*. London: RoutledgeFalmer. This offers some insights into the experiences of children working with trainee teachers in all areas of the curriculum.

SECTION ONE
PLANNING AND ASSESSMENT

2
Planning for excellence and enjoyment
Pam Banks

By the end of the chapter you should:

- **understand the contribution of planning to effective teaching and learning;**
- **appreciate the inter-relationship of long-term, medium-term and short-term planning;**
- **be able to write a lesson plan and an outline medium-term plan.**

This chapter addresses the following Professional Standards for QTS: Q3, Q5

The importance of planning for effective teaching and learning

Planning is fundamental to sustained effective teaching. Good planning gives you the freedom to be creative and spontaneous while being thorough and systematic. As you become more experienced, the process will become an integral part of your professional thinking, but effective planning has to be learned.

Experienced teachers carry all kinds of information about learning objectives and children's needs in their heads. Nevertheless, the most effective teachers, however experienced, do plan carefully what they are going to do in the classroom. Good teaching is planned thoroughly, both from day to day and in the longer term.

Why is it important to do this?

REFLECTIVE TASK

Make a list of all the reasons why you think it is useful to plan lessons in advance. Compare your list with the one below.

1. It gives you the opportunity to think carefully about what exactly you want the children to learn, taking into account the different needs of individuals and groups in your class and the context of the lesson.

2. You can look at your ideas for teaching and learning activities logically and decide the best order and timing for each part of the lesson.

3. It gives you the confidence to teach without having to worry about what comes next.

4. You can make sure that you have prepared all the material and resources you need for the lesson.

5. It gives you the basis for reflection after the lesson, and also documents what you did for future reference.

(adapted from Kyriacou, 1998, p19)

Remember: having a clearly laid out lesson plan next to you as you teach will reassure you and give you confidence.

Levels of planning

Every school has to have a policy document outlining its approach to the curriculum. While many aspects of the curriculum are laid down by government, *Excellence and Enjoyment* (DfES, 2003, pp16–17) lists the different kinds of freedom that schools and teachers have in choosing how to teach different aspects of the curriculum. These include being able to decide:

- **teaching methods;**
- **the emphasis placed on different aspects of a subject;**
- **the amount of time spent on a subject, both in the weekly timetable and over the school year.**

Choices such as these are likely to be made by teachers at different stages of the planning process.

Planning in most primary schools operates on three levels:

- **long-term;**
- **medium-term; and**
- **short-term.**

Exactly what these plans look like, and who creates them, varies from school to school. Except in very small schools, the general rule is that the longer the period covered by the plans, the greater the number of people who will have been involved in writing them.

In broad terms:

- **long-term planning tells you what to teach in a particular age phase;**
- **medium-term planning tells you when it fits into the school year;**
- **short-term planning helps you work out how to tackle it in the classroom.**

See Further Reading on page 24.

Long-term planning sets out the overall content of the curriculum for each year group in the school for a one- to four-year period. Medium-term planning looks in more detail at the work for each class over a year, in units of terms or half-terms. 'Short-term' variously applies to weeks, days or individual lessons and is specific to the needs of the children in the class at that time.

Long-term planning

A school's long-term plans are written and agreed by the team of senior staff and will remain in place, perhaps with minor alterations, for a considerable period of time. This ensures that over a key stage the children will cover the specified work with coherence, continuity and progression built into the plan. Long-term plans identify what topics in different curricular areas will be covered by the different key stages.

Long-term plans for Key Stages 1 and 2 are provided in two core subjects in the Primary Framework for Literacy and Mathematics which is part of the Primary National Strategy. The majority of English schools have adopted these in one form or another. Examples of long-term planning for the Foundation Stage are to be found in *Planning for Learning in the Foundation Stage* (QCA, 2001).

Here are the long term plans prepared by one school for their Year 5 class:

	Science	D & T	Art	History	Geography	Music	PE	RE
AUTUMN	Separating soils Materials Earth and beyond	Shelters	Lines and shapes		Local study: our village	Rhythm patterns	Games: net/court Gym Games: invasion	Places of worship
SUMMER	Electricity and magnetism Victorian science and technology: light, electricity, variation and classification	Cushions	Art in the home	Victorians: country life and town life (inc. local)		Musical shapes and sounds: sound inventions	Gym Dance: creative Games: invasion Dance: trad./folk	Putting faith into practice
SPRING	Life processes Animals Forces	Biscuits	Advertising and illustration		UK locality: National Park/ seaside	Music that tells a story	Games: strike/field Athletics Swimming	Stages of life

Table 2.1 Example of long-term planning (Year 5)

It is important as a trainee teacher to be aware of the long-term planning for your class but we shall focus here on medium-term and short-term planning with which you will be more likely to engage.

Medium-term planning

It is usually the role of year leaders or key stage co-ordinators to develop medium-term plans to ensure that the long-term plans are successfully implemented. The Primary National Strategy documents provide the basis for medium-term planning in English and mathematics. As well as setting out the overall aims and structure of teaching and learning for each year group, they give details of learning objectives and suggestions for activities which may help achieve them. For other subject areas, a variety of guidance is available, including the QCA schemes of work, widely used by teachers and freely downloadable from the web at **www.qca.org.uk**. The QCA schemes have done much to standardise the delivery of the National Curriculum across England and have also influenced primary teachers in other parts of the United Kingdom. It is important to remember that they are not statutory and do not have to be used; however, good teachers will adapt them freely to meet their own requirements.

Medium-term plans in schools are likely to come in one of two basic forms:

1. subject-based,
2. topic-based or cross-curricular.

Subject-based medium-term planning is exemplified by the QCA schemes of work. These address each subject separately and give a detailed account of learning objectives, activities and assessment opportunities for units of work in that subject. A complete set of medium-term plans for a key stage covers the whole of the curriculum for that key stage.

Topic-based or cross-curricular medium-term planning involves organising learning around a theme which draws on several different subjects simultaneously. Done well, this can provide a more holistic approach to the development of a series of learning episodes and allow for creativity and problem-solving. The importance of rigorous planning for the relevant subject knowledge must not be overlooked if this approach is to have impact.

In addition, many teachers find it useful to have a one-page outline to give an overview of what a class will be doing over a period of several weeks.

SEPTEMBER	Week beginning 4 Sept	Week beginning 11 Sept	Week beginning 18 Sept	Week beginning 25 Sept
Literacy	Traditional stories: beginnings	Characteristics of traditional stories	Describing places	Describing characters
Numeracy	Revision of basic operations			Symmetry
Science	Living and non-living things in our school grounds	Characteristics of living things	Investigational skills: sorting and grouping	Caring for our environment
D & T	Playgrounds			
ICT	Word processing: revision	Text and graphics: Harvest invitations	Storybook Weaver: creating own 'traditional' stories	
History	(not this half term)			
Geography	Our school and its grounds (explore; draw)	Our school and its grounds (mapping)	Describing our school grounds	How could we improve our school grounds?
Art	Using natural materials in art			
Music	Traditional songs from different world traditions			
PE	Outdoor: ball skills, small invasion games Indoor: dance – Rain Dance			
RE	Experiencing/valuing the natural world (walk)	Responsibility towards the natural world: Hindu story	Christian/Jewish story of the Creation	The work of environmental groups
Other			Harvest Festival Fri.	Anne B. (National Parks) Thurs.

Table 2.2   Example of outline (medium-term) planning (Year 2)

REFLECTIVE TASK

Look at the example of outline medium-term planning above. How many links between subjects can you identify? Can you see how this teacher has carefully timed the learning activities in different subject areas to maximise their effect? (Look both vertically and horizontally.)

Some schools take this approach one stage further and integrate learning objectives from different areas of the curriculum and teaching without subject boundaries. This works where a whole-school policy is in place which allows the necessary flexibility in both resourcing and timetabling.

Choose one of the following topics and devise an outline plan for a four-week unit of work in Foundation Stage or Key Stage 1 or Key Stage 2, which links as many different areas of learning or curricular areas as you think appropriate:

- **animals around our school;**
- **healthy living;**
- **a class story book;**
- **an international sporting event;**
- **a school visit.**

What are the challenges and opportunities of this kind of planning as compared with subject-based planning?

You may find that integrating learning across subject areas brings a fresh approach to planning.

- **In some cases, the same content already turns up in different parts of the prescribed curriculum (e.g. healthy eating is part of science, design and technology, and PSHE) – so 'joined-up thinking' allows teachers to cover different subjects simultaneously.**
- **Complementary work can be carried out in several areas at once (e.g. Year 2 work on a theme like Harvest might include creative writing, science, music, art and dance).**
- **One set of resources can be used to the full, in different ways (e.g. a Year 4 class examined and drew historical artefacts before going on to design and make packaging that could be used for posting them back to the museum).**
- **It gives an opportunity for developing 'transferable skills', enabling skills learned in one context to be practised in another (e.g. Year 5 work on data-handling and graphs in maths was put into action when recording a science investigation).**

Good medium-term planning, in whatever format, is likely to include certain features:

- **details of the year group for whom the planning is intended;**
- **the main content areas to be covered;**
- **over-arching learning objectives, often accompanied by expected learning outcomes on several levels (e.g. 'Most children will... Some children will... Some children will go further and will... ');**
- **possible teaching and learning activities, including differentiation; often in sequence;**
- **notes on cross-curricular links generally, and on how it may be appropriate to integrate ICT and/or primary languages into the learning activities;**
- **a list of resources needed in connection with each activity, and often a note of where these are available;**
- **suggested timing for each group of learning objectives and activities (i.e. how many lessons);**
- **a note of when and how achievement of each learning objective may be assessed.**

Given a set of learning objectives for a unit of work, the 'trick' is to devise a variety of learning activities so that the learners gain a really thorough understanding of the concepts without getting bored. You need to be aware of the qualitative differences in the types of activities you plan. Ask yourself, 'What is the purpose?' Is it:

a. revisiting old skills and knowledge prior to starting a new topic?
b. acquiring new skills or knowledge?
c. consolidating pupils' knowledge and skills under the teacher's guidance?
d. applying their knowledge or skills in a different context, with decreasing amounts of support?
e. being challenged to solve problems, make new discoveries or draw their own conclusions, using all their knowledge and skills independently?

The above list is broadly developmental and activities may be planned in this kind of order.

PRACTICAL TASK PRACTICAL TASK **PRACTICAL TASK** PRACTICAL TASK **PRACTICAL TASK**

A Key Stage 2 class studied their own locality (Painscastle) in the spring term, and are preparing to look at a contrasting locality (Dale) in the summer term. The overall learning objectives are:

- **to use geographical skills and sources to answer a range of questions;**
- **to describe and compare human and physical features in different localities;**
- **to explain the location of some features;**
- **to show awareness of similarities and differences between places;**
- **to give reasons for some observations and judgements about places.**

Here are a few of the activities the teacher has in mind to do with the children during the unit of work. How would you classify them in terms of points a–e in the list above? In what order would you plan to carry them out?

1. Search for Dale on the internet (site address provided) – what kind of place is it?
2. Write some sentences to compare the two places, using the structure 'Painscastle is . . . and/but Dale is . . .'.
3. Use aerial photos, maps and brief written descriptions to 'follow a trail' around Dale. Discuss points arising.
4. Read about different people's views on the new car park in Dale. Divide into groups and role play the public meeting.
5. Work in pairs to recall and make brief notes on what we learned about Painscastle (prompts provided at different levels).
6. With reference to aerial photos, other photos and maps, work as a class to describe the main physical features of Dale.

To plan a logical and effective pathway through National Curriculum content you will need:

- **thorough familiarity with the National Curriculum documents;**
- **sound subject knowledge;**
- **imagination and creativity in devising motivating teaching and learning activities to match sets of learning objectives;**
- **ingenuity and problem-solving capabilities, not only to track down appropriate resources but also to juggle with all the different variables until the most favourable sequence is achieved.**

Writing medium-term plans clarifies for you the direction in which you want to go and where you want to take your class. Working with colleagues improves the planning process and the benefits of teamwork are professionally rewarding.

Short-term planning

We come now to the critical part of your everyday job. Short-term planning may refer to planning for a week, a day or for one lesson. It is immediate. Experienced teachers may work from a combination of these, as well as from annotated medium-term plans, in their own classes. You will need, however, to prepare every lesson in detail, and to learn to write effective lesson plans.

Lesson planning is part of a cycle which also includes teaching, assessing children's progress and reviewing what has happened, before going on to the next round of planning. When teachers plan lessons they ask themselves the questions in Figure 2.1.

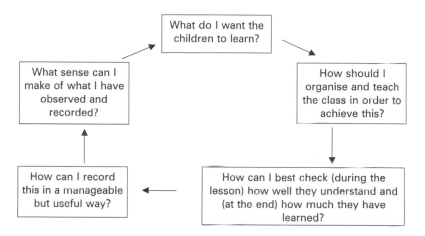

Figure 2.1 Questions to ask when planning lessons

Many schools, as well as teacher training institutions, have a standard lesson planning format which reflects these questions. This helps teachers to understand one another's plans more easily, and helps senior managers, mentors and tutors to check more quickly that everyone is remembering to include all the important things that need to go into a lesson plan. One possible layout for a lesson plan is given on pages 19–20. If the proforma is produced electronically, it is easy for teachers to adapt it to fit their particular needs.

In Early Years classes short-term planning very often covers a day or a whole week rather than a single lesson time-slot, but will normally include detailed notes on the learning intentions, key vocabulary, resources, possible adaptations for different children and assessment opportunities, in respect of each activity planned. Teaching in the Foundation Stage, even more than in Key Stage 1 and Key Stage 2, is usually very individualised and often there is an immense range of activities to which children are directed at different times during the week.

See Chapter 5 for further points on Foundation Stage teaching.

Teachers have plenty of guidance on what to teach:

- **the National Curriculum (long-term planning);**
- **the Primary National Strategy framework for literacy and mathematics (long- and medium-term planning);**
- **other national frameworks (e.g. the Key Stage 2 Framework for Primary Languages, 2005) (long-and medium-term planning);**
- **for Early Years children, the Curriculum Guidance for the Foundation Stage (long- and medium-term planning);**
- **medium-term planning produced by individuals or teams of teachers in school (medium-term planning);**
- **QCA schemes of work (available on *www.qca.org.uk*) (medium-term planning);**
- **commercially-published schemes of work (e.g. pupils' textbooks and, more importantly, the teachers' guides that accompany them) (medium-term planning).**

With the exception of the National Curriculum, none of these is statutory and schools can choose not to use them. However, within a school, teachers must abide by the curriculum policy agreed by the governors, the head teacher and the senior management team.

Lesson planning

Practical considerations that influence short-term planning include:

- **what other classes in the same year group are doing (there may be implications for the movement of children between classes as well as for resources and deployment of teaching assistants and other adult helpers);**
- **resources available in the school or that can be borrowed at the right moment from elsewhere;**
- **what else may be going on in the school in that week or on that day, e.g. trips, visitors, or special events (these may disrupt the normal timetable but they also provide special learning opportunities).**

The focus of each lesson is distilled into a number of achievable learning objectives or learning intentions. These are crucial because everything else about the lesson depends on them. It is vital to share learning objectives and learning intentions with everyone in the classroom. Teaching assistants and the children need to know your intentions if they are to understand where their learning is going and when it will have been achieved. Shirley Clarke's influential books (Clarke, 1998; 2001; 2005) on assessment for learning include useful advice on ways of sharing learning intentions with children, and the benefits to them in terms of focus, self-esteem and motivation.

Learning intentions or objectives state what the learners will know, understand or be able to do by the end of the lesson. Objectives need to be very specific and describe the learning outcomes, not the activities.

REFLECTIVE TASK

Trainees sometimes say that they know children have achieved an objective because 'they all finished the activity'. What is wrong with this argument?

In many cases the objectives for the half-term or term will already have been set out in broad terms in the medium-term planning, and it is your job to select the ones you intend to address in any given lesson or sequence of lessons. The objectives may need further refinement to fit the time available.

PRACTICAL TASK PRACTICAL TASK **PRACTICAL TASK** PRACTICAL TASK **PRACTICAL TASK**

How well do these learning objectives for lessons meet the criteria outlined above? (Make your own decisions before looking at the possible answers below.) If they are not suitable objectives for a lesson, can you improve them?

1. Know numbers to ten.
2. Understand why the Romans invaded Britain.
3. Be able to make a greetings card.
4. Complete a worksheet on adjectives.
5. Learn how to play football.

The following are possible answers.

1. Too broad and not specific: are the children learning to recite numbers, recognise figures, write them, count objects...?
2. An acceptable objective, as long as you are clear how you will be sure that the children really do understand.
3. Seems to describe the activity rather than the learning. What will the children actually learn from making the card?
4. Definitely an activity, possibly to reinforce or test the learning.
5. Far too broad, and describes an activity. Which skills will this lesson focus on?

How will the teaching and learning be organised?

When you are clear about what you want to achieve, you can start to plan the activities for the lesson. There is a well-tried tripartite structure which you can use for most of your lesson planning.

1. Good lessons start with a whole-class introduction. You should capture the children's interest with a surprise, a challenge, an intriguing question or an interesting artefact to gain and maintain their attention. Failure to grab everyone's attention right at the start will cause problems later, so take the time to get everyone involved at the outset. Then you need to remind the children of prior learning or a previous lesson which relates to the day's focus and share the learning objectives with the class in clear, child-friendly language. You can write them on the board, whiteboard or a poster and read them along with the children. With younger children the introduction can take place with children sitting 'on the carpet' and in a typical 45–60 minute lesson will last between 5 and 10 minutes.

2. Next you will develop a range of learning activities designed to enable all children to met the lesson objectives. Activities will need to be differentiated to accommodate the needs of the various children in the class. (Differentiation is an integral part of lesson planning, and will be discussed further in Chapter 3.)The menu of activities will take into account different styles of learning (e.g. visual, kinaesthetic, auditory) though in practice these may be addressed at different

times over several lessons in the day rather than within a single lesson. But children do need variety, and there may be changes of activity within this time, particularly for younger ones. In any case you will find it essential to call the class to attention at intervals, to re-focus them and review progress to date. It is these teacher interventions during the middle part of the lesson which should ensure successful learning. Activities might involve the whole class, small groups or individuals. The activities should focus on the learning objectives.

You may choose to plan in such a way that you can concentrate attention on particular children or groups of children, while the others can get on with work independently. Where children are working in groups, you need to decide how they and any other adults in the classroom will be deployed to best advantage. Teaching assistants need to be thoroughly involved and deployed to best advantage. It is your job to guide them. You should be mobile in the class, 'dropping in' on different groups to monitor, question and challenge as the children work.

3. The third part of the lesson is the **plenary**. Allow 5–10 minutes to put the seal on the children's learning, review with them what has been achieved and celebrate their achievement. This will help them to fix it in their minds, as well as boosting their self-esteem. The plenary gives you an opportunity to double-check through your questioning that the objectives really have been met. You can end by looking ahead to future lessons, whetting the children's appetites for their next learning adventure. Remember, a good finish is as important as a good start.

In addition to the overall shape of the lesson, your lesson plan will note a number of other things which are central to making it work.

- **Timing for different phases of the lesson (important for ensuring appropriate pace. May be modified as you go along, but consciously as you monitor the children's progress, rather than by accident).**
- **How you are going to manage transitions between different parts of the lesson (e.g. will children leave the carpet in groups or all together? how much warning will they need in order to clear up before the plenary?).**
- **Key questions that will be asked, together with possible or hoped for answers. This gives you a framework for your input and helps you guard against disconcerting surprises.**
- **Organisation of groups. It is generally advisable for teachers to be in charge of who works with whom, rather than letting children choose for themselves. The way you group them can be quite significant for the way they engage with the activities.**
- **Deployment of adults in the classroom.**
- **Organisation of resources, including when and how they will be distributed.**
- **Any hazards associated with the activities or resources planned, and a note to yourself of what you will do to avoid them.**
- **Key vocabulary that you intend to use or teach.**
- **Homework you are going to set. This needs planning just as much as the activities with the lesson itself – 'finish it for homework' is not an effective strategy for motivating children.**

LESSON PLAN		
Class/group Year 3	**Subject** Design and technology	**Date** 5 June

Main topic of lesson Photo frames (focused practical task) – how do they stand up?	**Relationship to other lessons** Introductory session

Reference **(NC/NLS/NNS/CGFS)**	**Objectives** *(up to three)*
NC 4b	Gain understanding of what makes a structure stable
NC 1a, 1b	Begin to generate ideas for a photo frame taking into account 'fitness for purpose'

Resources needed Mug tree – music stand – tripod – stool – trophy – easel – book rest – book end – clothes airer. Various photo frames. A4 card, sticky tape, glue, stapler, rulers, pencils. Prepared photo frame cards – two sizes.	**Key vocabulary to be used/taught** Stable – wide base – structure
Risk assessment *(specific activities etc. marked with an asterisk on detailed planning, overleaf)* Usual care with scissors and sharp pencil – remind children.	**Homework planned** Look at photo frames and other things to see how they stand up. Make 3 sketches. [Also look for suitable photo and bring to school for next time.]

After-lesson notes

Informal assessment of children's learning Beverley – no help was needed with cutting. Pete and Shaheen worked very well together – some imaginative solutions. Children excited about making frames. Anwar unsure about how frame would stand up. Some children (Rose, Dwain) doubtful about bringing photos.	**Brief evaluation of own teaching** Children enthusiastic about hands-on investigation and practical task. Intro. overran because all wanted to come out to demonstrate. Some good questions and answers while children were working on task – could have planned to do more in plenary.

Implications for future lessons
Recap on stability and wide base – check Anwar especially. Bring digital camera in case some children do not have photos. Allow enough time for practical tasks – keep an eye on time when on carpet. Another time, talk through best solutions with whole class at end?

Detailed activity planning			
Timing	**Learning activities** *(including deployment of other adults, groupings and special arrangements for individual children, as appropriate)*	**Assessment opportunities** *(refer to learning objectives: what may children do, say or produce at each stage which shows they have achieved these objectives?)*	**Additional notes** *(e.g. safety notes; particular points to be highlighted; specific teacher action needed at this point; use of spaces outside the classroom; use of ICT, etc.)*
10 mins	Introduction: Show selection of free-standing items. (Can we name them all? Who uses them? What for?) Do they stand up well? (Vocab: stable) Why is this important? What makes them stand up well? (importance of wide base) ***TA to interpret for Martha – make sure she sits where she can see easily.** Selection of photo frames – how do these stand up? (can children see parallels with other items?)	Do all children grasp this idea? (If not, allow further experimentation with TA.) **Return to this point in plenary.**	
25 mins	Introduce/explain task: to try out different ways of making things stand up. Quickly review what we have seen. Task: work in pairs (talking partners; **Martha + Michael with TA**). Cut A4 card in half, find a way to make an A5 piece stand up. Explain we are interested in: • Solutions to the problem • Elegance of solution • Joining techniques (ease, strength, appearance) **Help Sam, Beverley with ruling lines and cutting.** Pairs to try out as many different	Circulate – listen to conversations; who is focusing on task in ways instructed? Remind children of focus: what makes a structure stable?	Materials ready on tables. **NB LH scissors for Nazeem.** NB links with maths – remind ch. what half means! Stop class to show good work in progress.
10 mins	ways as possible. Clear up; each pair to choose ONE best structure to show. One from each pair to remain at table to explain; other from each pair to circulate to look at all solutions. Then swap.	How good are the explanations?	Leave structures on tables (to be moved to exhibition area before going out to play).
5 mins	Plenary: congratulate children on solutions to the problem. Introduce task for this half term: to design and make a photo frame to give as a present (who to?) Everyone will use same basic strong card frame (show – choice of two sizes). Task: a) to make it stand up, and b) to finish it to make it look attractive. (We will start to plan next week!) (Explain **homework** and how it relates to the task. Children also to look out for ideas for their frames.)		

Table 2.3   Example of a plan for a Year 3 Design and Technology lesson

REFLECTIVE TASK
REFLECTIVE TASK

Read carefully the lesson plan on the previous two pages. Note how each section has been completed by this experienced teacher.

Return to the plan after you have read the rest of this chapter. How does it compare with lesson plans you yourself have made or seen elsewhere?

Look back to the 'reasons for planning' in the reflective task on page 9. How well does this lesson plan illustrate those reasons?

Can you imagine yourself teaching from this plan? What parts would you find particularly useful? Do you think anything is missing?

How will learning be monitored?

Lesson planning proformas often include a column headed 'assessment opportunities'. You should consider before you begin what evidence there will be that children are learning what you want them to learn. You should be able to articulate this in terms of what you expect them to **do, say** or **produce** by the end of the lesson. Shirley Clarke (2001, pp22–23) suggests that success criteria can be worked out with children once they have had time during the lesson to fully digest the learning objectives and to make a start on the activities which are going to help them achieve those objectives. Either way you need to have in advance a clear idea in your own mind about what you are looking for, and this will be linked to the learning objectives you set at the start.

Monitoring of understanding (to check that your teaching is on course) and formative oral feedback are integral parts of every lesson. More structured summative assessment may not be appropriate every time. It may instead be specified in medium-term planning and appear in short-term plans only as units of work near their completion.

Where will assessment outcomes be recorded?

Minute-to-minute monitoring of children's progress is not normally written down, but is responded to immediately in the context of the lesson. If there is a pattern of misconceptions or achievement beyond expectations for any individual child or group of children, you will want to make a note of this so that you can take it into account in future planning. The easiest place to write it is somewhere on the lesson plan or you could have a sheet ready drawn up with the learning objective in a prominent position, on which you can write the names of children who have failed to demonstrate the intended learning and of those who have exceeded expectations.

When you plan for the next lesson, you can assume that the children in the group or class whose names are not noted have achieved the objectives more or less as planned and are ready to move on.

Making sense of recorded assessment

Somewhere on the lesson plan, or on another sheet close to it, you need to develop the habit of recording a brief evaluation of the lesson. You may choose to do this in relation to a specific aspect of the teaching (such as management of transitions or questioning); it will often be informed by a discussion with your

Teaching	Learning
What specific thing(s) did you do that helped or hindered the children's learning? How do you know?	Were the learning objectives met? How do you know? What did the children actually do? What did they learn?
Why did this happen?	**Why did this happen?**
Were your objectives sensible (in number, scope, level of challenge)? Was your explanation clear? Did you keep the children's attention throughout? Was the content presented in manageable steps, in the most appropriate sequence? Did you use your voice effectively? Was your timing satisfactory? Did the children have enough time to apply and to practise new skills? Did you help the children express and organise their own ideas? Were you able to make use of and build on the children's contributions? Did you have sufficiently high expectations of all the children?	Did the children really know what they were doing and why they were doing it (were not just 'told')? Did the tasks match the children's capabilities? Were the children interested and involved? Were they able to handle the equipment safely and purposefully? Did each child perform as expected? (Have you made a note of exceptions?) Were they pleased with what they achieved?
	What evidence do you have for your judgements?
	Did you see the kind of learning behaviour you expected? Did children respond orally in the ways you expected? Did you see the kind of written outcome or product you expected? Did you have any difficulty in deciding what an individual child had achieved? (And if so, what do you plan to do about it?)
What are the implications for future planning in terms of: 1. progression in learning; 2. your teaching skills?	

Table 2.4 Evaluating teaching and learning

mentor or university tutor and, together with the record of assessment of the children's learning, will inform your planning for the next lesson. Writing things down helps to crystallise thinking and also provides evidence for that all-important Standards profile.

Proctor et al (1995, p144) provide a framework of questions which you may find useful to guide your reflection on learning and teaching within a lesson: (see Table 2.4).

As a trainee you will often have the opportunity of discussing the implications of your reflections with your mentor. In terms of your teaching, they will help you to set yourself specific targets for improvement. In respect of the children's learning, they may lead you to think carefully, before next time, about:

- **the suitability of the learning objectives you decided upon;**
- **the appropriateness of the activities you devised, for every individual in the class;**
- **the way you explained things to children, questioned them and gave them instructions;**
- **the way you grouped the children;**
- **the quality of the resources;**
- **the different amounts of support and challenge that you provided for individual children and groups of children;**
- **any unexpected outcomes (things children said or did that you had not anticipated – and what to do about them in future lessons).**

What you decide to do next is, of course, crucially dependent upon your evaluation of the lesson and your response to the evidence provided by your assessment of children's learning (as discussed in detail in Chapter 4).

Conclusion

All teaching should have a clear purpose and motivate the learners. Often lessons are exciting and thought-provoking for both teachers and children. Sometimes teachers are nothing short of inspirational. But contrary to some lay belief, none of this happens by accident. Underpinning every really good lesson is sound planning at a number of different levels.

As *Excellence and Enjoyment* reminds us:

> *Inspectors will not expect to find a particular model or format for planning: they will be much more interested in the impact of planning on your teaching and the children's learning.*
>
> (DfES, 2003, p78)

School inspectors evaluate:

- *how well teaching and resources promote learning, address the full range of learners' needs and meet... requirements;*
- *the suitability and rigour of assessing in planning and monitoring learners' progress;*
- *the [...] provision for additional learning needs.*

> (Ofsted, 2005a, p19)

Thoughtful advance planning allows you to incorporate all of these features into your lessons, teaching them effectively and enjoying them as much as the children do. At the same time you will feel confident in the knowledge that you are doing all you can to meet their different learning needs and to inspire them to become lifelong learners.

Moving on

The difference between a good teacher and an excellent teacher rests to a large extent in the quality of their planning. As you gain experience and confidence, you will become increasingly creative with your plans and more expert at identifying the levels at which your pupils are operating, so that you can always challenge them appropriately. Your capabilities as an effective teacher will include:

- planning from assessments made in earlier (but still recent) lessons;
- incorporating a wide range of resources including ICT where it enhances the lesson;
- varying the 'shape' of lessons so that the children are eager to know what will happen today;
- keeping yourself sufficiently alert and informed so that you can make the content of lessons both topical and relevant to the lives of the children;
- making cross-curricular links where appropriate, including introducing other languages and cultures;
- being aware of how you can develop key skills such as literacy, numeracy, ICT and thinking and learning skills in all areas of the curriculum;
- organising resources (including adult helpers) to best advantage;
- being able to foresee potential problems and planning ways of avoiding them;
- being so sensitive to the children's potential responses that you can accurately plan for pace and timing, while allowing enough flexibility for when the unexpected happens.

PRACTICAL TASK PRACTICAL TASK PRACTICAL TASK PRACTICAL TASK PRACTICAL TASK

Find out how planning at all levels is carried out in your placement school.
Look to see how many things from the above list are evident in the planning and teaching of an experienced teacher.

FURTHER READING FURTHER READING FURTHER READING

Go to the Standards site **www.standards.dfes.gov.uk** and the QCA site (see below) for further guidance. See, for example:

DfES (2007) *Statutory Framework for the Early Years Foundation Stage*. London: DfES.

QCA (2001) *Planning for Learning in the Foundation Stage*. London: QCA. This supplement to the Curriculum Guidance for the foundation stage will be invaluable to anyone working in an early years setting. It can be downloaded from the QCA website.

QCA (2002) *Designing and Timetabling the Primary Curriculum: A Practical Guide for Key Stages 1 and 2*. London: QCA.

Clarke, S. (1998) *Targeting Assessment in the Primary Classroom*. London: Hodder & Stoughton.

Clarke, S. (2001) *Unlocking Formative Assessment.* London: Hodder & Stoughton. These two teacher-friendly books show clearly how successful planning is related to day-to-day assessment, and give practical examples of how this can be managed.

Hayes, D. (2003) *Planning, Teaching and Class Management in Primary Schools.* London: David Fulton. As the title suggests, this takes you step-by-step through the purposes and processes of planning for effective teaching.

Useful websites

www.nc.uk.net: Downloadable files of all the National Curriculum documents

www.qca.org.uk: The website of the Qualifications and Curriculum Authority. Downloadable schemes of work for guidance in all National Curriculum subjects.

www.standards.dfes.gov.uk: Standards site

www.teachernet.gov.uk: The government website for teachers

3
Planning for all abilities: inclusion and differentiation
Nicola Ivett
with thanks to Nicky Edwards who wrote the original version of this chapter for earlier editions

By the end of the chapter you should:

- **understand the use of the term differentiation;**
- **recognise different types of differentiation and their strengths and weaknesses;**
- **appreciate the importance of differentiation in your approach to teaching and learning;**
- **be aware of some teaching strategies used to differentiate the curriculum in the primary classroom;**
- **know how to select the most appropriate type of differentiation for a particular child in a particular context;**
- **understand the relationship between assessment, planning and differentiation.**

This chapter addresses the following Professional Standards for QTS:
Q10, Q12, Q18, Q19, Q25, Q26, Q27, Q28

This chapter explains the context of differentiation in Section 1 and examines some of the factors which affect differentiation in Section 2. Section 3 looks at different types of differentiation commonly used in the classroom and Section 4 broadens its perspective, examining the relationship between assessment, differentiation and planning. The final section summarises the importance of the differentiation process for effective teaching.

Does Every Child Matter? The challenge of differentiation

One of the biggest challenges that will face you as a teacher in the primary classroom is to cater for the variety of children with their wide range of learning needs and capacities that you encounter daily. All children do not arrive in your lesson with the same experiences, knowledge, skills and aptitudes and yet you must teach so that all can learn, so that all can 'enjoy and achieve' (ECM DfES, 2004a).

Removing Barriers to Achievement: The Government's Strategy for SEN (2004) states:

> All children have the right to a good education. All teachers should expect to teach children with special educational needs and all schools should play their part in educating children from the local community whatever their background or ability.

> (DfES, 2004b, Introduction)

This is one of the biggest challenges that face teachers in the primary classroom today.

Kerry and Kerry (1997) explain that differentiation rose to prominence after the 1988 Education Act. The Schools Examination and Assessment Council (SEAC) identified two methods of differentiation: by task and by outcome. They go on to describe the disparity between what is contained within the official documents about differentiation and what was actually needed in the classroom.

Since that time the Government has highlighted the importance of differentiation by giving it a new identity. The National Curriculum (2000) stated the need for all teachers to have due regard for the principle of 'inclusion'. This includes the three principles of:

- **setting suitable learning challenges;**
- **responding to children's diverse learning needs;**
- **overcoming potential barriers to learning and assessment for individuals and groups of children.**

Recent legislation has further championed the importance of inclusive education. In May 2003 *Excellence and Enjoyment – A Strategy for Primary Schools* was launched. This set out a vision for the future of primary education. It emphasised that in order for every child to succeed, they must be provided with an inclusive education. Kerry and Kerry (1998) note that some teachers may have low expectations of those they label as 'low ability'. This in turn denies them the opportunity to prove that they are able to achieve more. The Strategy continues to describe how inclusive education can only be achieved within a 'culture of high expectations'.

Every Child Matters: Change for Children in Schools (DfES, 2004a) identifies that a child's well-being and achievement at school is closely linked.

What is differentiation?

Recently on the TES website a message was posted on its Graduate Teacher Programme (GTP) Staffroom explaining that differentiation,

> ... is basically adjusting the main activity of your lesson to make it more difficult/simple for the different levels your children will be at. You would use the same activity for your lower groups and then challenge your high achievers.
>
> (TES Staffroom, 25 March 2006)

Kershner and Miles suggest:

> We seem to be looking for a global definition of differentiation. I don't think we can have one ... it's a term that ... like a bar of soap ... you try to grasp it and suddenly it shoots out of your hand.
>
> (1996, p17)

As a trainee you may be helped by a simple definition.

Moss (1996) says differentiation is *essentially about matching pupil, task and teaching method*.

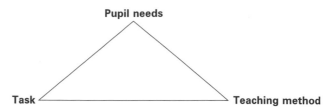

Figure 3.1 Triangle of needs

As a teacher I must make sure that the individual needs of the child, the specific nature of the task or activity and the way I teach are considered carefully when planning an individual lesson or series of lessons. When looking at the triangle of needs (see Figure 3.1) it becomes apparent that differentiation is not a simple concept – a one-off – which can be conveniently added to a lesson plan written earlier. It is an ongoing concept – an evolving process – which appears relatively simple on first inspection, but has a habit of growing and developing in complexity, alongside your teaching experiences and expertise. You develop a working definition of differentiation which expands and metamorphoses during the different stages of teaching development. It must start life in the form of a differentiated work sheet for different ability groups and gradually transform itself into an entire way of thinking and approaching the planning and delivery of the National Curriculum. Differentiation is:

> *not a single event, it is a process. This process involves recognising the variety of individual needs within a class, planning to meet those needs, providing appropriate delivery and evaluating the effectiveness of the activities in order to maximise the achievements of individual students.*
>
> (Dickinson and Wright, 1993, p3)

Already the concept has changed and developed, transforming from a triangular into a rectangular process shown in Figure 3.2.

Figure 3.2 Rectangle of needs

While the teacher must plan for individual needs, choose an appropriate teaching style and plan suitable learning activities, the accompanying reflective process, after the lesson has been taught, comes into its own. It is here that the teacher can analyse whether the differentiation has supported, stretched and enriched the children or challenged and motivated them by providing the best opportunity for learning. Without this evaluative process the teacher would never be sure how effective the selected differentiation was. With it the teacher is able to provide the children in the class with a variety of activities and approaches to learning that suit both educational and emotional needs.

Webster stresses the flexible nature of differentiation which must be understood if the teacher is to maximise the learning potential of each child.

Differentiation is:

> *An ongoing process which needs to be planned for and is characterised by flexibility. It is the means of maximising learning for all children, by taking account of individual difference in learning style, interest, motivation and aptitude, and reflecting these variations in the classroom.*
>
> (Webster, 1995, p34)

It is a flexible approach to learning, using a wide range of teaching strategies which make learning accessible by embracing the diversity of all the children (Bearne, 1996).

PRACTICAL TASK PRACTICAL TASK PRACTICAL TASK PRACTICAL TASK PRACTICAL TASK

A: Differentiation is about

B: Differentiation is not about

A: Differentiation is about	B: Differentiation is not about
INCLUSION	SEGREGATION
DIVERSITY	SELECTION
COLLABORATION	COMPETITION
VARIETY	UNIFORMITY
SOLUTIONS	PROBLEMS
OPTIMISM	PESSIMISM

Do these contrasting attitudes help or hinder approaches to differentiation? Which methods of differentiation would teachers with values A and B employ in the classroom?
(Adapted from Moss, 1996)

Visser is concerned about the lack of understanding surrounding the term differentiation, despite its popularity. *Differentiation has become one of the educational jargon words of the mid 1990s – used by many, understood by some, and put fully into practice by a few* (1993, p4).

A lack of teacher understanding has an impact on the practical application of differentiation in the classroom. And if differentiation strategies do not meet the needs of individual children, then learning opportunities are lost, preventing children from maximising their learning potential. Teachers, then, must concentrate on gaining an in-depth understanding of differentiation. Table 3.1 below details some of the key terms which are associated with differentiation which will help to clarify understanding and implications for application.

Key terms	Meaning
It is an ongoing process	• The teacher assesses what the children can do, then plans and differentiates the curriculum accordingly. It is part of an ongoing cycle of assessment, planning, differentiation and evaluation. • The process involves a continual dialogue between child and teacher about their learning needs (Stradling et al, 1991).
It is planned	• It is not an extra which is added to planning as an afterthought – it is intentional. • It can be used in medium-term planning (half-term plans) when the teacher uses different teaching/ organisational strategies to meet the different learning styles of the children in the class. • In short-term planning – weekly, daily or individual lesson plans – differentiation tailors the curriculum to specific individual learning needs (see Section 3).
It is the teacher's responsibility	• It is important not to blame the children if they cannot understand the learning objective. • The teacher is responsible for matching the diverse needs/abilities to appropriate activities using a range of teaching styles (Convery and Coyle, 1993).
It is a flexible tool	• There are numerous different ways to differentiate learning opportunities ranging from the task set, resources used, organisation of groups and the level of teacher support. See Section 4 for details.
It values each individual	• Individual children, whatever their ability, must feel valued. The type of differentiation must not undermine self-esteem or a sense of self-worth.
It celebrates diversity	• Differentiation is a way of providing equitable access to a diverse range of children's needs. It celebrates not accentuates the differences (Bearne, 1996).
It centres on entitlement	• Each individual child is entitled to have his or her learning needs and abilities catered for. • A teacher must provide opportunities for each pupil to have access to the National Curriculum (Visser 1993).
It maximises learning potential	• Differentiation aims to maximise the learning of individual children. • It is the difference between where the child is now and where the child has the potential to be (Dickinson and Wright, 1993).
It is contextually embedded	• The context of the classroom plays a vital role in helping the teacher to select and use subtle and appropriate differentiation (Kerry and Kerry, 1997, p3).

Table 3.1   Key terms associated with differentiation

Factors affecting differentiation

Differentiation, the school and you

In Section 1 differentiation was identified as part of an ongoing process which does not occur in isolation. When a teacher is planning a lesson additional factors must be taken into consideration. Each of these factors will affect the types of differentiation which you plan to use in the classroom. Table 3.2 below highlights these factors which have a substantial impact on differentiation options and teaching strategies available to you.

Factors for consideration	
1. Children's diversity	• Cognitive, educational and developmental factors • Biological, gender and maturational factors • Physical, neurological, sensory motor and perceptual motor • Cultural, family, ethnic and economic factors • Social, interpersonal, emotional, personality and motivational factors • Moral, religious and ethical factors (Moss, 1996)
2. Curriculum requirements	The ever changing demands of the National Curriculum and the latest educational developments: • Curriculum 2000 • The Primary Framework for Literacy and Mathematics • Primary Strategy • Every Child Matters 2004
3. Assessment methods used in schools	• Teachers under pressure to prepare children for Key Stage 1 and Key Stage 2 National Tests and spending more time preparing them for National Tests assessments • Summative assessment often narrow focus – written only • Some assessment publications are unreliable (multiple choice); the data might not give a valid benchmark of added learning
4. School context	• School self-evaluation • Inspection evidence • Attitude towards differentiation can be determined by school ethos and policies, e.g. setting of children in maths and English/organisation of SEN • Ethos in schools – valuing others and collaborative learning or winner takes all • The School Improvement Plan will prioritise the budget which might have recurring resourcing limitations for differentiation
5. Teacher style and management style	How teachers: • present tasks – diversity/quality of approach • support children – praise, feedback, frameworks • set high expectations – consistency • organise classroom – whole class/groups • organise resources – independent learning • value individuals – listen and value

Table 3.2   Factors which affect differentiation options

Types of differentiation

It is hardly surprising to discover that the types of differentiation are nearly as prolific as the number of definitions. While Lewis (1991) identifies 11 possible types of differentiation, Kerry and Kerry (1997) identify 15 methods and those are only for the more able learners. Table 3.3 below identifies six main types of differentiation.

Type of differentiation	Examples
Input (content) Contents of the teacher contribution	• Amount of factual information/content of teacher input • Number of concepts introduced or explained • Specific vocabulary chosen • Length of time used for teacher input • Delivery of input – clear/lively, etc.
Resources Variety of resources to fit individual needs	• Choice of text – layout/readability • Choice of visual resources/artefacts • Variety of writing materials – whiteboards/pens/paper • Organisation of classroom for ease of access to materials and for groups of children • Framework for writing/organisation • ICT – interactive whiteboard, laptops and related software, e.g. talking books, speech software, spell checkers, overlay keyboards and rollerballs
Support Additional support for children to enable learning outcomes to be met	• Teacher support for individual children • Additional adult works with a child or a group of children, e.g. acts as a scribe • TAs and LSAs • Peer tutoring or group work where chldren assist one another • Technological support – concept keyboard, spell checkers, tape recorder, computer, CD Rom and video • Praise achievement
Task	• Series of graded tasks of increasing complexity • Separate task set for each ability group • Verbal presentation of learning • Written format – fiction/non-fiction/first draft or final • Artwork/display • Choice of task • Problem solving tasks • Use of role play and drama • Homework
Outcome Common task set but outcome of task or end product will differ from child to child	• Summative assessment – all do the same test and achieve different marks, SAT or school report • Formative assessment – a piece of work marked identifying a target of the next learning step for the child • Answer to a question/verbal presentation • Piece of drama • Written outcome – first draft or final copy

Response	• Praise for particular achievement/attitude • Setting of specific learning targets • Constructive feedback • Set clear DLOs for individuals • IEPs for children with SEN • Using partner children to evaluate achievement/needs • Self-assessment by children

Table 3.3   Types of differentiation

Source: Adapted from Cheminais, 2006

Learning styles – understanding how different children learn and adopt appropriate teaching strategies	Auditory learners' characteristics – good listeners, expressive talkers, quick to learn from listening to others Teaching strategies: • Group discussions • Opportunities for oral feedback • Use investigative, reporting and interviewing Visual learners' characteristics – observant, quick to see things others miss Teaching strategies: • Need time to watch and think things through • Respond best to visual materials • Introduce flow charts, mind maps and diagrams Kinaesthetic learners' characteristics – enjoys teamwork, doing practical activities and enjoys concrete experiences Teaching strategies: • Provide opportunities to touch/manipulate objects • Build models • Participate in activity-based learning Logical/theorist characteristics – enjoys knowing and applying theories, concepts, enjoys problem solving Teaching strategies: • Provide step by step plans and instructions • Use data in a variety of forms

Table 3.4. Different learning styles

REFLECTIVE TASK

- Which types of differentiation have you used in the classroom? When did you use it and why?

- Examine one of your lesson plans. What type of differentiation did you use and why?

- Examine one of your lesson evaluations. What does it tell you about your current approach to teaching and learning?

Interpretation of teaching responsibility could lead to lost opportunities and children who, lacking in self-confidence, do not have the motivation to learn. Alternatively the teacher, in trying to cater for individual need and learning style, could get lost in a field of uncertainty over the selection of a suitable differentiation strategy. Too many strategies could be employed at once, clouding the learning objectives and clarity of teaching. Figure 3.3 looks at the implications and considerations and implications perceived by teachers when considering the notion of differentiation (Kerry and Kerry, 1997).

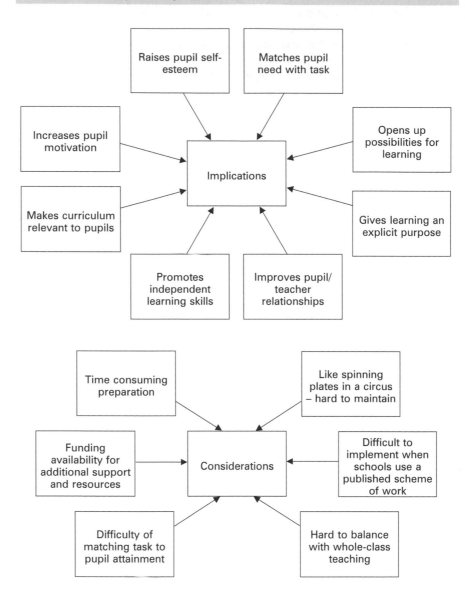

Figure 3.3   Implications and considerations of differentiation

Support staff and differentiation – a heavenly combination

Ofsted suggest that teaching assistants provide important support for up to one in four primary school children (Ofsted, 2003d). In her article 'Providing learning support in a mathematics lesson', Colloby (2005) describes how a teaching assistant (TA) Caroline works with a low ability group.

> *She enables learners to engage with the learning objectives of the lesson... She also mediates between learners and their sense of achievement by ensuring that her children can access the tasks through her additional explanations, encouragement and support... she reacts by reinforcing, redirecting and consolidating the links between knowledge and understanding.. Finally she supports the teacher's management of teaching and learning.*

(Colloby, 2005, pp52–53)

When planning for differentiation, think carefully about how you will deploy the TA in order to maximise the children's learning potential. Working in partnership with the TA benefits the whole class including you. In essence it is your responsibility to ensure that before the lesson, the TA understands the learning objectives and how these relate to the lesson. Also clear up any confusion that may arise from specific activities, for example definition of subject specific vocabulary, use of resources or how a lesson relates to a child's individual education plan (IEP). Finally, at the end of the lesson discuss any issues that have arisen during the lesson.

Matching differentiation to individual needs

Matching the differentiation to individual needs is a difficult task, especially when you don't know the children at the start of a placement. You will feel unsure of the children's personal qualities, needs and levels of attainment. Similarly there will be an uncertainty over the contextual factors within the school. You will not know the expectations for work and behaviour or, for example, the level of independent learning. Because of this early attempts to differentiate, however carefully prepared, often lead to frustration and perceived failure. It is the same for experienced teachers, every September, who struggle to find effective differentiation techniques until they know the children as individuals and can cater for their quirks and idiosyncrasies. The summative assessment helps, and is a starting point, but nothing beats the wealth of inside knowledge which accumulates as the teacher and the class build trust, sharing teaching and learning experiences together.

Effective matching of individual needs to an appropriate task is a subtle business, a skill which develops with the practical experience of the classroom. For this there is no substitute. The following section outlines the needs of five children. The original tasks set do not match the children's needs.

PRACTICAL TASK PRACTICAL TASK **PRACTICAL TASK** PRACTICAL TASK **PRACTICAL TASK**

- Using Table 3.3 on types of differentiation on pages 33–34, consider how you might differentiate for the following children to make the outcome of their work more successful.
- Look at Table 3.5 and see if you agree with the possible solutions suggested

John, age 8, has got to throw and catch a tennis ball with one hand. He says to his class teacher, 'Miss, do you need any jobs doing? I noticed the class library has got really messy,' and thinks to himself: 'Maybe I can forge a note from my Mum, I hate PE. I'm useless at it.'	**Identification of John's needs** • Lacks confidence in PE, frequent avoidance tactics • Lack of hand–eye co-ordination • Poor spatial awareness
Sarah, age 9, has been asked to write a description of a special object using adjectives. She thinks to herself, 'Quick, quick, quick one more sentence ahh, I'm the first to finish. I even beat Jane. Look, she hasn't even done a page!'	**Identification of Sarah's needs** • Rushes every piece of work – wants praise for completion • Poor listening skills • Hates re-drafting or checking work
Taj, age 9, refuses to answer comprehension questions in a literacy lesson. When working with a bilingual TA, it is obvious that he understands the questions. The TA also points out that he reads and communicates well in his first language.	**Identification of Taj's needs** • EAL • Good communication in mother tongue • Lack of confidence
Chantel, age 11, is in the top maths group. During a numeracy lesson on division, she thinks to herself, 'I'm bored. This is too easy. I can't be bothered.'	**Identification of Chantel's needs** • Gifted and talented • Does not find work challenging
Clare, age 7, must write a story about a holiday that went wrong. She thinks to herself, 'I know, we could be on a journey in the car to France. We could break down on the motorway, then we could get stuck on the ferry. After that we could run out of petrol in a deserted country lane.'	**Identification of Clare's needs** • Quick to understand new concepts • Extensive vocabulary • Good sequencing skills

Child's age	Possible problems	Possible differentiated solutions
John, age 8	• Will be unable to catch the small ball • Will lose even more self-confidence • Hand–eye co-ordination will not improve • He will develop a sudden stomach ache	**Resources** – larger, lighter ball with textured surface which is easier to grip **Task** – catching with two hands or with one **Support** – teacher to partner John during paired activities to teach catching sequence
Sarah, age 9	• As Sarah has poor listening skills she might not understand the task • The description will lack detail with few adjectives and little evidence of checking for errors • Disappointment when praise is not given • She hates redrafting and checking words	**Input** a) Teacher to check through questioning that Sarah has clear understanding of the task b) Task can be written on whiteboard **Task** – split into several units a) Sarah and partner to carry out brain storm on adjectives and create a list b) Sarah and partner to write an opening sentence using three of their adjectives c) Pair to read sentence out loud and continue **Resources** – a) Dictionary on table b) Specific word bank for piece of work c) Use of computer for redrafting purposes
Taj, age 9	• Will start to misbehave/ become withdrawn • Over-reliance on support staff • Will lose interest quickly in lessons	**Resources** a) Use dual language texts, word banks and bilingual dictionaries b) Use visual clues **Support** a) Model answers for Taj to repeat b) Ensure individual support is allocated to Taj c) Taj can also be supported by peer group who will model English language skills **Task** a) Allow Taj to use his first language, but at the same time encourage him to transfer this knowledge into English
Chantel, age 11	• Negative attitude may develop impacts on future lessons • Might begin to misbehave through frustration	**Input** a) Keep instruction to a minimum b) Delivery of input should be enthusiastic. This will encourage Chantel to take an active role **Task** a) Set her a challenge b) Give her a time limit **Support** a) Allow her to work collaboratively **Outcome** a) Give her time to explain her findings
Clare, age 7	• Will produce a good story without stretching her writing ability – won't improve • Will become complacent • Will get bored or lose interest	**Input** – introduce a more complicated story framework and ask Clare to model her story on this framework. **Task** – several stages a) Write a plan using a structure b) Produce a first draft c) Check spelling and punctuation d) Redraft into book e) Read to audience

Table 3.5 Differentiated solutions to children's problems

The big picture

The ADP (assessment, differentiation and planning) process

In Section 1 differentiation was identified as an ongoing process or cycle which takes place continually in the classroom to check that individual social, emotional, physical and learning needs are being met. The process of differentiation is interwoven with both assessment and planning. In isolation each area can only function partially. Unless the teacher links the three processes, the information provided is fragmented, making it difficult to plan the delivery of the curriculum in an informed and relevant way. Figure 3.4, the ADP model, shows the relationship between the three areas of teaching.

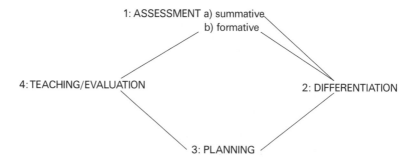

1a: Assessment (summative)
This provides the teacher with a starting point for planning. The teacher can plan what to teach because he/she knows what the children have previously learned and which levels of attainment have been reached.

2: Differentiation
Specific types of differentiation can be chosen to meet children's learning styles and individual needs planning is differentiated – unique to the context of each class.

3: Planning
The lesson is planned meeting the requirements of the National Curriculum and each child.

4: Teaching/evaluation
The lesson is taught.
Evaluation of the lesson in terms of learning environment and meeting desirable learning outcomes.

1b. Assessment (formative)
Use of formative assessment of the outcomes (the work produced) to see if the differentiation has helped to maximise learning. The whole process then starts again.

Figure 3.4   The ADP model

The ADP model in classroom use

To clarify understanding of the ADP process, the model has been applied to a classroom situation. The ongoing cycle of assessment, differentiation and planning is followed through to show the interdependence of the three processes.

The cycle starts with Stage 1, Summative Assessment, where the teacher gains information about the children's level of attainment in speaking and listening. This helps the teacher to differentiate the planned learning in Stage 2 through resources, input, task and response. The lesson plan is written in Stage 3 and delivered in Stage 4. The evaluation which follows the lesson allows the teacher to reflect upon the teaching strategies and classroom organisation. This, combined with the formative assessment of the learning outcomes which occurs in Stage 1b, helps the teacher plan and differentiate the next lesson successfully.

Stage 1a: Summative assessment

Key Stage 1   Age: Year 1 Class   Number in class: 29

- **Six children are working towards Level 1. They have difficulty in:**
  i. listening to others;
  ii. speaking audibly;
  ii. explaining their ideas in detail.
- **Twenty-one children have achieved Level 1. This means they can:**
  listen to other people;
  answer questions or offer ideas which are usually appropriate to the subject/lesson;
  speak audibly, using simple vocabulary to convey meaning, explain or extend an idea.
- **Two children have achieved Level 2. This means they can:**
  listen carefully to other people showing an awareness of others;
  adapt their vocabulary and tone of voice so that it is appropriate to the context;
  explain their ideas using relevant details.

Stage 2: Differentiation

Resources

(a) Classroom organisation
  i. Children organised, sitting in a semi-circle – good view of teacher and artefacts.
  ii. Each child can turn easily to a partner for later paired activities.

  - **Eye contact helps to keep concentration and listening skills.**
  - **By turning to a partner concentration and time are not lost through reorganisation.**

(b) Equipment
  i. Artefacts positioned on raised display next to teacher – easy access.
  ii. Labels/vocabulary noticeboard prepared with pictures of accompanying artefacts.
  iii. Mini whiteboards/pens beside teacher for later paired work and activities.

  - **First-hand experience of artefacts keeps interest and uses other senses in addition to sight.**
  - **The labels reinforce new vocabulary.**
  - **Mini whiteboards cater for children whose preferred response is not through speaking.**

Input

(a) Choice of vocabulary teacher decides to use.

(b) Type of expression teacher uses to help all the children listen.

(c) Use of artefacts while talking to maintain interest.

(d) The amount of time taken to give the input.

- **More able children must be extended and the needs of the National Curriculum Speaking and Listening programmes of study must be met.**
- **Clear speech with good intonation is a role model for children and keeps them listening.**
- **Children with poor listening skills will be visually stimulated.**
- **Too much talk is hard to listen to!**

Task

(a) Verbal tasks

i. Answering of open or closed questions as an individual in a class discussion.

ii. Expressing an idea or opinion and justifying it in class discussion.

iii. Discussion in pairs about most important artefact.

- **Increase pupils' confidence.**
- **Give pupils opportunities to use appropriate vocabulary.**
- **Encourage pupils to clarify their ideas and explanations when speaking.**

(b) Physical tasks

i. Coming to the front of a class to match a picture/artefact to a label.

ii. Matching new vocabulary with pictures in pairs.

iii. Passing round artefacts to look at and feel at first hand.

iv. Jotting ideas, diagrams or pictures on a mini whiteboard.

- **To allow the children who lack confidence in speaking in front of class to take part in the lesson.**

Response (outcome)

(a) Type of response

i. individual verbal response – extended or simple/use of vocabulary

ii. verbal response in pairs

iii. written

iv. diagram or picture form

- **To cater for and value individual learning style.**

(b) Verbal teacher response

i. praise for individual contributions

ii. repetition and extension of answers given by children

iii. varying amount of constructive feedback

(c) Non-verbal teacher response

i. eye contact

ii. nodding of head

iii. pointing to artefacts

(d) Time – giving children different amounts of time to respond

- **Increase children's confidence.**

- **Make individuals feel valued.**
- **Extend/enrich children's understanding/thinking skills.**
- **Allow time for children to think for themselves and organise their thoughts into words.**

Stage 3: Short-term planning

The teacher can plan the lesson with confidence ensuring they meet both the demands of the curriculum and the individual needs of the children.

Stage 4: Teaching/evaluation

(a) Input/Response

i. The teacher felt confident in the class discussion and was able to react in a flexible way to children's comments and extend their responses and confidence.

ii. Children were focused and listened during teacher input.

(b) Task

i. Children gained confidence when chatting over possible answers in pairs before responding.

ii. Children were interested to listen to the ideas of others.

iii. Paired activities worked well – talking/matching pictures.

Activity	PoS
• Class discussion about different types of mountaineering equipment – discovering its use in cold climates • Paired activity matching pictures to vocabulary • Paired talk to discuss most useful piece of equipment	Speaking and Listening, English 1a Clarify/explore ideas 2a To speak with confidence and use relevant detail/vocabulary to express ideas 3a Extension of vocabulary
Duration 40 minutes	**Class** KS1, Y1 Total 29
Desirable Learning Outcomes i. To understand and use new vocabulary in speech ii. To speak with increasing clarity expressing ideas/reasoning in a variety of contexts iii. To gain increasing awareness of audience as a speaker and a listener	**Assessment** Look at learning outcomes i. Did everyone contribute individually in whole-class discussion? ii. Did the matching pair activity consolidate understanding? iii. Did the paired talk increase confidence and clarify children's speech?
Differentiation Teacher input Resources Tasks Response	**Resources** Mountaineering equipment Labels on display Paired activity pictures and vocabulary words Small whiteboards and pens – one between two

Table 3.6 Lesson planning

Time	Lesson content	Key teaching points	Your role/other adults
10 minutes	**Introduction** i. Talk about cold climates re expedition ii. Show children equipment/ introduce vocabulary	Vocabulary Give clear answers – Reasons/ explanations	Effective role model while speaking Ask open questions to promote thinking
20 minutes	**Main activity** i. Label equipment as a class ii. Paired activity matching new words and pictures iii. Touch/look at equipment iv. Talk in pairs deciding most useful piece of equipment and why?	Listen to your partner Take turns	Praise for positive learning atmosphere/ learning skills
10 minutes	**Conclusion** Share ideas on useful equipment. Check vocabulary retention	Listen to others Speak giving reasons for your choice	Assess if DLOs have been met

Table 3.7 Detailed lesson planning

BUT

(c) Resources
i. Children were excited to see artefacts and found it difficult to wait their turn and tempers flared!
ii. There was insufficient time to use whiteboards – needs developing.

(d) Organisation
i. Children had to wait too long to touch the artefacts.

Stage 1b: Formative assessment
(a) Speaking as an individual: some children who do not normally participate in class discussions spoke when they were holding the artefacts.
(b) Speaking in a pair: the paired talking activity got more children involved, talking to one another and enthusiastic to feedback verbally to the whole class.
(c) Matching pictures with new vocabulary: each pair successfully matched the artefacts with the labels.

Stage 2: Differentiation
How does the next lesson plan need to be altered to ensure that the learning opportunities are maximised?

(a) Classroom organisation
- **Organise class into groups so that they can pass one artefact around a table at a time and reduce the waiting time.**

(b) Task
- **Use different paired task diagrams, notes and pictures.**
- **Role play using equipment in cold environment.**

(c) Input
- **The length of teaching input should stay the same as the children listened.**
- **Change the content to revise the meaning of new vocabulary – play riddles where teacher gives clues and children guess which artefact it is.**

Using questions to ask in each stage of the ADP cycle

Stage 1a: Summative assessment
- **What level of attainment have the children achieved?**
- **How were the children assessed?**
- **How diverse were their individual needs?**
- **Select a starting point for planning.**

Stage 2: Differentiation – selection of teaching/organisational strategies
- **Which specific individual differences must be matched to the curriculum through differentiation?**
- **Which method(s) of differentiation will it be most appropriate to use?**

Stage 3: Planning
- **Has the plan met the curriculum requirements from the programmes of study?**
- **Has the plan catered for individual needs?**

Stage 4: Teaching the lesson
- **Have the teacher strategies been used flexibly and responsively?**
- **How did the children respond during the lesson?**
- **Did the differentiation enable equal access to the curriculum?**

Stage 1b: Formative assessment of learning outcomes
- **Do the outcomes reveal new information about the children?**
- **Do the outcomes reveal an area of subject knowledge/concept that children need support with?**

Stage 2: Differentiation
- **What kind of adjustments need to be made to my next lesson?**
- **What kind of differentiation – what is its purpose?**
- **How will I know if this is successful?**

Conclusion

There are, however, wide ranging implications if teachers are to put differentiation into practice successfully, that is, catering for the sheer diversity of children's learning needs, which Thomas describes as *the phenomenally difficult process of making learning come alive for all children*. (McGarvey et al, 1996, pp69–70)

When, as an initial trainee teacher, you are suffocating with total information overload, surviving all-night planning marathons, making classroom resources that any *Blue Peter* presenter would be proud of and suffering from an accumulation of sleep deprivation, it might be difficult to judge whether the individual teacher really does make a difference. When the difference you make is couched in educational jargon and removed from the context of the classroom it becomes even harder to appreciate. It is hoped that this chapter will have helped you see that differentiation is a way of making a difference to the individual children in your charge.

Differentiation matters because:

- it caters for a diverse range of interests, characteristics and learning styles, celebrating 'the differing talents of children';
- it is child centred and considers how best to suit the learning needs to children;
- it breathes life and purpose into the National Curriculum;
- it makes every child feel valued, sensing pride in their achievements;
- it shapes the quality of learning opportunities offered to children;
- it encourages them to become involved and gain responsibility of their own learning.

Differentiation is important because:

- the National Curriculum requires it;
- Ofsted inspectors demand it;
- effective teaching embraces it;
- children gain curriculum entitlement through it;
- children develop a sense of value because of it;
- independent learning springs from it;
- individual learning potential is maximised by it;
- it brings learning to life!

Differentiation matters because it is your job, as a teacher, to make learning an engaging and purposeful activity. You have to breathe life into the curriculum, motivate children and set them challenging objectives which advance their learning at an appropriate pace. It is a vital teaching tool and an essential part of your planning, teaching and assessment.

Moving on (and moving up!)

As an NQT you must demonstrate your effectiveness as a classroom teacher. Here are a few ideas for future development.

- Have high expectations of all the children.
- Do not forget to involve them in their learning.
- Get to know their needs and interests. This will take time but be patient.
- Recognise that children do not learn in a vacuum. Parents and carers play a vital role in the development and attainment of their child.
- Continue to reflect on your practice. Highlight areas that need to be addressed. In terms

of your professional development, it may mean attending courses or just observing excellent practitioners.

- Think creatively in order to meet the needs of the children in your class.
- Do not be afraid to take risks.
- Remember you are not alone.
- Finally, do not forget that you never stop learning!

FURTHER READING   FURTHER READING   FURTHER READING

Bearne, E. (ed.) (1996) *Differentiation and Diversity in the Primary School*. London: Routledge. The different authors in this collection of articles, edited by Eve Bearne, discuss a wide range of general issues concerning differentiation and also their application in specific areas of the primary curriculum. The chapters range from 'Hearing impaired children in the classroom' to 'Differentiation in physical education'.

Cheminais, R. (2006) *Every Child Matters: A Practical Guide for Teachers*. London: David Fulton. This is a practical guide to understanding the impact of Every Child Matters in the primary classroom.

McNamara, S. and Moreton, G. (1997) *Understanding Differentiation: A Teacher's Guide*. London: David Fulton. This is a very practical guide which explores different forms of differentiation and suggests how they may be implemented in the classroom.

4
Assessment for learning
Andrea Raiker

By the end of the chapter you should:

- **understand the different purposes and forms of assessment;**
- **understand the principles underpinning assessment for learning;**
- **understand the application of assessment for learning in the class-room;**
- **be aware of the relationship between planning, assessment, recording and reporting.**

This chapter addresses the following Professional Standards for QTS:
Q12, Q19, Q25, Q26, Q27, Q28

Introduction

By reading this chapter, and working through the practical tasks, you will come to an understanding of how assessment relates to learning and teaching focused on individual children. It is important that you understand the significance of effective assessment for learning; only then will you see assessment as an essential and integrated element of your teaching.

Section 1 considers the nature of assessment and its essential components. Section 2 presents the rationale for assessment and discusses the differences between assessment *of* learning and assessment *for* learning. Section 3 considers forms of assessment, including the Foundation Stage profile and National Curriculum. Section 4 discusses the key principles of assessment for learning (AfL). Section 5 looks at putting AfL into practice through sharing learning goals, using effective questioning techniques, peer and self-assessment, and using marking and feedback strategies. Section 6 presents different ways of recording assessments, both formal and informal. There is an increasing emphasis on electronic information management and transfer so the concept of e-portfolios is introduced. The chapter concludes with a discussion on reporting.

Section 1: What is assessment for?

REFLECTIVE TASK

Consider the different types of assessments which you have experienced as a learner.
- **What is assessment?**
- **What different forms and purposes of assessment can you identify?**

Assessment involves gathering information and making judgements about learning. As a teacher you will do this both formally and informally. You will sometimes participate in assessing children to make formal judgements about their progress and achievement, as in National Tests, for example. In every lesson, however, you will continually be assessing children's learning as an ongoing part of your teaching. How else would you know when you need to adapt an activity, explain something that is unclear, or make any other adjustment to your planned lesson?

Excellence and Enjoyment: A Strategy for Primary Schools clearly links assessment with planning, learning and achievement:

> *Good-quality assessment is essential for planning children's learning, based on their performance, so that they are stretched to achieve to their full potential.*
>
> (DfES, 2003, p22)

The assessment of a child's progress in all the subjects of the National Curriculum is a demanding task. However, by carefully considering what is to be assessed and for what purpose, collecting the right evidence and considering it alongside other information known about the child, reasonable judgements can be made about the learning that has taken place.

Consider some features of the underlying structure of a typical lesson:

- there are learning objectives;
- there is input involving questioning by the teacher and engagement of the children in activities which enable them to achieve the learning objectives;
- there is assessment of achievement;
- there is feedback on the assessment.

REFLECTIVE TASK

Think of a classroom activity at school in terms of the four bullet points above. Write down the learning that occurred. Now consider, how do you know that the learning occurred? How sure can you be? What other evidence might you need to be able to make an informed judgement? This is important because learning in schools tends to be structured in schemes of work, with one lesson going on from where the last finished. If the children's learning has been faulty, or incomplete, their subsequent learning will be adversely affected.

As you will read, AfL takes each of the bullets and focuses on making each an effective tool for learning.

Section 2: Why assess?

Assessment has different forms and purposes. You will have heard of such tests as the Key Stage National Tests, GCSEs or QCA tests. This kind of assessment is called summative assessment and usually takes place at the end of a school year or key stage. These are formal assessments *of* learning; they have well-established grading and reporting procedures linked to them. The results of summative testing inform not only teachers but parents, members of the senior leadership team, governors, the local authority and government. This form of assessment contributes to the wider monitoring of standards as well as to the judgement of the progress of individual children.

In this chapter we are focusing on assessment *for* learning, or formative assessment. In the classroom, formative assessment of individual children is made to ascertain the degree to which learning objectives have been met. Future teaching can then be tailored to the learning needs of each child. In the past this kind of assessment was undertaken solely by teachers. Children, however, have some understanding of what they do and do not know; they must be brought into the assessment process so that teaching activities can be modified to stretch them towards fulfilling their potential. The teacher and the child can both give feedback on the assessment with the teacher taking the lead as the 'expert' on what is needed to meet the learning objective. It is the child's task to achieve the learning objective. Research by the Gillingham Partnership Formative Assessment Project 2000–2001 (Clarke, McCallum and Lopez-Charles, 2001; Clarke and McCallum, 2001a, 2001b) has demonstrated that this approach increases children's learning.

So assessment in the classroom has several functions.

- **It enables each child to learn more effectively because he/she is given feedback that is targeted on individual needs and is meaningful.**
- **It enables the teacher to teach more effectively because focused information is produced on each child. Those who need extra support are identified as well as those who need more challenging work.**
- **Teachers are able to give parents detailed information on their child's progress.**
- **Should a child move school, accurate records of progress and attainment can be forwarded to ease transition and prevent regression in learning.**
- **School leadership teams will have evidence on which to base targets aimed at whole-school improvement.**
- **Government, both local and national, will be able to assess the performance of individual schools and identify where the best of good practice is to be found. This practice can then be disseminated with the aim of increasing overall school improvement.**

Section 3: Forms of assessment

You have been introduced to formative and summative assessment. These can be thought of as part of the same continuum.

Formative ──▶ Summative

Figure 4.1 Assessment continuum (1)

Much formative assessment will be **informal**. For example, the teacher as part of a quick-fire mental starter asks children in a Year 4 class to write on their ro-ro boards the answers to multiplications in the 7 × table. When the children show their boards, the teacher can quickly assess whether individuals, a group or the whole class need to revisit that table. Informal assessment comes to the left of the assessment continuum.

Figure 4.2   Assessment continuum (2)

As part of your school experience you will be asked to evaluate your lessons. This will take the form of written reflection, usually within the structure of the lesson plan. Teachers also evaluate their lessons. This can take many forms and constitutes the recording section of this chapter. For the moment suffice it to say that **evaluative** assessments are informal but are recorded to inform future planning. So they appear on the assessment continuum to the right of informal assessment.

Figure 4.3   Assessment continuum (3)

As has been said, assessment must be focused on individual children's needs and abilities. Many children will be enabled by having individual targets within the structure of class lessons based on learning objectives and differentiated activities and tasks. However, there will be some children who need more than this. The Primary Strategy (2003, 4.5) states that *increasing the focus... will be the single most important force in mainstreaming (without diluting) the support that is given to pupils with special educational needs*. When individual assessment reveals that further assessment is needed to identify a particular educational need, **diagnostic** tests are carried out. These tests are summative in the sense that the results from them will inform stakeholders outside the classroom, for example parents, the senior management team, etc. They are, however, also formative in that strategies will be put in place to enable the child to close the gap between his/her achievement and class learning objectives. So diagnostic tests can be placed in the middle of the continuum.

Figure 4.4   Assessment continuum (4)

Occasionally teachers administer interim tests to their classes, such as table tests, spelling tests, end of project/half-termly/termly tests and past test papers for National Tests and QCA tests. These are not formal tests in so far as the results will not be published. The results will be used to identify areas of development for individual children, a group of children or the class as a whole so that gaps in knowledge and understanding can be addressed before the children sit their summative tests in which they will receive grades. However, these class tests are clearly summative in nature. So they are positioned on the assessment continuum just to the left of the national standardised tests which are truly summative.

Informal   Evaluative   Diagnostic   Class tests   National tests

Formative   Summative

Figure 4.5   Assessment continuum (5)

PRACTICAL TASK PRACTICAL TASK **PRACTICAL TASK** PRACTICAL TASK **PRACTICAL TASK**

Consider a recent module you have undertaken at university, school or college. Draw an assessment continuum and position on it the assessments you undertook. Which assessments were most useful to you? Which assessments were of most use to the wider society? Can you draw any conclusions?

Section 4: Assessment for learning

Assessment for Learning is the process of seeking and interpreting evidence for use by learners and their teachers to decide where the learners are in their learning, where they need to go and how best to get there.

(Assessment Reform Group, 2002)

The purpose of AfL is to raise achievement. As discussed in Section 2, it is now recognised by government that children construct their own learning. Therefore they need to be included in the assessment of their learning and take ownership for it. If children understand what it is they are learning, and how far along that learning journey they have travelled, with help from their teachers they will be able to complete the journey.

Arising from their research, the Assessment Reform Group (2002) have identified ten principles for AfL.

1. *AfL is part of effective planning.* Planning, including assessment, should be focused on learning objectives but should not be rigid. There should be opportunities for emerging ideas and skills to be fostered and assessed. How children and teachers are to assess learning should be fully integrated into lesson planning.
2. *AfL focuses on how students learn*. Children should be encouraged to understand that how they learn is as important as what they learn.
3. *AfL is central to classroom practice*. Teachers should become aware that much of what they do is assessment. Activities, observation and questioning are all directed towards providing information on which teachers can make informed judgements about the learning that is taking place.
4. *AfL is a key professional skill.* Analysing and interpreting verbal and visual information and giving appropriate feedback to learners are key skills. Opportunities must be given to trainees and teachers to develop these.
5. *AfL is sensitive and constructive*. Feedback, whether marks, grades or comments, can result in feelings of confusion, anxiety, guilt and failure that will affect a child's confidence and enthusiasm. Teachers should devise means of giving constructive and sensitive feedback.

6. *AfL fosters motivation*. Research by the Assessment Reform Group demonstrated that children's motivation was raised when they felt in control of their learning and could choose how to improve their work. Assessment methods should embrace children's enthusiasm for learning and need for autonomy by promoting progress and achievement rather than failure.

7. *AfL promotes understanding of goals and criteria*. Learners need to understand what it is they are trying to achieve. Understanding and commitment to learning are enhanced when children and teachers have mutually understood goals, ways of achieving them and clear criteria for success.

8. *AfL help learners know how to improve*. Teachers should give children direction in how to build on their strengths and address their area for development, and provide opportunities for them to do so.

9. *AfL develops the capacity for self-assessment*. This is an essential life skill. As adults we are independent learners of knowledge, skills and understanding. Children must be given the opportunity and guidance to reflect on their work and develop skills of self-assessment to move from being dependent to independent learners.

10. *AfL recognises all educational achievement*. Achievement in all areas of education, within school and outside, should be recognised and celebrated. All learners should have their efforts recognised.

Section 5: AfL in practice

To put AfL into practice in the classroom the ten principles above can be concentrated into the following four areas:

- sharing learning goals;
- using effective questioning techniques;
- peer and self-assessment;
- using marking and feedback strategies.

Sharing learning goals

The learning objective (sometimes called a learning intention or learning goal) is what a teacher plans children will know, understand or be able to do at the end of a lesson or project. The activities planned will enable the children to fulfil that learning objective. By the teacher sharing the learning objective, the children know the point of the lesson. As they are the ones doing the learning, much of the responsibility for its achievement is passed to them. The objective also gives direction as to where most effort should be made. For example, if the learning objective is 'to apply the use of multiplication tables to everyday problems', most effort should not be placed on the use of description of the settings to these problems. However, it would be different if the learning objective was 'to use adjectives effectively to describe settings'. Lastly, the learning objective generates key points that the children need to understand as steps towards its successful achievement, known as success criteria. This encourages self-evaluation.

To share learning objectives effectively with the children, the teacher should:

- have the learning objective written where all the children can see it;
- share it with the children, using child-friendly language;
- discuss with the children what they will be able to do as a result of the lesson;
- identify the *success criteria* that will enable the children and you to know when they achieve the learning objective and involve the children in producing them;
- ensure that children know what these criteria are by writing them down or reading them back to you;
- tell the children the reasons for the learning objective. This should be related to everyday life or further learning. This is sometimes termed an 'aside' and is given verbally, as it would be too time-consuming to write down.

Many teachers now use WALT (We are learning to . . .) to express a learning objective and WILF (What I am looking for . . .) to express success criteria. Research by Shirley Clarke (2003) has demonstrated that linking these acronyms to characters, such as animals, confuses some children. She suggests keeping language simple and focused and recommends such phrases as *We are learning to . . .*, *Remember to . . .* or *What you need to do to achieve this is . . . .*

It is important to remember that the aim of AfL is the promotion of a learning culture where learning can be transferred to solve problems. This means that learning must not be identified with activities. Activities are the vehicles of learning, not the learning itself. Therefore we should be using language such as that given above rather than 'Today we are going to play a game to find out about multiples.'

Effective AfL strategy demands that learning objectives and success criteria should be closely linked. The language used for both should refer to learning, thinking, knowing and using skills. Here are some examples to clarify what we mean.

- Learning objective: We are learning how to draw an object so that it has a 3-dimensional appearance.
- Success criteria: What I am looking for are drawings that show you have *looked carefully* at the object and used *different hardnesses of pencils* to create a 3-dimensional effect.

PRACTICAL TASK PRACTICAL TASK **PRACTICAL TASK** PRACTICAL TASK **PRACTICAL TASK**

Are learning goals/intentions/objectives being used in your school experience classroom? Are the children being encouraged to use success criteria?

If they are, assess their effect on the children's learning.

If they are not, what would your success criteria be to judge the effectiveness of the lesson? Assess the work of some children by your success criteria. Would the children's learning have been enhanced if your success criteria had been used?

Using effective questioning techniques

Research by the author (Raiker, 2002) has shown that most questions asked by teachers are closed. Teachers often have one answer in mind when asking a question and are looking for children to confirm their own thinking. AfL encourages teachers to move away, where possible, from closed questioning to open-ended questions that require children to respond having thought more deeply about the way they understand ideas and concepts. In doing so they will have to demonstrate their use and understanding of subject specific language.

The QCA Website gives an illuminating example of the liberating effect of open-ended questioning in comparison with closed questioning. A teacher asks if 7 is a prime number, to which the answer is either 'Yes', 'No' or 'Er ... I don't know.' This gives little clue as to the child's thinking or depth of understanding. A right answer might have been a fortunate guess! In contrast, a response to the question 'Why is 7 a prime number?' will engage their thinking.

- **The children will have to recall the properties of prime numbers and judge whether these accord with the properties of 7.**
- **The children are more likely to use subject specific language, such as 'primes', 'factors', 'tables', 'products, 'multiply' etc.**
- **The children will have to explain their reasoning. This externalisation of thought processes will enable the teacher to ascertain the extent and depth of understanding.**

The QCA document *Using Assessment to Raise Achievement in Mathematics* suggests the following question introductions would be useful.

- *How can we be sure that ...?*
- *How would you explain ...?*
- *What does that tell us about ...?*
- *What is the same and what is different about ...?*
- *How do we know ...?*

(QCA, 2003: 9)

This list is not exhaustive. Such questions can be applied to any subject area.

It is interesting to note that the average response time to a question allowed by teachers before choosing a child to answer is about a second. This is not enough for most children to understand the language in which the question has been given, relate the question to their prior learning, select the prior learning which is going to enable them to formulate their reply, structure their reply and put their hands up. Some teachers find difficult the silence that occurs between a question being asked and a response being given, and will make that span of time as short as possible. However, there are various strategies that can be used to keep the quick thinkers engaged while giving others the time they need. The thumbs-up-close-to-the-chest strategy for children who have the answer works well. Slowly counting to 5 before asking for hands up is another. Research has demonstrated that about five seconds is a reasonable length of time for most children to construct responses to questions.

Peer and self-assessment

Self-assessment tackles children's feelings of failure, which we have seen is a significant inhibitor to learning. It does this by encouraging the children to judge their own work and not compare its quality, and hence themselves, with that of others. An integral aspect of the concept of ranking is failure.

AfL's approach includes introducing the children to the inevitability of finding difficulty in learning and giving them strategies to overcome these difficulties. We have already met the principal strategies – shared success criteria linked to shared learning objectives. With self-assessment, a child applies these to judge the quality of their own work. QCA has recommended that children need to:

- *reflect on their own work;*
- *be supported to admit problems without risk to self-esteem;*
- *be given time to work problems out.*

www.qca.org.uk/296.html

Then, with feedback from the teacher or another, children decide what has to be done to improve the quality of their work to meet the success criteria which will lead to the learning objective. Athletes use this approach regularly when they train to achieve their 'personal bests'.

One method of increasing children's understanding of how to use success criteria to improve work is to give them examples of other, preferably unknown, children's work that does or does not meet learning objectives. The children are then asked to decide what they would do to improve the work. Another advantage of this peer assessment is that children become aware that there is more than one way to improve work.

Of course, teachers must ensure the children know the meaning of self-assessment, or self-evaluation as it is sometimes termed. They can do this by having a list of self-help suggestions or prompts on display and referring to it throughout the lessons. This list could contain the following.

- *Don't worry or panic.*
- *Solving problems = learning.*
- *Read again, think it through.*
- *Ask a friend.*
- *Use class resources – number squares, dictionaries, etc.*
- *Ask an adult.*

(Clarke et al, 2001, p61)

Another important aspect of counteracting the fear of failure is sympathetic use of language. The Formative Assessment Project revealed that teachers became aware that, as a result of using explicit language to help children see difficulty as part of the learning process, their children stopped being afraid of making mistakes and were more able to admit to finding work difficult. In particular, children with special needs demonstrated increased confidence.

Using marking and feedback strategies

You will have realised by now that these four areas, of which marking and feedback is the last, interlink and are part of a whole approach. Feedback has two elements, oral and written. The written element is more commonly known as marking. Both oral and written feedback should be closely linked to learning goals and give clear direction to improvement. Giving a mark of 6 out of 10, or writing 'good work!' on a piece of writing, is no longer appropriate. Feedback should always include diagnostic comments so that the child knows how to improve a piece of work next time.

Feedback can be given to individuals, a group or to the class as a whole. However, it is not a one-way process. AfL needs children to respond to the feedback with positive comments on how that feedback reflects on their work and with suggestions for its improvement. This means that time must be built into the activities and plenaries of lessons for children to be encouraged to be reflective, communicative and responsive while the feedback is still relevant. For children to be able to reveal themselves in this way means that there has to be mutual trust between teachers and their classes. This should be part of the school's ethos but takes time to establish between teacher and child. The following guidelines applied systematically will enable effective feedback to be embedded in practice.

- **Find the positives about a child's work. Discussions on improvement are more likely to succeed if the child believes that he/she is on the way to achieving the learning objective.**
- **AfL is not about giving a child the complete solution as soon as he/she meets difficulties. By 'scaffolding' the child with appropriate support and prompts while he/she reflects and finds his/her own way forward the teacher will promote independent learning.**
- **If a child continually makes the same mistake following feedback, he/she should be encouraged to consider alternative solutions. Being repeatedly 'stuck' invites feelings of frustration and failure leading to decline in motivation.**
- **In working towards meeting individual success criteria, children should not be allowed to lose sight of the overall learning objective. Learning should not be compartmentalised, as can often be observed, for example, in the lack of transfer of skills learned in literacy lessons to creative writing. Having completed a worksheet, a child can know what an adjective is, but then not be able to use adjectives in writing a story.**
- **Oral feedback can be more effective than written feedback as it allows for further discussion and clarification.**

Recording

Although much formative assessment is made and kept in the teacher's mind, formal records will have to be kept for various purposes. Firstly, there is a legal requirement for individual attainment targets to be kept in each curriculum subject. Records of formative assessment inform the planning of future lessons based on individual children's learning. They provide evidence of what a child knows, understands and can do, and the progress the child has made. Analysis of formative records enables judgements to be made on target setting, gives information for reports to parents and the child's next teacher and/or school, and can form the basis of discussion with parents at consultation evenings. Formative records also enable teachers to make summative judgements for their teacher assessments. It is useful to remember that formative and summative assessments are closely connected. Summative assessment should be used formatively to support future learning. Your records of formative assessments will eventually be given to the class teacher so that the child's records on work covered and progress made can be updated. You can see that your records of formative assessment have a summative element too, in that they record work has been completed at a particular standard.

Different schools have different record keeping systems that all teachers in the school are expected to use. Some schools have sophisticated information management systems which can be used to record assessment data; others have more basic approaches. Having a record keeping system at school level ensures that all teachers are recording evidence in a similar way. This is essential for reliable judgements to be made on progress from year to year. In some cases, teachers will supplement these with their own systems. You may be given a record format to complete, or you may be expected to produce your own. Whatever you record, it is worth remembering that under the Freedom of Information Act 2000 parents can ask to look at any records kept on their child.

Field diary

A very useful and simple tool for recording the formative assessment that we do instinctively is a notebook. As you are teaching or working with the children, you will notice something. During the oral/mental starter of a numeracy lesson you notice that Simon has begun to reverse his 3s and 5s. In PE, Anne shows surprising eye/ball/hand control when practising netball throws. In science, Toby brings some insects he found near the pond in his garden. All these observations can be noted down during lessons and added to a more formal record later. Through such means you will achieve greater depth of understanding of individual children and be able to tailor more effectively your teaching to their needs.

Annotating your lesson plan

Another simple record of assessment is the lesson plan itself. Very quickly you note points that have surprised you about individual children's learning. Most children will learn as you have planned, because you will have differentiated your lessons according to their prior learning and abilities. However, there will be children who perform better than or not as well as you anticipated. Noting this down at the time ensures that these important pointers towards effective future planning and learning are not lost.

Tables

Records vary according to the nature of the learning goals. For example, records on multiple tables known can be very straightforward, as in Table 4.1 below.

Name		7/9	14/9	21/9	28/9	5/10	12/10			
James	ABBOT	5×6	8	10	6×3	5	8			
Eliza	BOLAN	8×9	10	9×8	10	M	M			
Michael	CORUS	6×7	9	10	7×3	7	10			
Nasreen	SINGH	6×4	7	9	10	7×5	6			
Alicia	WHITE	M	M	M	M	M	M			

Table 4.1   Grid for recording tables known

Here the number followed by an x is the table being learned. Single numbers are marks out of 10. M stands for 'mixed'. When children have shown they know all their tables, they have a weekly test of mixed tables to keep their skills sharp.

Simple grids like these can be created in any word processing package and can easily be adapted for different purposes.

Spreadsheets

A more sophisticated record can be created using a spreadsheet. There can be up to 65,536 rows and 256 columns in each worksheet, or page. Much detail can be stored on a spreadsheet. Also, with a spreadsheet information can be manipulated and extracted according to purpose. For example, the spreadsheet in Figure 4.6 has been created using Excel. The record charts the progress of a Year 4 class of children during a week working on fractions/decimals and percentages.

Group			DOB	SEN	Recgnise 04-Jan	Identify 2 fr 05-Jan	Link simple 06-Jan	Identify 2 de 07-Jan	Link f/d/p to £p/m&cm 08-Jan	11-Jan	12-
C	Joseph	Abbott	03/10/1997		A	A	A	A	A + TA		
A	Susan	Andress	06/06/1998	School Action Plus	Abs	Abs	R	R	R		
C	Tracey	Anson	26/09/1997		A	A	A	A	A		
C	Neil	Barton	11/12/1997		A	A + ext	A	A	R		
D	Lewis	Cocklow	15/12/1997		A + ext	A + ext	A + ext	A + ext	A + ext		
A	Diana	Collins	31/05/1998	Statement	R + TA	R + TA	R + TA	R + TA	R + TA		
D	Kurt	Geenlea	11/06/1998		A	A	A + ext	A + ext	A + ext		
B	Desmon	Hall	15/09/1997		A	A	A	WT	WT		
B	Reese	Handma	28/01/1998		A + TA	A + TA	A	A	A		
A	Christop	Jefferies	06/05/1998	School Action Plus	WT	WT	WT	ML	R		
B	Aman	Johni	01/07/1998		A + TA	A + TA	A + TA	A + TA	R		
D	Deena	Johnston	14/08/1998		Abs	A + ext	A	A + ext	A + ext		
C	Charles	Kiler	25/04/1998		A	A	A	ML	A		
A	Petra	Lewis	11/10/1997	School Action	A	A	WT	WT	WT		
D	George	Liddle	21/11/1997		A	A	A + ext	A + ext	A + ext		
D	Kristen	Michel	01/08/1998		A + ext	A + ext	A + ext	A + ext	A + ext		
D	Hadyn	Miles	13/04/1998		A + ext	A + ext	A + ext	A + ext	A + ext		

Figure 4.6   **Excel spreadsheet recording progress of Year 4 class**.

The teacher has a code:

A   achieved
WT   working towards
R   repeat
TA   working with teaching assistant support

ext   extension materials given
abs   absent
ML   music lesson

The codes can be chosen to fit the subject, but A, WT, R, TA and ext. or equivalent will be useful for most records.

The advantage of working electronically is that, once a master has been created, the basic structure of pages can be copied and pasted into new worksheets and so serve for other subjects and topics. Using the sort and filter tools, details on groups of children can also be extracted for analysis. There are many publications and websites that will guide you through the use of Excel. There will also be ICT specialists in your university or college whom you can ask for support if necessary.

Portfolios and e-portfolios

You might also find that your school has a portfolio for each child's work. A portfolio is a folder or box into which go examples of a child's achievements, a profile of personal issues, assessments and records. This forms the evidence used to write reports to parents. Your records and work with the children will feed into each child's portfolio. Growing interest is being shown in e-portfolios, and e-assessment. According to the British Educational Communications and Technology Agency (Becta), *within a few years, e-assessment and e-portfolios will be integral parts of modern learning and teaching* (Becta, 2006: 1). Priority 2 of Becta's e-strategy is to *ensure integrated online personal support for learners*. The intention is to *provide a personalised learning space for every learner that can encompass a personal portfolio*, and by 2007-2008 for every school and college to have a *personalised learning space with the potential to support e-portfolios...* (Becta, 2006, p2). Into an individual learner's e-portfolio would go pieces of writing, examples of mathematical problem solving, PowerPoint presentations of humanities projects, video clips of dance and drama, digital photographs, pieces of music, scanned artwork, details of assessments, CVs. The e-portfolio would grow over time, be amended and some items would be deleted. It will be able to be passed electronically wherever and whenever it is needed.

Reporting

There is a statutory requirement that schools send at least one written report out to parents each year. This report must cover:

- **a summary of the child's achievements over the year, including strengths and areas for development in all foundation stage or curriculum areas;**
- **comments on general progress;**
- **details of attendance;**
- **a revised IEP if appropriate;**
- **details of the arrangements the school will be making for parents to discuss their child's report with his/her teacher, the Special Educational Needs Co-ordinator (SENCO) and the head teacher;**
- **the results of any statutory assessment. These are the National Tests that take place at the end of Key Stages 1, 2 and 3.**

This is regarded as a minimum. End-of-year and half-termly reports are now common. Many schools include suggested targets, comments by the children on their progress and opportunities for parents to respond. Whatever the detail of their content, reports must be focused, constructive and clearly understood. Generalisations like 'Jenny has worked hard this year' are not very helpful. Parents will want to know how their children are achieving in terms of their perceived abilities. They will also want to know how well they are performing in relation to the class. It is to be hoped that the schools where you have your practical experiences of learning and teaching have held information evenings for parents on AFL and the philosophy that underpins it.

PRACTICAL TASK PRACTICAL TASK **PRACTICAL TASK** PRACTICAL TASK **PRACTICAL TASK**

Imagine you are a parent of a Year 3 child. Read the end-of-year report below on the child's achievement in history, taken from an actual report. Does it tell you what you want to know in terms of your child's abilities, progress and achievements? How could it be improved to reflect focused judgements on the child's learning?

Jane likes history and produces neat work with lovely pictures to illustrate her stories. She enjoyed writing about our trip to the museum and could describe varying aspects of the historical period we are studying.

Conclusion

AfL is central to good classroom practice. Research supports it and the DfES has acknowledged the importance of AfL to fostering the learning of all children: *Assessment for learning is a powerful tool for making sure that learning fits individual needs* (DfES, 2003, p39). Using AfL will enhance your teaching and enable more children to excel and enjoy.

Moving on

AfL is a key area of development in schools. Look for training events and conferences on this theme.

FURTHER READING   FURTHER READING   **FURTHER READING**

Assessment Reform Group (1999) *Assessment for Learning: Beyond the Black Box.* Cambridge: University of Cambridge School of Education. **http://www.qca.org.uk/ downloads/beyond_black_box2.pdf**

Becta (2006) Becta's view: E-assessment and e-portfolios. Coventry: British Educational Communications and Technology Agency. **http://ferl.becta.org.uk/content_files/acl/ resources/keydocs/Becta/e-assessment%20and%20e-portfolios.pdf**

Briggs, M., Martin, C., Woodfield, A. and Swatton, P. (2003) *Assessment for Learning and Teaching in Primary Schools*. Exeter: Learning Matters.

Clarke, S. (2001) *Unlocking Formative Assessment: Practical Strategies for Enhancing Pupils' Learning in the Primary Classroom.* London: Hodder & Stoughton.

Clarke, S. (2003) *Enriching Feedback in the Primary Classroom*. London: Hodder & Stoughton.

Clarke, S. (2005) *Formative Assessment in Action*. London: Hodder Murray.

DfES (2003) *Excellence and Enjoyment: A Strategy for Primary Schools.* London: DfES.

Gardner, J. (ed) (2006) *Assessment and Learning*. London: Paul Chapman.

McCallum, B. (2000) *Formative Assessment: Implications for Classroom Practice*. London: Institute of Education. Available via QCA website: **http://www.qca.org.uk/downloads/ formative(1).pdf**

Useful websites

QCA Assessment for Learning: **www.qca.org.uk/7659.html**
Assessment Reform Group: **www.assessment-reform-group.org/**
Association for Achievement and Improvement through Assessment (AAIA): **www.aaia.or-g.uk/index.htm**. This site has useful material including a booklet: *Primary Assessment Practice: Evaluation and Development Material.*

SECTION 2
MANAGEMENT, ORGANISATION AND DELIVERY

5
Foundations for learning: Early Years
Jennifer Lovesey

By the end of this chapter you should:

- recognise the role of the Foundation Stage;
- understand the content of the Foundation Stage curriculum;
- recognise the importance of practitioners' knowledge, skills and understanding of children in the Foundation Stage;
- understand how to plan, teach and assess for this phase of education;
- appreciate the value of play in children's learning;
- recognise the links between the Foundation Stage and the ECM agenda.

This chapter addresses the following Professional Standards for QTS: Q10, Q11, Q12, Q14

Introduction

Early Years education is widely recognised as the phase of care and education that precedes the start of statutory education in England. Children are required by law to attend school at the start of the term following their fifth birthday. For many children this means that they may start in a Reception class in either the autumn, spring or summer term of one academic year. Some children who have their birthday following the end of the spring term may not begin statutory education until the beginning of Key Stage 1. In reality, however, many children attend either a Reception class, Nursery class or a foundation unit on either a part-time or full-time basis during the year, or in some cases two years, prior to starting in Year 1. It is very important that early years teachers appreciate the fact that there may be children in a Reception class who may have just had their fourth birthday, as well as children who may be about to turn five. A good understanding of child development is therefore crucial to meeting the physical, intellectual, emotional and social needs of all the children in the class.

Since the introduction of the National Curriculum, there has been an increased understanding of the distinct nature of development and learning for children aged under five. Significant contributions from authors such as Bruce (2004), Moyles (2005) and Whitebread (2003), to name but a few, have helped to formulate a much more child-centred approach to teaching and learning in the Early Years.

The Foundation Stage

The first part of a child's life is known as 'birth to three' and this precedes the Foundation Stage. It has its own framework set out in *Birth to Three Matters* (DfES, 2002). The Foundation Stage was introduced in September 2000 and is a distinct phase of Early Years care and education that encompasses children aged from three years to the end of the Reception year. It has been the first point of the National Curriculum since 2003. The introduction of the Foundation Stage was generally warmly welcomed by those working with children in the Early Years. Prior to its introduction, teachers and other adults working within this age phase could refer to the National Curriculum for Key Stage 1. However, this was not always appropriate and there was always the concern that children were engaged in the types of activities that were not relevant to their stage of development.

The main document that supports the Foundation Stage is the *Curriculum Guidance for the Foundation Stage*, although this is set to change in 2008, with the introduction of the Early Years Foundation Stage. (This will be discussed in more detail later in the chapter.) This guidance is underpinned by the following 12 principles that reflect the increase in the depth of knowledge and understanding regarding how young children develop and learn.

> 1. *Effective education requires both a relevant curriculum and practitioners who understand and are able to implement the curriculum requirements.*
> 2. *Effective education requires practitioners who understand that children develop rapidly during the Early Years – physically, intellectually, emotionally and socially.*
> 3. *Practitioners should ensure that all children feel included, secure and valued.*
> 4. *Early Years experience should build on what children already know and can do.*
> 5. *No child should be excluded or disadvantaged.*
> 6. *Parents and practitioners should work together.*
> 7. *To be effective, an Early Years curriculum should be carefully structured.*
> 8. *There should be opportunities for children to engage in activities planned by adults and also those that they plan or initiate themselves.*
> 9. *Practitioners must be able to observe and respond appropriately to children.*
> 10. *Well-planned, purposeful activity and appropriate intervention by practitioners will engage children in the learning process.*
> 11. *For children to have rich and stimulating experiences, the learning environment should be well planned and well organised.*
> 12. *Above all, effective learning and development for young children requires high-quality care and education by practitioners.*
>
> (QCA, 2000a, p11)

As can be seen from these principles, there is an emphasis on learning through activities that have been both child and adult initiated in environments that are stimulating and which provide structure. There is also an emphasis on the opportunities that are provided through play. It is important that practitioners are familiar with these principles, as they form the basis for what happens in practice.

There are some terms that are used that are specific to this phase of education.

- *Setting refers to Local authority nurseries, nursery centres, playgroups, pre-schools, accredited childminders in approved childminding networks, or schools in the*

Area of learning	Areas and aspects of learning	Links with KS1 subjects
Personal, social and emotional development (PSED)	1. Dispositions and attitudes 2. Self-confidence and self-esteem 3. Making relationships 4. Behaviour and self-control 5. Self-care 6. Sense of community	PSHCE
Communication, language and literacy (CLL)	1. Language for communication 2. Language for thinking 3. Linking sounds and letters 4. Reading 5. Writing 6. Handwriting	English
Mathematical development (MD)	1. Numbers as labels and for counting 2. Calculating 3. Shape, space and measures	Mathematics
Knowledge and understanding of the world (KUW)	1. Exploration and investigation 2. Designing and making skills 3. Information and communication technology 4. A sense of time 5. A sense of place 6. Cultures and beliefs	Science DT ICT History Geography RE, PSHCE
Physical development (PD)	1. Movement 2. A sense of space 3. Health and bodily awareness 4. Using equipment 5. Using tools and materials.	PE
Creative development (CD)	1. Exploring media and materials 2. Music 3. Imagination 4. Responding to experiences and expressing and communicating ideas	Art and Design Music Dance/Drama Drama/Dance

Table 5.1. The six areas of learning

independent, private or voluntary sectors, and maintained schools (QCA, 2000a). This
means that children can be receiving a similar experience in terms of care and education
as each setting works within the framework of the *Curriculum Guidance for the
Foundation Stage*.
- *Practitioner refers to, the adults who work with children in the settings, whatever their
qualifications...* (QCA, 20000a). This means that the person who has QTS in an Early
Years setting is not differentiated in terms of title. The role of the Early Years
professional will be discussed later.

The Curriculum

The curriculum is divided into six areas of learning, although there is an acknowledgement that one learning activity may cover more than one area of learning. The
six areas of learning are:

- personal, social and emotional development (PSED);
- communication, language and literacy (CLL);
- mathematical development (MD);
- knowledge and understanding of the world (KUW);
- physical development (PD);
- creative development (CD).

The abbreviations in the brackets are useful as you may often see these on planning sheets.

The curriculum looks quite different from the more distinct subject areas of the
National Curriculum for older children.

A brief overview of each area is given in Table 5.1. (The areas and aspects of
learning are taken from the guidance for planning in the Foundation Stage.)

The table on page 65 only provides an overview of the curriculum and it is necessary to read further for a full understanding of the content of each area.

Stepping stones and Early Learning Goals

Because the *Curriculum Guidance for the Foundation Stage* is for children within
quite a wide age range and because it is acknowledged that within this range there
could be vast differences in terms of levels of development, each area of learning is
divided up into what are known as stepping stones. These are colour coded and
while there are no specific ages linked to each stepping stone, it is nonetheless
generally accepted that the younger children are likely to 'fit' the guidance for the
yellow and blue stepping stones while children nearer the end of the Foundation
Stage are more likely to 'fit' the green stepping stones and the Early Learning Goals
(ELGs) (QCA, 2000a).

The stepping stones demonstrate a continuation of progress within each area of
learning and cover three main areas:

- **stepping stones;**
- **possible learning activities;**
- **what the practitioner needs to do.**

The example in Table 5.2 is taken from the Communication, Language and Literacy area of learning.

Stepping stone (green)	Examples of what children might do	What does the practitioner need to do?
Know that information can be retrieved from books and computers.	Yen asks the practitioner to read the ingredients for making Chinese dumplings.	Use books, other reference material and computers with the children to answer their questions and provide instructions.

Table 5.2 Example of a stepping stone
Source: QCA 2000a, p63

From these examples, it can be seen that the planning for specific learning activities, as well as any decision regarding the resources used, is the choice of the setting. Many settings have many years' experience of teaching very young children and provide contexts that they know produce optimum conditions for learning.

Planning

In October 2001, the QCA published guidance for 'planning for learning in the foundation stage'. In this guidance there are examples of long-, medium- and short-term planning. This guidance emphasises the recognition that certain areas of learning may have more of an emphasis at certain times of the year than at other times. For example, there may be more of an emphasis on personal, social and emotional development in the autumn term, as this reflects the developmental needs of the children as they settle into a new environment with new routines, adults and experiences.

Planning in the Foundation Stage tends to begin with a topic or theme that is closely linked to the experiences, interests and developmental needs of the children. Practitioners may often begin with a theme that focuses on the children themselves. This then provides a common point of reference for all children. The six areas of learning can then be planned around this theme. However, it is also important to remember that as with all planning, the starting points will be the learning objectives, rather than the activity that is being experienced or resource that is available. It should also be remembered that planning for children in the Foundation Stage is often developmental. This means that short-term planning, that is the week-to-week, or even day-to-day plans, may be influenced by the ongoing, formative assessment of the children. This might mean that adjustments may be necessary for individuals or groups of children.

Examples of planning

Long-term plans

Practitioners should aim to have a long-term view of the knowledge, skills and understanding that they anticipate children in the Foundation Stage should be learning. The *Curriculum Guidance for the Foundation Stage* helps both with long-term and more immediate planning. The supplementary guidance on planning includes, *areas and aspects of learning for the foundation stage*. These aspects provide a numerical code for each of the areas of learning so that they can be 'mapped' across planning for the whole year. The national Literacy and Numeracy Strategies should also be a point of reference for planning over the course of a term or even the whole year.

Medium-term plan

This plan would probably be for a half term. The ideas in Table 5.3 are examples of what could be included and are by no means exhaustive.

Theme: **Myself** Autumn Term (first half)			
Area of learning	Themes	Broad examples of activities	Specific examples
PSED	My family My friends My pets My toys	Circle time activities, talking about families, sharing experiences	Talk about favourite toy
CLL	My name Names of people in my family	Recognising own name Beginning to form the letters for own name Recognise other family names, Mum, Dad, etc.	Bring name card to pocket for register
MD	Mathematics linked to my home – people, rooms, pets	Maths linked to people in family counting, sizes, shapes	Counting the number of people in my family
KUW	Finding out about myself Using my senses to find out	Using a range of objects and tools to explore using the senses	Magnifying glasses, different materials in sand tray, sound lotto
PD	My body	Identifying and naming parts of the body	Talcum powder footprints/ handprints
CD	My home and family	Recreating home life Representations of family Musical representations	Role play area Family portraits Songs about 'myself', e.g. 'I've got a body.'

Table 5.3   Medium-term plan

From this overview, it is now possible to generate a weekly plan that incorporates more detail for each of the areas of learning.

Weekly plan

Learning intention	Context	Specific knowledge, skills and understanding
PSED, Talk freely about homes and communities. Links to: CLL	Circle times – talk about the members of their family, incorporate home experiences into the discussion	Speaking and listening Taking turns Being part of a group
CLL Begin to recognise some familiar words Links to PSED	Bring name card to pocket for register	Visual discrimination Memory of routines
MD Say and use number names in familiar contexts Links to CLL	Counting the number of people in my family	One to one correspondence Comparisons Cardinal aspect of number
KUW Links to CD, PD	Different tactile experiences – clay	Using senses Describing Fine motor skills – manipulation
PD Links to CLL	Talcum powder footprints/ handprints	Using senses Describing textures Naming parts of the body
CD Links to CLL, PSED	Role play area – home corner Family portraits – paintings Songs about 'myself', e.g. 'I've got a body.'	Recreating roles Use of objects to represent Fine motor control Observing (features) Spatial awareness Awareness of rhythm and rhyme Group cohesion

Table 5.4   Weekly plan

Differentiation

It is important to recognise that there could be a wide range of abilities within any group of children in the Foundation Stage. Mention has already been made of the possibility of nearly a year's age difference between children and the potential effects that this may have on a child's maturational level in a Reception class. There may also be children who have the cognitive ability to learn certain concepts but may not possess the levels of concentration that would enable them to sustain this type of thinking for long periods of time. Consideration needs to be given to those children who have been identified as being particularly able in one or more areas of learning.

There also needs to be a consideration of children who may have an identified SEN. The introduction of a Common Assessment Framework, closely linked to the ECM agenda, now helps to provide early information regarding any perceived need for individual children. A child's needs may then be provided for within the context of the setting, or in liaison with other agencies such as speech and language therapists or educational psychologists.

An acknowledgement of the range of individual factors is important when planning the curriculum. It may be an idea to have a column on a plan where details for provision for individual children can be noted. In addition to this, planning ought to reflect the recognition that groups of children, who have not been identified with a particular need, also require careful consideration. Sometimes, inclusion of learning intentions that reflect the progressive nature of the stepping stones and ELGs, will provide information regarding differentiation.

Learning intention	Context	Differentiation
MD:1 Count an irregular arrangement of up to 10 objects (green stepping stone) Links to: **KUW: 1** **PD: 5**	**Outdoor area** (Paired activity) Digging area – tell children we need to check how many of each tool we have. Put tools into groups. (classification) Model counting activity as necessary. Children count amounts and tell practitioner who records this.	JL – needs helps to hold tools as she counts. NR, CB – encourage very careful 1–1 counting RA, ST, DM – already secure counting to 10, extend to amounts above this Children who are able to record amounts can do so on a clipboard.
Assessment opportunities Checklist of children who are secure with this concept. Note ability to count accurately.	**Resources** Selection of trowels, pots, dibbers, plant labels, etc.	
Next steps: *This would be completed after the activity.*		

Table 5.5 **Planning for a practitioner-led activity – from a medium-term plan that is focused on the theme of growing**

This activity plan shows that the differentiation is through both the possible different adult support needed, and potentially different outcomes.

Assessment

Formative assessment

This reflects assessment for learning and is part of the 'plan, teach, assess' cycle that you may already be familiar with. Practitioners constantly monitor children's learning, either through planned observation, or through incidental occurrences in the setting. The information that parents and other adults provide can also be extremely useful in developing an understanding of a child's progress in one or more areas of learning. As children of this age tend not to produce pages of written work or mathematical calculations, there must be methods for recording what they know, understand and can do. One example of this might be a practitioner scribing a child's story. Children often have wonderful imaginations, but lack the cognitive skills linked to using words to represent ideas, as well as the necessary fine motor skills linked to writing. Another example might be the use of sticky notes to note incidents that occur but have not necessarily been planned as part of an assessment.

The information generated by formative assessment should form the basis for discussion among practitioners in the setting to determine the next steps for children and their learning. In 2005 the QCA published a practitioner's guide to aid this, *Seeing steps in children's learning*. The document, along with an accompanying DVD, provides examples of children and where they are in terms of the stepping stones or ELGs. The next steps in terms of learning are then described.

Summative assessment – Early Learning Goals (ELG)

These are the sets of criteria that most children are expected to reach by the end of the Foundation Stage. Some children with particular special needs may not meet the goals while others may show evidence of skills, knowledge and understanding that extends beyond the goals.

Children's achievements, as defined by the criteria of the ELGs, are recorded in a booklet known as the Foundation Stage Profile. Practitioners use a variety of methods, primarily observation, to assess children and enter this information on the profile. This information is shared with parents and may be used to generate a further report at the end of the Foundation Stage. Information from the profiles is also forwarded to the local authority.

One example of an Early Learning Goal is, 'Orders numbers up to 10' for mathematical development. Another is, 'Asks questions about why things happen and how things work', for knowledge and understanding of the world. From these two examples, it is possible to see that some goals may be more straightforward in terms of assessment than others. Experienced practitioners are constantly observing and assessing children, as well as ensuring that learning objectives reflect assessment opportunities against both the stepping stones and the ELGs. Guidance for assessment according to the ELGs is provided in a separate document that gives examples of children's achievements that demonstrate that particular goals have been met, or that children at the end of the Foundation Stage are achieving according to the criteria from the stepping stones.

PRACTICAL TASK PRACTICAL TASK **PRACTICAL TASK** PRACTICAL TASK **PRACTICAL TASK**

Make a list of the different ways of recording children's achievements. This may include children's own representations of this, but may also include the practitioner's methods.

The significance of play in children's learning

Children in Early Years education spend a great deal of their time in a setting playing. Some people, including parents and some adults involved in education, sometimes find it difficult to understand that play is the context in which young children learn. Over seventy years ago, Vygotsky acknowledged the importance of play in the development of thought processes:

> *The child moves forward essentially through play activity. Only in this sense can play be considered a leading activity that determines the child's development.* (Vygotsky, 1978, p103)

A more recent advocate for the inclusion of a play-based curriculum is Tina Bruce. She devised a list of 'features of free-flow play'. These include a focus on the motivational factors involved and the deep concentration that is often involved in play. There are also features that describe differing levels of social interaction as well as the role that play has in learning. Bruce asserts that if seven or more features are present *we are likely to see effective learning* (Bruce, 2004, p149).

A child engaging in a self-chosen play activity can be deeply involved in the development of concepts, some of which may have been introduced through a context that was led by the adult. For example, the practitioner may have been working with a group of children on ordering numbers to ten, as part of the mathematical development area of learning. Children may then play at vets in the role play area. If each child has to take a numbered ticket to wait their turn to see the 'vet', this helps to reinforce the concept of ordering numbers in a relevant context. The skill of the practitioner involves seeing these learning opportunities and providing the resources to facilitate them.

Sometimes the practitioner plans to become involved in play activities and sometimes plans to observe the play in order to inform those activities that are adult-led.

As children progress through the Foundation Stage, they become more able to develop knowledge and understanding in contexts that are not always play based. The ability to think in more abstract ways starts to become apparent and the concrete experience that was previously needed to embed the learning in a meaningful context often becomes less necessary for many children. However, it is important to recognise when individual children are ready for this transition; the introduction of more 'formal' types of learning activities too soon can lead to children becoming less motivated and bored. This can then lead to behavioural problems which may require a different type of teacher input. Equally, those children who are clearly ready to move to the types of activities that require more abstract thought, and perhaps formal recording of understanding, need to be provided with this opportunity so that they are motivated by challenging and enjoyable learning situations.

The role of the practitioner

Practitioners need to ensure that interactions with children, either through adult- or child-led activities, should be effective and meaningful. Constantly asking questions of children is not necessarily an effective way of taking their learning forward. Often, a more conversational approach that engages children in a dialogue can be more fruitful. Adults who commentate on the activities of children are supplying the vocabulary that young children may not possess, but may then learn through the context of the activity. Where children are trying to solve problems, adults can offer possible solutions that children may then select from based on their knowledge of what they think might work.

Allowing children time to work through their ideas is important. We want to encourage sustained concentration in young learners. Providing opportunities that allow children to follow something through to its natural conclusion aids this.

Children often have very clear ideas about the direction that their activity is going in. Adults need to recognise the appropriate opportunities for scaffolding the learning that can occur, or provide opportunities for children's more able peers to provide this.

The learning environment

Children in the Foundation Stage learn in an environment that reflects the principles of learning through play. You are unlikely to see as many tables and chairs in a Foundation Stage setting as you might see in a Key Stage 1 class. Equally, you are unlikely to see a variety of exercise books for children to record their work in.

Edgington (2004) suggests, *A list of provision for Foundation Stage children should include the following if children are to have access to a broad, exciting curriculum.*

For the indoor environment:

- *a comfortable self-contained book area;*
- *sand (wet and dry) and water;*
- *malleable materials (e.g. clay);*
- *a graphics area (for early attempts at writing);*
- *role play areas;*
- *music and movement opportunities;*
- *small and large construction materials;*
- *specific mathematical and scientific equipment;*
- *interactive displays;*
- *a creative workshop area.*

For the outdoor environment:

- *a defined quiet area;*
- *spaces to be active and/or noisy;*
- *places to hide in;*
- *shady areas to shelter from the sun;*
- *areas to explore natural interests.*

(Edgington, 2004, p132–135)

PRACTICAL TASK PRACTICAL TASK PRACTICAL TASK PRACTICAL TASK PRACTICAL TASK

1. Use these lists to investigate the provision in a Foundation Stage setting. Does the setting provide for all of these areas? If not, what do you think are the reasons for this (for example, space, resources, number of adults)?

2. Observe one child's use of the provision. Does the child spend a long time at one activity or does he or she move frequently from one activity to another?

Every Child Matters

The Early Years curriculum has clear links to the ECM agenda.

The five outcomes for children are:

1. being healthy;
2. staying safe;
3. enjoying and achieving;
4. making a positive contribution;
5. achieving social and economic well-being.

The first two outcomes have very close links to the PSED and PD areas of learning. Children are involved in learning that focuses on their health and well-being. There are well-planned opportunities for children to engage in discussions of, and activities linked to, aspects of their lives that relate to their physical and mental health. The teaching and learning processes promote positive attitudes to these two outcomes. The principles clearly focus on the need for children to feel safe, secure, valued and that they are the starting point for their own learning.

Outcome 3 links to the desire for each child to realise his/her own potential. The stepping stones provide a framework for practitioners so that children are provided with appropriate challenges that match their abilities. The skills of the practitioner enable children to engage in high quality learning experiences that enable them to make progress through this stage of their learning.

Outcomes 4 and 5 may be aspects that will be more evident later, although there are opportunities for even very young children, given the right circumstances, to make positive contributions. One example of this could be making up baskets of food at Harvest Festival, or filling a shoebox with gifts that can be sent to less fortunate children. These types of activities also engage the participation of the parents and help to develop relationships between home and school.

Some settings are very explicit in identifying where the outcomes for ECM occur in terms of planning. You may be required to write this on lesson plans, so it is a good idea to look for further connections between the outcomes and the principles and content of the Foundation Stage Curriculum.

New developments in Early Years education

In 2008, *Birth to Three Matters* and the *Foundation Stage* will be replaced by a single framework called the *Early Years Foundation Stage* (EYFS). This single framework will cover the care and education of children from 0–5 years. Training will be provided to settings to enable practitioners to work within the new framework.

The areas of learning will change to:

1. personal, social and emotional development;
2. communication, language and literacy;
3. problem solving, reasoning and numeracy;
4. knowledge and understanding of the world;
5. physical development;
6. creative development.

The main change is to area 3, which is currently mathematical development.

The EYFS takes the outcomes for ECM as well as the Children Act 2004 as the starting point for the framework. This reinforces the position in Early Years education that the needs of the child, rather than the content of 'subjects', is the primary consideration for this phase of learning.

Conclusion

Teaching in Early Years settings can be very rewarding, if not tiring! The notion that because the children are very young (many may not be of statutory school age), less consideration needs to be given to teaching and learning, is not a valid viewpoint. The distinct nature of learning in this phase requires teachers who are highly skilled in the pedagogy of early learning.

Moving on

Early Years education is the focus of considerable interest and is constantly developing. It is important to keep abreast of new developments in both the curriculum and the wider context. As the Every Child Matters principles, the Common Assessment Framework and the new Early Years Foundation Stage are implemented you will be involved with a wide range of other professionals. It is important to understand their roles in relation to you as a teacher and to the children whose education and well being is increasingly seen as a shared responsibility. There are many active groups and networks for Early Years practitioners. Look for these in your local area and take advantage of opportunities to understand the contribution of all those involved with young children.

FURTHER READING   FURTHER READING   **FURTHER READING**

Baldock, P., Fitzgerald, D. and Kay, J. (2005) *Understanding Early Years Policy.* London: Paul Chapman.

Bruce, T. (2004) *Developing Learning in Early Childhood Education*. London: Paul Chapman.

Cheminais, R. (2006) *Every Child Matters: A Practical guide for Teachers.* London: David Fulton.

DfES (2007) *Statutory Framework for the Early Years Foundation Stage*. London: DfES.

Edgington, M. (2004) *The Foundation Stage Teacher in Action: Teaching 3, 4 and 5 year olds.* London: Paul Chapman.

Moyles, J. (ed.) (2005) *The Excellence of Play,* 2nd edn. Buckingham: Open University Press.

Pugh, G. and Duffy, B. (2006) *Contemporary Issues in the Early Years* London: Sage.

QCA (2000) *The Curriculum Guidance for the Foundation Stage*. London: QCA.

Whitebread, D. (ed.) (2003) *Teaching and Learning in the Early Years,* 2nd edn. London: Routledge.

Useful websites

www.everychildmatters.gov.uk
www.standards.dfes.gov.uk
www.surestart.gov.uk

6
An introduction to children's learning
Ray Potter

> **By the end of this chapter you should;**
>
> - **have an understanding of what constitutes 'learning';**
> - **know that children may think about concepts in very different ways to adults;**
> - **have an overview of some of the psychological theories that are applied to teaching and learning.**
>
> This chapter addresses the following Professional Standards for QTS:
> **Q14; Q18**

You will know by now from your time in school that teachers do very much more than simply teach children. You may have seen them act as accountants, social workers and even surrogate parents. Indeed, with so much going on in the modern primary classroom it is easy to forget sometimes that the fundamental task of any teacher is *to organise learning*. This chapter will help you to understand how children learn and to manage learning more effectively in the classroom. This awareness is fundamental, not only to skilful teaching, but also as an aid to behaviour management.

But firstly, it has to be admitted that human learning is highly complex and far from fully understood. Indeed it is probable that this entire book could be filled with what we don't know about learning! Take a moment to write down what you understand by *learning.*

A fairly simple but enduring psychological definition of learning is: 'Relatively permanent changes in behaviour or in potential for behaviour that result from *experience.*' (Lefrançois, 1999, p41)

Of course when psychologists refer to behaviour they include not only overt, that is observable, actions but also changes in thought patterns that are internal or covert. The keywords in this definition are *relatively permanent* and *experience*.

Although it is the field of psychology which has provided the clearest insights into children's learning it is worth bearing in mind that psychology is unusual in several respects. First, of course everyone is an amateur psychologist and secondly, unlike the physical sciences, people form part of their own data. Therefore we can never be too exact and many statements remain problematic.

Inevitably over the years numerous theories have been advanced to explain how children learn. Perhaps the two most widely regarded are behaviourism and cognitive approaches. Each, in its own way, has something to offer to the prac-tising teacher and each views humans in a fundamentally different way.

Behaviourism

If you recall that learning involves a relatively permanent change in *behaviour*, then it is not surprising that for much of the twentieth century psychologists sought to understand learning by looking at actual behaviours. The theory of behaviourism is modelled firmly on the physical sciences and, although particularly popular in America until the 1960s, it has had an enduring influence on the British primary classroom. According to behavioural theory we should seek to rid psychology of words such as mind, feeling, sensation and instead concentrate on what can be readily observed and measured. Behaviourists claim that we are what we are, not because of innate intelligence or genetic factors, but solely due to our life experi-ences. This suggests a just and equal view of people, a society in which literally anyone can aspire to be a doctor or a judge.

Since 'experimenting' with the human mind is ethically undesirable and rightly frowned upon, behaviourists have often gathered information from animals, parti-cularly rats and pigeons. Although, of course, in these enlightened times the ethics of this approach may also be debatable, it has often been said that the rat is the hero of twentieth-century psychology!

One such behavioural theorist was B. F. Skinner (1968). One of his many techniques was to place a rat in a cage known as a Skinner box. A Skinner box typically contains one or more levers which an animal can press, one or more stimulus lights and one or more places in which reinforcers like food can be delivered. The animal's presses on the levers can be detected and recorded and a contingency between these presses, the state of the stimulus lights and the delivery of reinforcement can be set up. The cage may be regarded as a stimulus for behaviour and the result is that the rat moves around, initially randomly, until it accidentally depresses the lever, which results in being rewarded with a pellet of food. Not surprisingly, the rat comes to learn that the lever is associated with a reward and this can lead to frantic lever pressing. The situation may be represented diagrammatically:

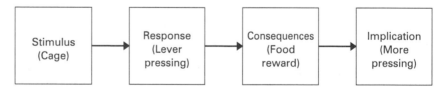

Figure 6.1a Operant conditioning in rats

The procedure is referred to as **operant conditioning.**

It appears that humans are also susceptible to this type of conditioning, but thankfully not involving cages. Indeed, although it is deeply unpalatable to some teachers, the classroom may be seen in some ways to resemble a giant Skinner box.

Why do you think this should be so?

It is a relatively self-contained unit where commonly there are in place reward systems which are intended to bring about certain given behaviours and eradicate others. Of course children are more intelligent than rats and classrooms are far more variable than the Skinner box but nevertheless similarities do exist.

A simple analogy is:

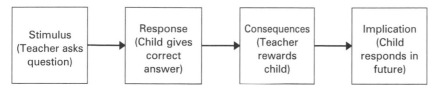

Figure 6.1b   Similarities to the classroom

The converse is where the child's response is met with ridicule. In this case she is unlikely to respond in the future! Classroom reward systems often include teacher praise, house points, gold stars, extra privileges, merit certificates and the like. These are collectively referred to as extrinsic (external) motivators.

But it is possible to overuse rewards systems and this can have negative consequences. In a study by Amabile (1983) children, while happily playing together, were offered certificates if they continued interacting in a similar manner. This had the rather surprising effect of not reinforcing the desired behaviour but extinguishing it. The children became less active and less creative. The reason for this may be that the children were already motivated intrinsically (internally) and needed no further encouragement. Furthermore, they may have interpreted the adult intervention as interference; that they were being manipulated in some way and what was enjoyable became simply another adult led task.

Generally speaking, children do enjoy receiving external rewards but they tend not to lead to the promotion of what Lepper and Hodell (1989) describe as 'a learning culture'. Children may come to see the goal of learning not as achievement but as reward.

It is important therefore to maintain a balance between intrinsic and extrinsic motivators. During the early stages of learning a new task or topic, learners need plenty of encouragement to succeed. Later, completion of the task itself and the associated satisfaction derived from it may be all the motivation that is needed.

Skinner's theories have had a major impact on schooling, particularly with regard to managing children's behaviour. Skilful teachers reward pupils on a daily basis in the hope that desired behaviours will be repeated. This theory does, however, cast the learner in a relatively passive role. It suggests 'traditional' teaching methods where the teacher is firmly in control, both of the content to be learned and of the pace of learning. Lesson content is broken down into small manageable chunks that can be reinforced when learning has occurred. It may have scant regard for the child's existing knowledge or interests and can therefore prove de-motivating for children.

Implications for teaching and behaviour management

- Teacher controls what is to be learned and the pace of learning.
- Children can be taught in relatively large groups.
- Desired learning and behaviours are rewarded, often extrinsically.

Cognitive theories

The theory of behaviourism as outlined above might be thought of as a 'black box' approach since it makes no attempt to explain what is actually occurring in the mind. Recall that behaviourists are only interested in observable actions. Words such as understanding, thinking and memory are considered unimportant since they cannot be 'seen' – but these ideas are the very stuff of the next generation of theorists, the cognitivists.

Cognition loosely means knowing, involving information or ideas, or more precisely the kind of thought which involves perception, intuition and reasoning. Now this thinking is largely frowned upon in schools. I still recall vividly an incident from my early, somewhat tentative years of teaching.

One day, as I was working from the board, in sound behaviourist fashion, a boy at the back of the room sat silently staring out of the window. This was an unusual thing to do in that particular city so I interrupted the lesson and asked what he was doing. He responded quietly, 'Thinking'. My reply, which shames me to this day, was 'Well stop it and get on with your work!'

Jean Piaget

Piaget proved to be the most prolific and influential child development researcher and theoretician the world has ever known. His career spanned more than 60 years and his findings have proved influential to both psychologists and educationists alike. The scope of his work was wide; his theories are contained in more than 30 books and several hundred articles. Nevertheless his work is not without its critics and many researchers believe that they have discovered serious flaws in Piaget's original theories.

Piaget questioned hundreds of children aged between three and twelve using a technique he called the 'clinical method'. This involved listening to the child's answers and, where possible, pursuing the immature thoughts without distorting them. This led him to the theory that the child's adaptation to the world may be described in terms of two different ways of interacting with the environment. These he termed *assimilation* and *accommodation*. Assimilation involves the incorporation of new knowledge in existing mental structures and making a response which has previously been acquired, sometimes ignoring novel aspects of the situation, in order to make it conform to the child's existing mental system. Accommodation describes the process by which the existing mental system can be modified in order to take account of conflicting external stimuli.

A rather crude metaphor for this might be a stranger visiting a town for the first time. Initially every street and shop is new and he struggles to make sense of it all. One wrong turn may result in total confusion. He is accommodating to his new environment. Later, as roads and landmarks become more familiar, he is able to form a mental map of his surroundings and is unlikely to be perplexed by the sudden discovery of a new street or alley. He simply assimilates this to his existing mental picture.

Of course Piaget recognised that the division between the two is not always clear cut and all activity inevitably involves both assimilation and accommodation. Flavell (1985) refers to assimilation and accommodation as two sides of the same coin – both must occur together if an individual is to adapt.

Piaget developed a *stage theory* that suggests that the development of logical thinking in children can be broken down into a series of steps. Each stage derives from and builds upon the previous stage. This concept has inevitably received a great deal of attention from educators since it claims, in part, to explain the contrasts between children of differing stages which parents and teachers experience daily.

The stages are as follows:

Stage	Age
1) Sensorimotor	0–2 years
2) Pre-operational	
a. Pre-conceptual	2–4 years
b. Intuitive	4–7 years
3) Concrete operations	7–11 years
4) Formal operations	11–15 years.

The exact details of the stages may be found in any introductory educational psychology book (Child, 2007; Fontana, 1995; Lefrançois, 1999) but the second, or pre-operational, is particularly interesting since this is a period in the child's development when many of Piaget's investigations took place.

Some of Piaget's more formal experiments involved assessing children's understanding of conservation. These varied in detail but essentially all involved presenting children with two matching sets or quantities, then manipulating one of them in some way and asking the child to compare the results. Typically children during the intuitive stage appear fooled by the transformation and answer that the amounts are now different. Piaget concluded that the child was relying on perception rather than thought and that this is one of the key differences between the thinking of children and adults. This may be true but Piaget's theories are not without their critics and other, possibly more plausible suggestions to explain this behaviour have been put forward (Bryant, 1974; Donaldson, 1978).

Before turning to these readings you might like to consider for yourself the profound implications of stage theory. How might this concept affect teaching?

This section has tried to give a flavour of Piaget's work with particular reference to the experiments involved during the intuitive stage of development. Piaget recognised that the stages are only approximate and that the more mature child will enter a new stage perhaps two years earlier than average. Nevertheless the stages are referred to as being *invariant*, that is, they are the same for all children. But was Piaget right? Are these stages *real*, are children younger than a certain age dominated by perception and simply incapable of logical thought or conservation? Or, are there alternative, more acceptable, explanations for these phenomena?

Implications for teaching

Although Piaget himself was not concerned with drawing educational implications from his general theories they do provide teachers with some useful pointers.

- First, when setting tasks for children we need to bear in mind the balance between accommodation and assimilation. For example when teaching a new concept in science we must ask how closely related this is to the child's previous learning (assimilation) or is it entirely new (accommodation).
- Secondly, Piaget has shown that children may think about concepts in entirely different ways to adults. His conservation investigations clearly demonstrate that children's minds are not simply the same as adults but on a smaller scale, their thinking is *qualitatively* different. Contrast this with the behaviourist view of the child's mind as simply that of an immature adult. This helps us to understand children's limitations but, importantly, should never lead teachers to set artificial boundaries for children.
- Finally, he emphasises the self-motivated, active role of the learner and the importance of meaningful interactions with the environment. This *constructivist* approach, has been developed by other cognitive psychologists.

Lev Vygotsky

It is very easy to believe that Vygotsky is a contemporary theorist but in fact he died over 60 years ago. However it is only in the last 30 years or so that his writings have been translated into English (e.g. Vygotsky, 1978). Unlike Piaget, Vygotsky stressed the importance of language and the role of the adult in the learning process. Naturally this has great resonance with the teaching profession.

Vygotsky describes a 'Zone of Proximal Development' or ZPD.

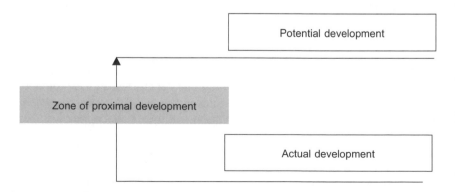

Figure 6.2   Vygotsky's Zone of Proximal Development

The ZPD is the gap between what the child can do independently and what might be achieved through the support of an interested adult. Imagine two pupils in your class who are working together at the computer. One is confident and takes the lead, while the other is more tentative and holds back a little. Later you discover that this is because the more assured child has a computer at home. Should we conclude that one child is simply more able? The ZPD model suggests that we are assessing the child's *actual* development rather than her potential. It is quite possible that the less confident child has equal or more potential and may, given appropriate guidance, show greater development.

The gap between actual development and potential development needs to be bridged by appropriate intervention.

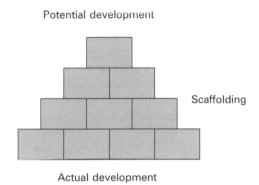

Figure 6.3   Bridging the gap between actual and potential development

The model suggests that during the early stages of learning the teacher needs to provide a great deal of help and encouragement. But later, as the learner begins to master the technique or task, this support can be gradually withdrawn, leading towards independence.

This technique is often referred to as 'scaffolding' and may take many forms in the classroom including:

(a)   providing clear and realistic objectives;
(b)   gaining the child's attention and focusing it on the requirements of the task;
(c)   providing written or actual models;
(d)   reducing the task to manageable subtasks;
(e)   drawing attention to the most relevant aspects of the task;
(f)   explaining procedures;
(g)   keeping the learner on track and motivated;
(h)   correcting on-task errors;
(i)   easing frustration associated with difficulties the child might experience.
(based on Lefrançois, 1999, pp108, 226)

Vygotsky's model is essentially an optimistic view which suggests that instruction promotes development and that teachers can set the agenda. Contrast this with Piaget who has been interpreted as saying that it is pointless attempting to teach a child something until they are at the appropriate stage of development.

Implications for teaching

- Teachers should encourage discussion in the classroom.
- Teaching should lead development not lag behind it.
- Teachers should carry out a careful diagnostic assessment of children's abilities – know your starting point!
- Learning activities should be appropriately sequenced and be within the child's Zone of Proximal Development.

Jérome Bruner

Another cognitivist theory to be discussed in this chapter is that of Jérome Bruner. In a similar way to both Piaget and Vygotsky and quite unlike Skinner, Bruner's theories view the child as an active processor of information.

According to this view, children are not simply *given* knowledge by a teacher or parent but actively *construct* their own knowledge. It follows therefore that, according to this view, children should not be presented with material in its final form but required to organise it for themselves, therefore schools should foster the discovery of relationships. Not surprisingly the teaching method most closely associated with this theory is known as 'discovery learning'.

Inevitably discovery learning requires far less teacher direction than some other methods but good teachers understand that teaching through discovery does not mean sending children away with the summary exhortation 'Discover!' No, the process of discovery must be taught and leadership given throughout. In order to emphasise the role of the teacher the term *guided discovery* is usually applied to this method.

It casts the teacher more in the role of a 'learning facilitator' – one who arranges appropriate learning experiences, guides and questions rather than merely directs. A good example might be a situation where primary school children are given an area to explore and are asked where they would establish a settlement. They are encouraged to discover that settlements need to be near rivers/harbours, etc.

Advocates of this method claim that it is more motivating and increases the child's problem-solving ability.

Bruner suggests a model of children's learning. He claims that all learning should move through three set phases:

- enactive (by doing – including motor and sensory experiences);
- iconic (pictorial representation);
- symbolic (abstract representation).

A good example might be when teaching about electricity in science. Children should first explore making a circuit with bulbs, batteries, wires, etc. (enactive). When they are quite familiar with these they should be ready to draw the circuit (iconic) and only later are they introduced to the concept of the circuit diagram (abstract representation). Sadly, and all too frequently, children are faced with circuit diagrams and the like without having had the requisite early practical experience. Often they appear to learn but this change in behaviour is only temporary and therefore does not fit in with our earlier definition of learning that referred to 'relatively *permanent* changes in behaviour.'

The notion of re-visiting topics but at a higher and more abstract level suggests what Bruner refers to as the *spiral curriculum.* So for example a topic such as fractions might be introduced by working initially with concrete materials like cakes, wooden blocks, etc. Children then move on to to other topics before returning to fractions but at a higher level, perhaps by using a pictorial representation of the blocks. Again children move to other topics before returning to the final abstract stage of $1/2 + 3/4$ etc.

Implications for teaching

- Children should not be given information in its final form but allowed to discover relationships for themselves.
- Learning should begin with motor and sensory experiences and only later move to the more abstract.
- Topics should be first visited and later re-visited at a higher level (the spiral curriculum).

David Ausubel

In direct contrast to Bruner's theory of discovery learning, Ausubel (1963; 1968) claims that children learn more speedily and easily when they receive the material in relatively final form. Ausubel sees Bruner's ideas as wasteful of the teacher's time and indeed discovery learning does take time. Of course this suggests a very different kind of classroom and a changed role for the teacher. Here we see a classroom where the teacher uses direct instruction and the pupils mainly listen. The emphasis being upon meaningful verbal learning.

Since the teacher's role is literally to *expose* the children to the material this method is usually known as *expository* teaching and can be seen in any primary classroom on almost any day of the week. Here the emphasis is on the teacher initially researching the topic, selecting appropriate material and sequencing the learning outcomes to make them accessible to the pupils. Since the child's role is merely to receive the information this is known as 'reception learning'.

However, Ausubel argues that there is no need for this method to lead to passive learning, nor should it encourage rote (without understanding) learning. Teachers who use this method (and we all do) must take particular care to ensure that the new material relates closely to the children's existing knowledge. Since it is the learner who constructs their own knowledge by creating links between the old and new material this method may also be categorised as constructivist.

Implications for teaching

- Teachers should organise the material for the children.
- New learning should be related to existing knowledge.
- New ideas and concepts should be 'potentially meaningful' to the learner.
- Lessons should begin by making links to previous learning.

Reconciling discovery and reception approaches

It may appear at first that the theories of Bruner and Ausubel are total opposites that can never be reconciled, but this is not the case. Ausubel would readily admit that discovery learning might be more appropriate, in the early years of schooling, to enhance problem solving and to establish intrinsic motivation. However, he claims that after the age of about eleven discovery learning is wasteful of time and effort. By that time most learners have sufficient background material to allow them to make their own links.

Recall that both theories are *constructivist,* learners are required to make their own sense of the material, and of course neither is behavioural. Nor should it be assumed that one method is to be preferred to the other. 'Scientific' comparisons between discovery and reception learning are full of methodological problems due to the many variables involved. For example:

- **different criteria are often used for assessing the effectiveness of learning, e.g. speed of learning, retention, transfer, motivation;**
- **children are different;**
- **teachers are different – the same lesson may not be as effective when delivered by dissimilar teachers.**

Good teachers should of course use both methods as appropriate to the subject material and the age group of the pupils.

Information processing models

While all of the aforementioned theories remain useful to teachers, a more recent metaphor in cognitive psychology is the information processing model. This theory has become more popular since the advent of computers and is not the work of a single theorist but has developed from the work of many researchers working in similar fields.

Information processing likens human cognitive functioning to the workings of a computer. The human mind, similar to the computer, takes in information, organises it in some way and then stores it for later retrieval.

	Input	Processing	Storage	Output
Computer	Keyboard, mouse, etc.	Central processor unit (CPU)	Hard disks, memory sticks, etc.	Screen, printer, etc.
Human mind	Eyes, ears, etc.	Short-term or working memory	Long-term memory	Action – movement, speech, etc.

Table 6.1   The information processing model

While this analogy can only ever hope to provide a fairly loose model, the distinction between 'working' or 'short-term' memory and 'long-term' memory is one which educators should consider. Short-term memory (STM) lasts a matter of seconds and is highly limited; Miller (1956) claims that its average capacity is only about seven items. Information in short-term memory needs to be processed or rehearsed within 5 to 20 seconds for it to be transferred to the permanent storage of long-term memory (LTM). Long-term memory is stable and enduring; indeed some psychologists claim that information entered into LTM is never forgotten – it is simply that, on occasion, we can no longer retrieve it!

Principle	Example
• Gain the children's attention	• Use cues to signal when you are ready to begin • Move around the room • Vary the way you use your voice
• Bring to mind relevant prior learning	• Review previous lesson related to the topic • Discuss material previously covered with children
• Point out important information	• Provide handouts • Highlight on whiteboard
• Present information in an organised manner	• Present concepts and skills. in a logical sequence • Move from simple to complex when presenting new material
• Provide for repetition of learning	• State important principles several times in different ways during presentation of information (STM) • Include items on each day's lesson from previous lesson (LTM) • Have periodic reviews of previously learned concepts and skills (LTM)

Table 6.2   The information processing model – implications for the classroom
Source: Adapted from Huitt, 2003

The information processing model views children as active learners who devise strategies to deal with novel situations. Mnemonics, repetition and concept maps are all widely used to facilitate the handling of new information.

Conclusion

This chapter has tried to give you an overview of some of the major theories that have been applied to teaching and learning since the early twentieth century. Inexperienced teachers do occasionally find it difficult to perceive how these ideas can be directly applied in the classroom. This is to be expected, as it is the interplay of theory and practical application that leads to understanding. Only daily contact with children in a range of learning situations can help here. As you spend more time with children you will begin to make connections and realise that learning situations can frequently be seen to have a theoretical underpinning.

For now it is simply worth recalling that you are not asked to embrace one method to the exclusion of others. None is inherently superior and each has its place in the modern teacher's repertoire. The best teachers are eclectic, that is, they select the appropriate method to fit the given situation.

Finally, please do not let this chapter blind you to the fact that you will teach children, not theories. Children are spontaneous, often humorous, open *people* who deserve to be treated with the tolerance, respect and understanding that you would accord to any member of society.

Moving on

For those new to learning theory, this chapter can only ever hope to provide a brief introduction to some key theories of learning. There are, of course, other ideas about learning that you may wish to consider. With the current interest in personalising learning and catering for individual differences you might look at some ideas about learning styles. Several theories have attracted attention. In one model which has been adopted by some schools, three learning styles are identified: visual, auditory and kinaesthetic (VAK). Individual children in your class may display a marked preference for a single learning style and skilful teachers will strive for a balance of approaches in order to ensure that all children have access to the curriculum. For further information and to discover your own preferred learning style – at least as identified in one particular model – see DVC Online at: **www.metamath.com/lsweb/dvclearn.htm**.

FURTHER READING   FURTHER READING   **FURTHER READING**

Child, D. (2007) *Psychology and the Teacher,* 7th edn. London: Continuum. A well-established introduction to psychology for teachers.

Donaldson, M. (1978), *Children's Minds*. London: Fontana. Widely regarded as ground-breaking. A critical examination of the work of Piaget. This book had a major impact in the education world.

Fontana, D. (1995) *Psychology for Teachers*, 3rd edn. London: Macmillan. An accessible introduction to educational psychology. Full of practical insights to aid the teacher in helping children.

Howe, M. J. A. (1999) *A Teacher's Guide to the Psychology of Learning,* 2nd edn. Oxford: Blackwell. Approaches children's learning in an interesting and accessible fashion. The suggested strategies present a stimulating challenge to all educators.

Leadbetter, J., Morris, S., Timmins, P., Knight G. and Traxson, D. (1999), *Applying Psychology in the Classroom.* London: David Fulton. Considers a range of issues for improving children's motivation and understanding social dynamics in the classroom.

Lefrançois, G. R. (1999) *Psychology for Teaching*, 10th edn. Belmont: Wadsworth. A comprehensive introduction to educational psychological principles, written in an entertaining style.

Pollard, A. (2005) *Reflective Teaching: Effective and Evidence-Informed Professional Practice*, 2nd edn. London: Continuum. Deals with most significant aspects of primary school teaching. Promotes skilful, imaginative teaching that is rewarding for both child and teacher.

Wood, D. (1997) *How Children Think and Learn*, 2nd edn. Oxford: Blackwell. Explores in detail the discussions surrounding how children think and learn, tracing the historical influences that have taken place over the past ten years. Wood acknowledges some of the difficulties teachers face when trying to put theory into practice in the classroom.

Website

Funderstanding, available at: **www.funderstanding.com/about_learning.cfm**

7
Managing the learning environment
Paul Frecknall, Uli Dunne, Barbara Leadham
With thanks to Andrew Waterson

By the end of this chapter you should:

- **be able to identify the ways a purposeful working atmosphere can be created through a classroom's physical layout, grouping of children, established routines and learning areas;**
- **understand organisational and management strategies that ensure effective teaching of the whole class, groups and individuals and that teaching objectives are met within the teaching time;**
- **know about implementing personalised learning plans.**

This chapter addresses the following Professional Standards for QTS:
Q2, Q4, Q10, Q21, Q25 (a–c), Q30

Classroom management looks deceptively simple but is highly complex. The effects of Workforce Reform (WAMG, 2003), the introduction of ECM and sophisticated technology make the management of the learning environment even more so. When you observe an experienced, effective primary school teacher you may not appreciate the range of complex manoeuvres inherent in the effective running of a successful learning environment. Moyles (2002) argues that the classroom is like a 'workshop' where teachers have to synthesise their own understanding of the children in their care and organise teaching into structured forms of organisation. If we believe that children learn best when they are in a position to construct their own learning, then we have to also provide an environment that supports and facilitates this approach. Therefore a classroom that enables discussion and collaboration as well as independent study and research is essential.

Laslett and Smith (2002) identified four basic 'rules' of classroom management.

1. Get them in!
2. Get them out!
3. Get on with it!
4. Get on with them!

This is a massive simplification of complex processes, but does offer a good starting point for the beginning teacher. The complexities begin to unfold when we start to ask the question 'How do we...?'

Most trainee teachers throughout their courses look forward to the day they have their own classroom. On school placements you will find yourself inheriting patterns of organisation designed by the class teacher. You may be given the opportunity to do some limited re-arranging of the furniture and groupings, but on these occasions it is more likely to be akin to 'cooking in someone else's kitchen'.

While working in classrooms and observing teachers 'at work' you may well have made notes, physical or mental, on how you would organise your own classroom when that day arrives. Every teacher in every school demonstrates their ideas, values and beliefs through the ways they 'construct' the classroom. What has to be considered? Classrooms have to support the curriculum and its current diverse requirements of the National Curriculum and the Primary National Strategy. Of course there needs to be flexibility, to promote 'fitness for purpose' and to allow a number of possible arrangements for tables, chairs and other resources including computers.

PRACTICAL TASK PRACTICAL TASK PRACTICAL TASK PRACTICAL TASK PRACTICAL TASK

Draw a plan of your ideal classroom. Show windows, doors, power points, computers, chairs, tables, etc. Think about different sorts of lessons that you might want to teach. How might you want to alter the learning environment to facilitate each? What else do you have to consider when organising the learning environment (e.g. constraints, opportunities in relation to behaviour management, health and safety, resource availability, TAs)?

The arrangement will also need to reflect your philosophy and preferred style of teaching. Which of these factors will come first, the curriculum or the philosophy of teaching and learning? What about the physical space as well? There may be things in this that are fixed (sink, power points, network connections, interactive whiteboard, etc.). There may be opportunities to develop particular strategies or worthwhile practices, for example children helping to display their own work. There may be particular resources that are needed for subject specific curriculum areas or children's needs. Then, of course, we must not forget Health and Safety. How far will these actually allow you to fulfil your list of ideals – and where to begin? The elements widely accepted that need to be considered fall into a number of categories. Moyles suggests that these are:

- **the physical environment both indoors and out;**
- **structures (including routines) and resource management ;**
- **rights, responsibilities and rules;**
- **communication.**

(2002, p39)

Recognising and accepting that classrooms are active, practical places that must support the learning needs of children, what other information is available to help us make our decisions and preferences?

Remember that trainee teachers will need to keep an open mind. There is not always an observable connection between a teacher's own educational philosophy and how the classroom is organised and the curriculum delivered. Frequently though there is a link and much can be understood about the teacher from the style of the environment. In this chapter we aim to enable you to effectively and realistically realise your favoured ideology in practice while at the same time acknowledging that effective teachers utilise a range of teaching styles often matched to the requirements of the curriculum and the needs of the children.

The Ofsted (2003a; 2003b) inspection framework guidance requires inspectors to evaluate whether:

- *the teacher's exposition is lively, informative and well structured;*
- *the grouping by ability promotes higher standards;*
- *the teacher's use and style of questioning probes children's knowledge and understanding, challenges their thinking and engages all the children;*
- *practical activity is purposeful and not stereotyped in that children are encouraged to think about what they are doing, what they have learned from it and how to improve their work;*
- *investigation and problem-solving activities help children to apply and extend their learning in new contexts;*
- *the choice of grouping of children, for example children working alone, in pairs or small groups, or all together, achieves the objectives for teaching and learning;*
- *the form of organisation allows the teacher to interact efficiently with as many children as possible;*
- *the use of resources stimulates learning and sensitively reflects different groups, cultures and background.*

(Ofsted, 2003b)

When you observe or work in someone's classroom you may consider these Ofsted criteria but you make judgements based on what you believe and what you feel about how children learn and consequently what classroom organisation best suits those learning needs. For example:

If the classroom is laid out formally with children seated in rows and the teacher using didactic, instructional approaches such as whole class teaching and teacher set learning objectives, we might suspect that the teacher (or school) favours a formal and traditional educational ideology. If, on the other hand, when we enter a classroom we see children working collaboratively in groups, involved in setting their own learning targets and devising their own approaches to tasks, we might suspect that a more progressive approach is favoured. These are two opposite or even alternative perspectives; they merely represent two points on a multidimensional scale upon which the whole gamut of educational ideas, values and beliefs are represented.

(Waterson, 1998)

Among current thinking and reports from central government, its various agencies and organisations, the most recent emphasis is the move towards a more creative approach to teaching and learning in our schools (DfES, 2003) including opportunities made possible with recent technological developments. You should therefore ask yourselves how we are to achieve a more creative approach once we have understood what we mean by the term. How will this impact on classroom organisation and management? What elements must we include to aid rather than hinder these creative approaches? Particularly in the Early Years curriculum the research (Woods 1990; 1993; 1996; Kessler, 2000) suggests that strategies supporting more creative learning include:

- *adequate space and time;*
- *the fostering of self-esteem and self-worth;*
- *using mentors in creative approaches;*
- *involving children in higher level thinking skills;*
- *encouraging the expression of ideas through a wide variety of expressive and symbolic media;*
- *encouraging the integration of subject areas through topics holding meaning and relevance to the children's lives.*

(Craft, 2001)

PRACTICAL TASK PRACTICAL TASK PRACTICAL TASK PRACTICAL TASK PRACTICAL TASK

List the routines in operation in a classroom that you know well. Try and place them into categories, e.g. start of the day, work routines, ending of sessions, interruptions, lunches, getting changed, assembly, moving from one place to another, milk/snack time, adult helpers, checking work, rewards and incentives, communication with parents, etc. Add to them as you move from one school experience to another. They could even be the basis of a check list.

Carefully read the following section from Waterson (1998) where he provides a clear outline with useful tasks to help you to reflect on how you might approach developing your own classroom organisation.

Planning for classroom organisation and management

Reflective action planning is a widely used and effective method of personal professional development. School experience allows you opportunities to be reflective and use your own observations or those of others to begin identifying targets for your personal development.

Reflective action planning can be represented in terms of a cyclical process as shown below in Figure 7.1.

Before, during and after school experience you are expected to:

- **Identify professional issues: you need to consider your strengths and weaknesses as a teacher and identify areas for development. You will need to prioritise these so that you work on the most important issue first.**
- **Construct personal action plans: you will need to plan targets and tasks for each of the professional issues that you have identified.**
- **Implement: this is where you implement your plans during the school experience.**
- **Record and evaluate: How successful was your plan? Did you achieve your target?**
- **Review: at the end of your placement, with your mentor you should review the progress you have made.**
- **Set future targets: you will need to set clear targets for your own future professional development either for your next school experience or your Career Entry and Development Profile.**

You need to begin identifying professional issues in terms of classroom management and organisation and then move on to areas for further development. Remember to include personal learning plans. Some children will depend on them.

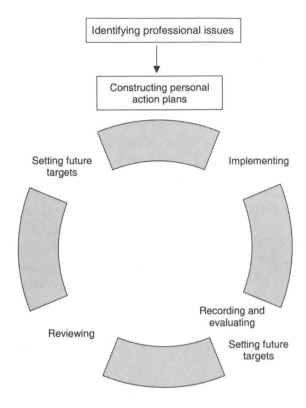

Figure 7.1   The cyclical process of reflective action planning

Identifying professional issues

What classroom environment do you want to create and how do you want children to use it?

Effective classroom environments contain a number of common features.

- They empower, stimulate and motivate children to learn effectively.
- They are workable and realistic given the available resources. Resources in this context include space, time, materials, learning resources and support staff as well as personal and professional resources you bring into the classroom. That is, the classroom organisation needs to be realistic given your current professional capabilities.
- They support children in taking responsibility for their own learning.
- They reflect theoretical perspectives that you judge effectively promote learning. (For example, Dawes et al's (2000) ideas of thinking together would be reflected in the use of collaborative group work.)
- They enable all groups of children to obtain equality of opportunity in the classroom.
- They support the provision of programmes which are suitably differentiated to meet the needs of the individual children.

Where are you now?

What is the current organisation and management of the classroom, its strengths and weaknesses and how does this relate to your ideas, values, beliefs and capabilities?

To develop effective classroom management you will need to review the current system in use within the class together with your own experience and abilities. You will need to consider the following questions.

- **What are the current systems of classroom management being used?**
- **Are the children used to working in groups? Are they used to working independently?**
- **How is the classroom laid out?**
- **What resources are available, e.g. display boards, display materials, computers and software, reference books, children's creative and investigative practical equipment and materials?**
- **What is the class timetable? How much flexibility is there to change and adapt this? How much time is actually available?**
- **What classroom management and behavioural skills do you have now?**
- **What classroom management skills do you need to develop?**
- **How much of your preferred strategy are you going to be able to put into practice within the available period of a school experience?**

PRACTICAL TASK PRACTICAL TASK PRACTICAL TASK PRACTICAL TASK PRACTICAL TASK

Reflect on a recent visit to a school. Answer as many of the questions in 'Where are you now?' as you can. Think about the implications of your answers in terms of how you might prepare for a future block school experience.

Constructing personal action plans

See Table 7.1 on page 96.

What kind of class organisation is going to help you achieve this?

The three most commonly utilised systems of class organisation are whole-class work, group work and individual work.

Whole-class work involves all children within the class undertaking the same activity leading to similar outcomes. The teacher commonly leads whole-class work although he/she may invite children to lead some aspects such as feedback on their work activities at the end of the lesson.

Teacher activities include:

- **introducing learning and contexts;**
- **explanation;**
- **instruction;**
- **questioning;**

Date	Issue requiring action	Action required (be specific about what you are going to do) What kind of class organisation is going to help?	When will this action be taken? (give start date/ finish date)	How will you know when you have achieved your target? (What evidence will there be that the action has been successful? What will be the result?)	Date action complete

Table 7.1. Action planning sheet

- demonstration;
- recapitulation;
- summarising;
- reinforcing learning.

Children are often relatively passive in whole-class work. Their activities include:

- listening and watching;
- answering questions;
- giving examples;
- reporting back;
- reflecting on and evaluating their work.

The management of whole-class work is relatively easy as each activity is distinct and separate and occurs consecutively. Two examples of whole-class work are:

(i) the beginning of a lesson where a teacher introduces the focus of the learning and the context in which it takes place;
(ii) the conclusion or plenary at the end of the lesson where the teacher and children summarise the learning.

Teachers also use whole-class teaching for certain curriculum areas such as story, music and physical education. In Early Years and Key Stage 1 classes children often sit in a specific area such as the 'carpet' during whole-class work.

Group work involves children being arranged in groups of between two and eight and seated around a shared workspace. There are several different activities that can be undertaken within group work. These range from children sitting at the same table working individually on their own activities (essentially individual work) to all the children in a group working collaboratively towards a common outcome. The emphasis here is much more on the children's rather than the teacher's activities.

Group work tasks involve children in:

- initiating an activity;
- seeking information and opinions;
- giving information and opinions;
- elaborating on ideas and concepts;
- co-ordinating a group's activity;
- summarising the learning outcomes.

Collaborative activities include:

- encouraging;
- allowing others to speak;
- setting standards;
- accepting others' decisions;
- expressing group feelings.

(Bennett and Dunne, 1992)

The management of group work can be relatively difficult as each activity may be made up of a series of interacting elements which occur concurrently. You will need to adopt a range of roles depending on the type of group work taking place. Your time will frequently be split between supporting groups and supporting individuals and a key issue here is the level of teacher support each group requires: in practice, most groups will need to work independently of you if group work is to remain manageable. Effective group work has been found to enhance the quality of child/teacher interactions.

Examples of group work include:

- **children working individually on mathematics with differentiated work being supplied to high, middle and low attainment, groups;**
- **children co-operating within a group to produce a newspaper by carrying out different tasks which build into a whole group outcome;**
- **children working collaboratively to investigate how to separate the materials in 'Alien Soup'.**

Individual work involves children working on their own on tasks which have individual outcomes. By carrying out individual work children learn independence and autonomy. Individual work can include a range of activities such as:

- **writing;**
- **drawing;**
- **investigating;**
- **planning;**
- **redrafting;**
- **evaluating, etc.**

By far the commonest activity involves a child working on his or her own with a paper-based task. The management of individual work is moderately difficult as each activity is individual and different and all occur concurrently. Teachers spend much of their time monitoring each child's work individually and interactions with the children are frequently short. Learners needing support may have to wait for the teacher's attention and this often involves queuing. Individual work needs to be carefully managed if both the children's time and the teacher's time is to be used effectively. For this reason tasks need to be designed so that the children are able to work independently for most of their time.

The strengths and weaknesses of each of these class organisations are summarised in Table 7.2.

Organising and managing ICT in the classroom

Research evidence suggests that ICT has a positive impact on teaching and learning. (Condie et al, 2007) and government initiatives (DfES, 2005a) indicate that it will continue to play a major part in teaching and learning. It is therefore essential that

Class organisation	Strengths	Weaknesses
Whole-class work	More time is spent in whole-class discussion. Interactions are more direct and efficient. More opportunity to stimulate children's thinking by exploring ideas, asking questions and sharing problems. Creative work is recognised and supported. Teacher's time is used efficiently. Very effective in some curriculum areas.	Difficult to meet every child's needs. Difficult to ensure that all children participate.
Group work	Can support differentiated learning. In appropriate groupings children of all attainment levels make good progress, e.g. mixed attainment Children learn social and affective skills. Can support progressive development and egalitarian ideologies. Teacher's time is used effectively when group work is appropriately structured.	It may be quite difficult to keep children on task as groups are often seen as being about friendship and fun. Monitoring of groups can be difficult, especially of collaboration. Children of middle and low attainment when grouped together make little progress. Children when grouped by ability can become demotivated. Children have to be taught group work skills.
Individual work and personal plans	All children can work on tasks differentiated to meet their needs. Children learn to work independently and autonomously. The outcomes of a task is unambiguously achieved by one child.	The same teaching point may need to be made on different occasions to different children. During monitoring and support there is a lot of movement either by the teacher or each child. Limited time is spent with each child. More time is spent monitoring work than developing understanding. Children often experience work cards or worksheets rather like a correspondence course.

Table 7.2 Strengths and weaknesses of different class organisations
Sources: Bennet and Dunne, 1992; McNamara, 1994; Reason 1993, Pollard, 1997

careful consideration is given to access to information technology within classrooms.

ICT can be organised in several ways for different purposes:

- **whole class teaching (with an interactive whiteboard or a projector displaying resources for all children to see and interact with);**
- **group work: one or several group(s) of children working collaboratively using one computer;**
- **in pairs: children working collaboratively or taking turns on one computer;**
- **individual work: each child using one computer either in an ICT suite or in the classroom, enabled by a set of laptops or taking turns on one or a small number of computers in the classroom.**

Each mode has its merits, but it is essential that the ICT based task is facilitating learning and is not just carried out in order to make use of the technology, for example to reward children who have completed their work quickly (Ager, 2003).

Teaching and learning styles will determine which mode is appropriate at any one time and the classroom needs to be set up in such a way that ICT can facilitate and support learning in a variety of ways.

PRACTICAL TASK PRACTICAL TASK **PRACTICAL TASK** PRACTICAL TASK **PRACTICAL TASK**

When next visiting a classroom take note of the ICT facilities available to the learners, their number and their position in the classroom. Make an assessment of how central the technology is to the learning process.

Observe how they are used and ask yourself: What are the children learning?

Conclusion

Classrooms are not passive environments in which teaching and learning happen to take place – they should be designed to promote and enhance learning. They should motivate and stimulate, and they should be planned to make the most efficient use of the most important resource – namely, the teacher.

(Clegg and Billington, 1994, p123)

Moving on

Developing personalised learning plans for children is now a key feature of teaching your class. Discuss with your mentor how you can realistically make this happen and maintain class cohesion.

FURTHER READING FURTHER READING FURTHER READING

Laslett, R. and Smith, C. (2002) 'Four rules of class management', in Pollard, A. (ed.) *Readings for Reflective Teaching*. London: Continuum.

Worton, C. (2005) 'Classroom approaches and organisation', in English, E. and Newton, L. *Professional Studies in the Primary School: Thinking Beyond the Standards*. London: David Fulton.

8
Creating a positive classroom climate
Pat Macpherson

By the end of this chapter you should:

- **recognise the importance of establishing a positive classroom climate with and between the children you teach;**
- **know that the relationship you have with children is an interpersonal one;**
- **understand how the ways in which you structure learning is as important as what you teach;**
- **understand that the 'hidden' curriculum is an important contribution to the overall experiences provided for children.**

This chapter addresses the following Professional Standards for QTS: Q1, Q2, Q3a, Q4, Q10, Q15, Q18, Q25a

Learning: more than an academic exercise

The National Curriculum is underpinned by a statement of entitlement for all children. Schools must:

- **promote the spiritual, moral, cultural, mental and physical development of children at the school and of society;**
- **prepare children for the opportunities, responsibilities and experiences of adult life.**

See Chapter 10 for further points on the aims of education.

This statement focuses not only on the academic aspect of school life, but also on personal and social development – both while at school and as a preparation for later life.

It is quite clear, then, that a major intention of education is to educate the child as a person (as well as a pupil), in terms of behaviour, roles and relationships in school and with regard to behaviour, roles and relationships outside of school and beyond the years relevant to a particular phase. This intention is strongly reflected in recent intiatives to promote citizenship. It is also a major feature of Every Child Matters and the five strands that make up the government's aim for every child.

How individual schools provide for this – and the extent to which they are successful – varies, but it should be remembered that schools are social communities and institutions as well as educational establishments. Much attention to what goes on in schools is directed at the subjects taught – the formal curriculum; but, because schools are communities also, the school's behaviour patterns, roles and relationships are of equal importance in the development, both academic and personal, of children.

All that a child experiences in school is part of his/her personal and social and health education (PSE). The teacher has a central role to play in this:

Parents have the major part to play, but the role of the teacher is vital because personal and social development and responsibility are intrinsic to the nature of education. It is something from which no teacher can opt out.

(HMI, 1989, p1)

This chapter in many ways brings together the key elements covered elsewhere in this book. You will understand already the need for teachers to have a sound grasp of subject knowledge, learning theory, assessment, differentiation and special educational needs. But the nature of primary education makes teaching in this phase very much an interpersonal activity, and one where the relationship established between you and the children can enhance or diminish the quality of learning that takes place. Therefore it is essential to match the 'whats' of your teaching with the 'hows'. The importance of this is made explicit in the introduction to the Professional Standards for QTS (DfES/TTA, 2002, p2):

Teaching is one of the most influential professions in society. In their day-to-day work, teachers can and do make huge differences to children's lives: directly, through the curriculum they teach, and indirectly, through their behaviour, attitudes, values, relationships with and interest in pupils.

Before you read the remainder of this chapter, think about *why* you have decided to become a teacher. The reasons often given by both students and qualified teachers include:

- **because I love working with children;**
- **because I want to do a worthwhile job;**
- **because I would get a lot of satisfaction from helping children develop;**
- **because I had difficulties at school and would know how such children feel.**

These all relate to and derive from the personal and social dimensions of the classroom and you, as the teacher, are not just an influence on these but are the director. It may help to think of yourself as the conductor and the class as an orchestra. The difficulty lies not in getting one person or section to play an instrument but in getting everyone to play in time, with the same feeling and expression and the same tune!

Just as a conductor needs to plan rehearsals, practices, discussions of the music etc., so you, the teacher, must plan for the interpersonal relationships which exist within the classroom. That is, you need to be clear about the type of relationship and classroom climate you wish to foster; how your behaviour and responses influence these; and how the children will know the sort of climate you want to establish and foster.

REFLECTIVE TASK

REFLECTIVE TASK

What do you consider to be the key influences/factors in achieving a positive classroom climate?

A positive classroom climate:
- **has attractive displays based on children's work;**
- **is tidy;**
- **has a purposeful atmosphere when children are working;**
- **promotes children's self-esteem.**

In a classroom with a positive climate children:
- **are generally happy and enthusiastic about their work;**
- **feel valued;**
- **want to do well, for themselves as well as for the teacher.**

See Chapter 15 for further points on what pupils expect.

The teacher in a classroom with a positive climate:
- **does his/her best not to have favourites;**
- **respects the children as people;**
- **has a good relationship with the children.**

The teacher–pupil relationship

When you are working in school, you probably want your pupils to like you – and why not? Depending on the length of a placement you are likely to spend many hours with the children and of course you do not want to be disliked. But the teacher–child relationship needs to be established carefully.

Extreme familiarity and/or informality does not, usually, make you more popular. Children know that the teacher is supposed to be 'in charge' and they will expect you to behave accordingly. So, while the relationship you have, and hopefully enjoy, is interpersonal, it must be professional also. There is a clear purpose to your being there with the children, you each have a role (teacher/child) and the power balance is not equal.

What you need to aim for is an approach which:

- **is friendly but not over-familiar;**
- **fosters a close relationship but is not cloying;**
- **has some professional distance so that you command respect but is not so distant that you seem aloof or indifferent;**
- **is challenging but not overly-critical or hostile;**
- **helps children feel secure but does not encourage their over-dependence on you;**
- **values the children as individuals but develops their own interpersonal skills and promotes co-operation;**
- **accepts the uniqueness of each child but requires some degree of conformity from all children.**

A tall order, especially for a student teacher in training!

However, if you are able to establish a good relationship with children and establish the right sort of climate then the rewards are plentiful. You will find that the majority of children:

- settle more quickly;
- are more motivated;
- enjoy being at school, and working hard;
- have a higher standard of behaviour;
- become much more co-operative, willing to share and sensitive to the needs of others;
- have a heightened self-image and self-esteem.

This links strongly to the Enjoying and Achieving strand in *Every Child Matters* (2004a).

Self-esteem

There are three important points which affect self-esteem:

- a comparison of one's self-image with an ideal self-image – the kind of person one would like to be;
- internalisation of society's judgements – self-evaluation is based on the evaluation of others and involves position, status and culturally learned standards;
- personal competence in relation to taking on various roles in life – every role embodies a set of expectations and is related to 'finding one's place in society', feeling that you are good at what you do and being able to express yourself through what you do.

(Tyler, 1992, p3)

There are two distinct areas in the day-to-day life of a primary school. The first of these is the stated or formal curriculum of subject matter, knowledge and skills. The second comprises attitudes, values and relationship and is usually called the hidden curriculum. Whether you plan it or not, the two operate side by side.

Consider: which will have the more lasting imprint on a child:

- the facts of a history (or any other) lesson;

or

- the humiliation of being an isolate;
- the fear of being teased;
- the confusion arising from being unexpressed;
- the ways that decisions are made and rules enforced;
- the partiality of a teacher towards other children?

Factors which influence self-esteem
It is important to remember that:

- **positive peer regard improves self-image;**
- **teaching and learning methods employed by teachers influence and affect achievement;**
- **a positive classroom climate enhances motivation and improves behaviour.**

If the classroom climate is right, then there is a much greater chance that children's self-esteem will be enhanced.

But there is no fairy dust available to help you establish the right climate. Besides giving serious thought to the sort of climate you desire in the classroom you need also to think through how you are going to achieve it.

Research shows that you as a student teacher are likely to have a clear, if idealistic, idea about the sort of teacher you want to be, the kind of relationships you want to develop with the children you teach, the physical appearance of the classroom and the classroom atmosphere you want to create (Furlong and Maynard, 1995, p74).

You may feel that the views of two students in their study reflect your aspirations.

> I want people to come into my classroom and automatically feel it is a really happy place to be. The kids know exactly what to do and are enjoying it and everyone is getting on with it.

> [It is important] that we care for each other, look after each other and are there for each other...I would like to be part of that sense of belonging.

> (Furlong and Maynard, 1995, p75)

However, only one student out of the eleven in the study made an explicit reference to the need for additional aims beyond giving pupils knowledge (Furlong and Maynard, 1995, p149).

It was evident from the students' classroom practice that they did make some connections between the formal and hidden curricula. But if you approach classroom climate in an ad hoc or unfocused way, there is a good chance that you will overlook or not develop sufficiently one or more important contributory factors.

You will need to consider the following factors.

- *Routines and procedures* **which form part of your classroom management –
  transition from one activity to another, movement from the classroom to a different part of the school, access to resources, tidying away at the end of sessions.**
- *Classroom habits* **that can discriminate unintentionally against some children –
  selecting children to undertake 'jobs'; identifying children for a special mention in assembly, focusing on academic achievement only when giving rewards (merit marks, table points, certificates); your responses when children 'tell tales'; the extent to which you model what you probably preach with regard to classroom tidiness (especially your desk and resources).**
- *Approaches to the management of learning* **which may enhance or diminish the climate you create –
  whether children contribute to the setting of classroom rules;**

whether positive personal skills and attributes are encouraged (co-operation, perseverance, collaboration, independence, a questioning approach, confidence);

how you respond to children's answers, especially if they are wrong;

the extent to which tasks and activities are interactive;

whether you share with the children what your learning aims are for lessons;

how you mark children's books (work which is incorrect, untidy, unfinished, of a different standard from usual, etc.);

whether there is consistency in each of these;

whether your behaviour offers a positive role model for the children.

- *Rapport –*

whether you pronounce and spell the children's names correctly;

whether you engage children in personal talk about their interests, hobbies, views, feelings, etc.;

the extent to which you do this with all of the class;

how you respond to an 'unlikeable' child (clingy, attention seeking, know-it-all, dirty, smelly, cheeky, unattractive, etc.);

whether the children have to 'read your mood' each day;

whether children feel able to approach you with personal information or questions about the nature of the work you have set.

PRACTICAL TASK PRACTICAL TASK PRACTICAL TASK PRACTICAL TASK PRACTICAL TASK

Focus on your current or last school placement and write a short evaluation of how well you managed routines and procedures, classroom habits, approaches to the management of learning and rapport. Indicate your strength(s) and areas for development. In preparation of your next placement (or your first class as a Newly Qualified Teacher), identify three targets which will help you in establishing a positive classroom climate with your next class.

In establishing a positive classroom climate you will need to weave together all of the elements covered in the other chapters of this book with each interpersonal element of your teaching so that a genuine congruence is built up; a congruence, or agreement, between what you say you want with what you do to bring it about.

In doing this you will be better placed to match the hidden curriculum of your classroom with the formal. The formal subjects taught cannot be separated out from the overall and complete interpersonal package experienced by the children, and it is the remainder which comprises the hidden curriculum.

- Accepted conduct towards and between each and every member of the class.
- How you organise and manage the formal curriculum.
- The teaching methods used.
- The learning styles promoted.
- The combination of attitudes, values and procedures.

Day-to-day relationships and interactions, then, all make an important and significant contribution, not just to personal and social education but also to learning and achievement in curriculum areas. Tattum (1988) suggests that these relationships and interactions are ongoing, reciprocal, lifelong and cumulative. The whole curriculum experience that you present either enhances or diminishes the very qualities and skills which are essential to growth as a person.

The implication for you as the teacher is to examine the ways in which the formal curriculum is planned and delivered so that it actually does help children acquire appropriate and positive attitudes and values and a healthy self-esteem.

Worthwhile learning approaches

In 1989, HMI identified the following worthwhile learning approaches as being features of quality education and of relevance to pupils of all ages:

- *pupils are encouraged to take responsibility for their learning; pupils develop self-confidence and judgement; from the earliest age, pupils are encouraged to exercise informed choice within and between activities;*
- *there are opportunities for all pupils to achieve, irrespective of their particular strengths and abilities;*
- *pupils understand that everyone's contributions – including their own – deserve attention; pupils are able to work in and help foster a supportive context;*
- *pupils have the opportunity to work in groups of different size and purpose as well as on their own; they experience leadership as well as membership of a group; they can offer and respond to ideas; they can argue a case and defend sensibly a decision or course of action;*
- *pupils have the opportunity to explore PSE through role play – roles perceived as good or bad; roles which explore different ways of life; roles which challenge views held in society; roles which reveal a range of feelings and beliefs;*
- *pupils have the opportunity to use their imagination and to develop personal ideas and insights.*

(HMI, 1989, pp5–6)

Although these were produced some time ago, they relate well to more recent publications: *National Curriculum 2000, Early Learning Goals, Personal, Social and Health Education and Citizenship,* the Primary National Strategy develops the social and professional aspects of teaching and general teaching requirements for inclusion.

The latter, the general teaching requirements for inclusion, show that aspirations for children's involvement in their own education are high and that establishing a proper classroom climate is essential for this. The guidance and directions on inclusion outline what teachers can, and, indeed, should do to achieve the following:

1. create effective learning environments in which:
- **the contribution of all children is valued;**
- **stereotypical views are challenged and children learn to appreicate and view positively differences in others.**

2. secure children's motivation and concentration by:
*   **using teaching approaches appropriate to different learning styles;**
*   **planning work which builds on their interests and cultural experiences;**
*   **using materials which reflect social and cultural diversity and provide positive images of race, gender and disability.**

3. adopt aapproaches that provide equality of opportunity by:
*   **taking account of the interests and concerns of boys and girls;**
*   **avoiding gender stereotyping when organising children into groups, assigning them to activities or arrangement access to equipment.**

4. help children to manage their behaviour, take part in learning effectively and safely:
*   **using positive behaviour management, including a clear structure of rewards and sanctions;**
*   **giving children every chance and encouragement to develop the skills they need to work well with a partner or a group;**
*   **teaching children to value and respect the contribution of others;**
*   **encouraging and teaching independent working skills.**

5. help individuals manage their emotions and take part in learning through:
*   **providing positive feedback to reinforce and encourage learning and build self-esteem;**
*   **creating a supportive learning environment in which the child feels safe and is able to engage with learning.**

www.nc.uk.net/nc-resources/html/inclusion.shtml

QCA guidance on Personal, Social and Health Education and Citizenship (2000) states that:

> *Children and young people need the self-awareness, positive self-esteem and confidence to:*
> *   *have worthwhile and fulfilling relationships;*
> *   *respect the differences between people;*
> *   *develop independence and responsibility.*

Further on, the guidance points out that a range of teaching strategies are needed if all children are to be provided with a breadth of effective learning opportunities – active learning, enquiry and discussion.

As discussed earlier, you will need to consider how you present and manage lessons so that your teaching strategies contribute to and promote a positive classroom climate.

It is worthwhile, at this point, to look at what teachers are asked to provide in terms of children's personal and social development.

At Key Stage 1, children:

*   **have opportunities to show they can take some responsibility for themselves and their environment;**

- **learn social skills such as how to share, take turns, play, help others, resolve simple arguments.**

At Key Stage 2, children:

- **become more mature, independent and self-confident.**

At neither key stage can you the teacher assume that such developments occur automatically. Even if you tell the children that these key stage statements are what you want to promote, there is no guarantee that you will be successful if you do not give equal attention to how you are going to promote them.

Towards the end of Curriculum 2000 you will find an extract from the Statement of Values by the National Forum for Values in Education and the Community. With regard to the values which underpin relationships, the forum agreed the following:

> We value others for themselves, not only for what they have or what they can do for us. We value relationships as fundamental to the development and fulfilment of ourselves and others, and to the good of the community.
>
> On the basis of these values, we should:
>
> - *respect others, including children;*
> - *care for others and exercise goodwill in our dealings with them;*
> - *show others they are valued;*
> - *earn loyalty, trust and confidence;*
> - *work co-operatively with others;*
> - *respect the privacy and property of others;*
> - *resolve disputes peacefully.*
>
> (DfEE/QCA, 1999, p148)

The 'we' referred to includes you the teacher because these values are considered necessary for all people. It is heartening to see this, a statement of values which is inclusive of all, teacher and children, because a climate which is based on these values, and which is promoted with what Pollard (1997, p101) terms 'genuineness', will be all the more positive and closer to the ideal.

REFLECTIVE TASK

Tyler (1992b, p4) offers a list of questions for teachers wishing to test their commitment to a good, interpersonal classroom climate.

- **Do children work in silence or can they collaborate?**
- **Is there an atmosphere of co-operation or competition in the classroom?**
- **Is all the work defined and imposed by the classteacher or can children sometimes develop their own interests?**
- **Does all work require close supervision or does it also involve initiative and independence?**

Other questions you may like to ask.

- **Do children take part in assemblies, helping to plan the content and delivery also?**
- **Are children actively involved in setting their own targets?**
- **Do children contribute to assessments of their performance, achievements and attainment?**

PRACTICAL TASK PRACTICAL TASK PRACTICAL TASK PRACTICAL TASK PRACTICAL TASK

When you are next working in school, ask your class teacher to tell you about his/her approach to fostering, establishing and maintaining a positive classroom climate.

When you evaluate this discussion think about whether you have noticed a congruence between what your class teacher said and what he/she actually does.

The climate in action

Three features of your practice which can reinforce the classroom climate and cross subject boundaries are:

1. circle time;
2. productive talk;
3. interactive tasks.

Circle time

One way of fostering and maintaining a positive classroom climate is through circle time. Circle activities can help to develop self-esteem, an understanding and appreciation of community and listening and speaking skills (Braddy, 1988). They also bring together the teacher and children in an enjoyable atmosphere of co-operation (Bliss and Tetley, 2006, p1).

The teacher and children sit in a circle so that everyone can see each other and take part equally. Simple ground rules should be established – such as everyone has a turn if they want one, that everyone is listened to, that there is only one speaker at a time, that all contributions are respected, there are no put downs, it's OK to pass.

Begin with a common phrase –

My good news is . . .
My favourite food is . . . (toy, game, story, TV programme, etc.)
Hello, my name is . . . (when there are new children or visitors)
I can hear . . .

This allows feelings, experiences, ideas and information to be shared. Children can be asked for their own suggestions for a 'circle'.

Once the children are used to circle time and a sense of trust is shared within the circle, it is possible to deal with issues of importance within the class/school.

For example:

> *In the playground, I feel unsafe...*
> *When I have to write a story, I feel...*
> *I think we should...to improve our school...*
> *A secret I can share is...*

Some of these statements relate to child protection and safeguarding children. It is important that you deal sensitively with the children and in response to their comments.

(You will find Jenny Mosley's book particularly helpful if you wish to read further on this – see Further Reading).

Productive questioning and talk

Teachers talk a lot, don't they? Routine talk, expositions, explanations and questions are all part of a teacher's job, so to speak. It has been suggested that teachers ask a question every 70 seconds on average, and that teachers themselves answer at least 40 per cent of them (Hargie, 1978 cited Fontana, 1995, p83).

You will have your own observations about the effectiveness of your placement-teachers in presenting expositions, explanations, questions and so on; and you will certainly have a view of your own effectiveness. If you can focus also on the type and purpose of the approach used and on your responses and the way in which you present them, you will be able to make explicit links between your oral/verbal skills and techniques and their impact on the classroom climate.

The type of talk you use will depend mainly on what information you expect in return, your purpose in framing your speech in the way that you did and how involved you want the respondent to be.

Remember, teachers ask lots of questions. That means you do, also, in your role as the teacher. The questions you pose may be productive or unproductive.

Productive questions are likely to be:

- **open – respondents answer as they see fit;**
- **probing – further information or clarification is sought;**
- **reflective – the respondent has to consider and evaluate;**
- **hypothetical – the respondent considers situations and conveys opinions, values and perceptions.**

Unproductive questions are likely to be:

- **several questions in one;**
- **closed;**
- **ambiguous;**
- **rhetorical;**
- **leading.**

The link between your approach to questioning and classroom climate is, I hope, obvious but it does need to be explicit. When you plan for your teaching, you need to think through not only what questions you are going to ask but also which children you are going to ask, and your likely responses. How you do this will be a manifestation of the classroom habits discussed earlier which impinge on your teaching.

Therefore, consider the extent to which your approach to expositions, explanations and questions:

- **is inclusive of all children;**
- **is clear and unambiguous;**
- **presents an encouraging tone;**
- **allows children time to think before they are expected to answer;**
- **is personable and incorporates humour when appropriate;**
- **motivates or sustains the children's interest/enthusiasm;**
- **accords dignity to children in how you phrase a question or accept an answer;**
- **allows them to 'have a go' at answering questions/contributing even though they may be wrong (no put-downs);**
- **displays consistency and fairness in how you respond to different children;**
- **models what you expect from the children when they talk to each other;**
- **recognises the interpersonal nature of the exchange.**

This list is not exhaustive and you will work with teachers who vary in their ability to mould this element of their practice with a positive classroom climate.

Interactive learning

It is probably true to say that we all learn in different ways but there are general principles about how we achieve this – and we tend to read, do, watch and listen. You need to ensure that a range of learning approaches is incorporated into the curriculum. A better learning atmosphere is secured if children are actively engaged, understand what they have to do and the purpose of an activity, and believe it matters that they do their best.

In most primary classrooms children sit alongside at least one other and in many they sit as a group, typically in 4s, 6s or 8s. The children more often than not do not have the opportunity to function as a group. This, according to Dunne and Bennett (1990), means that opportunities are lost to enhance children's social relationships. You will find further information on grouping children in Chapter 7. The purpose of including it here is to emphasise its link with classroom climate.

See Chapter 7 for further points on grouping.

Possible grouping patterns are:
1. working individually on different tasks for individual products;
2. working individually on identical tasks for individual products;
3. working individually on jigsaw elements for joint outcome;
4. working jointly on one task for joint outcome.

(ibid., pp10–14)

If children are provided with opportunities to participate in jigsaw and joint tasks, then they experience collaboration and co-operation, awareness of their own and others' needs, decision making, problem-solving and listening. Such experiences can help develop the classroom climate by promoting a 'spirit of co-operation' that goes beyond that found in many classrooms. However, group work is not a panacea for deficiencies in teaching, organisation or management and it requires proper planning and structure. So, you will need to think through:

- **ground rules;**
- **fitness for purposes;**
- **practice for children;**
- **incorporating group work into routines and procedures and classroom habits also.**

Again, further information on this can be found in Chapter 7.

Conclusion

The importance of classroom climate to children cannot be overstated. Children in the primary phase of education need to feel secure and valued as individuals so that they come to school willingly, are motivated to learn and develop appropriate social skills.

A congruence between what you say/expect as the teacher and what you do and how you do it will influence this greatly. You the teacher determine the classroom climate.

A final thought: how can children be expected to display:

- **even-handedness;**
- **tolerance;**
- **sympathy;**
- **politeness;**

if the teacher:

- **treats children with manifest inequality;**
- **is intolerant of some children;**
- **lacks sympathy for some children;**
- **sweeps past a door held open for them without a word of thanks?**

Moving on

Consider the extent to which a positive classroom climate helps children achieve their potential.

Can/does a positive classroom climate help children display or develop gifted work and talents?

Evaluate the contribution of a positive classroom climate to helping children develop self-control, independence and co-operation through developing their social, emotional and behavioural skills?

FURTHER READING FURTHER READING FURTHER READING

Barnes, P. (ed.) (1995) *Personal, Social and Emotional Development of Children.* Buckingham: Open University. An easy read about key aspects of children's development with particular reference made to children's self-esteem.

Best, R. (ed.) (2001) *Education for Spiritual, Moral, Social and Cultural Development.* London: Continuum. A book which examines the culture of teaching and the social aspects of education. It includes sections on developing social skills in children and moral education.

Best, R., Lang, P., Lodge, C. and Wilkins, C. (eds) (1995) *Pastoral Care and Personal and Social Education.* London: Cassell. A wide range of issues related to personal and social education is covered including the impact of a teacher's interpersonal style on pupil behaviour and the link between personal and social education and the whole curriculum.

Biott, C. and Easen, P. (1994) *Collaborative Learning in Staffrooms and Classrooms.* London: David Fulton. This book widens the definition of collaborative learning beyond formal group work in classrooms and promotes active forms of children's learning.

Bliss, T. and Tetley, J. (2006) *Circle Time.* London: Sage Publications. A very useful book on circle time which makes explicit links to Every Child Matters and healthy schools.

Bottery, M. (1990) *The Morality of the School.* London: Cassell. A book which poses teachers moral challenges. Attention is given to the roles of teachers and children and various co-operative group activities.

Briggs, A. R. J. and Sommefeldt, D. (2002) *Managing Effective Learning and Teaching.* London: Paul Chapman Publishing. A book covering a wide range of curriculum issues as well as aspects related to values, culture and ethos.

Clare, H. (2004) *Achieving QTS: Teaching Citizenship in Primary Schools.* Exeter: Learning Matters. A comprehensive guide to understanding and meeting professional standards related to citizenship in the primary school.

Collins, M. (2006) *First Choices – Teaching children aged 4 8 to make positive decisions about their own lives.* London: Sage Publications. This book provides opportunities for teachers to engage young children in decision making through recognising thoughts and feelings, considering consequences and choosing the best outcome. Reflection and discussion points are built into the text.

Cullingford, C. (1990) *The Nature of Learning.* London: Cassell. This book outlines the holistic nature of learning. Inner meanings and emotion, relationships with others and a sense of self are addressed in a practical way.

Dowling, M. (2000) *Young Children's Personal, Social and Moral Development.* London: Paul Chapman Publishing. A book which draws together the theory and practice of personal and social development in young children. Emphasis is placed on the need for sensitive interventions from adults who understand children's needs.

Edwards, J. and Fogelman, K. (eds) (1993) *Developing Citizenship in the Curriculum.* London: David Fulton. A collection of articles on how the cross-curricular theme of citizenship may be incorporated into the curriculum. Chapter 2 outlines how to create a climate for citizenship education and makes explicit reference to personal qualities and relationships, self-esteem and giving pupils responsibility.

Fontana, D. (1995) *Psychology for Teachers*, 3rd edn. Basingstoke: BPS/Macmillan. A comprehensive and practical guide to psychology. A number of chapters are of particular interest with regard to personal, social and moral development and teach attitudes and personality.

Furlong, J. and Maynard, T. (1995) *Mentoring Student Teachers*. London: Routledge. This book draws on research on students' school-based learning to analyse how student teachers learn to teach.

Galloway, D. and Edwards, A. (1991) *Primary School Teaching and Educational Psychology*. Harlow: Longman. The authors demonstrate how an understanding of teachers' day-to-day work in the classroom helps teachers tackle everyday problems related to children's learning and behaviour. The chapters on Interactions in Classrooms and Personal and Social Education are very useful.

Hunter-Carsch, M., Tiknaz, Y., Cooper, P. and Sage, R. (eds) (2006) *The Handbook of Social, Emotional and Behavioural Difficulties*. London: Continuum. A book which examines issues related to social, emotional and behavioural difficulties and which provides practical responses to these.

Inman, S., Buck, M. and Tandy, M. (eds) (2003) *Enhancing Personal, Social and Health Education*. London: RoutledgeFalmer. School ethos and the need for schools to be happy and caring is discussed. The book also includes case studies on PSHE, school councils and emotional literacy.

Kerry, T. and Tollitt, J. (1989) *Teaching Infants.* Oxford: Blackwell. A practical exploration of both the essential skills and the key issues involved in teaching infants. There is much of value for the teacher of juniors also, especially the unit on understanding social relationship issues.

Mosely, J. (1993) *Turn Your School Round: a Circle-time Approach to the Development of Self-esteem*. Wisbech: Learning Development Aids. A highly practical book which contains many suggestions for circle-time sessions supported by photocopiable handouts. Important links are established with behaviour management.

Muijs, D. and Reynolds, D. (2005) *Effective Teaching: Evidence and Practice.* London: Sage Publications.

Pollard, A. (1997) *Reflective Teaching in the Primary School*. London: Cassell. A comprehensive book dealing with all significant aspects of primary school teaching. It is full of practical ideas and support for reflection on classroom experiences. There is much of interest on the theme of classroom climate.

Prashing, B. (2005) *New Ways of Learning and Teaching through Learning Styles*. Stafford: Network International. A book which focuses on learners – children and teachers – and which posits the claim that how you learn and work is how you live.

Pring, R. (1984) *Personal and Social Education in the Curriculum*. London: Hodder & Stoughton. This book maps out personal, social and moral education and identifies practical implications for the curriculum. It is of relevance still, incorporating philosophical questions with a systematic consideration of personal, social and moral education.

Rae, R. (2006) *Good Choices – Teaching young people aged 8–11 to make positive decisions about their own lives*. London: Sage Publications. This book provides opportunities for teachers to engage young children in decision making through recognising thoughts and feelings, considering consequences and choosing the best outcome. A menu of stories related to real-life experiences is used and reflection and discussion points are built into the text.

Robson, S. and Smedley, S. (eds) (1996) *Education in Early Childhood*. London: David Fulton. A consideration of a wide range of early childhood issues that have relevance across the entire primary phase. Chapters of particular interest are those covering personality, professionalism and politics; roles and relationships; and meaningful interaction.

Rodd, J. (1996) *Understanding Young Children's Behaviour*. London: Allen and Unwin. A focus on teaching children to behave in socially acceptable ways whilst fostering self-esteem also.

Rowland, V. and Birkett, K. (1992) *Personal Effectiveness for Teachers*. Hemel Hempstead: Simon and Schuster Education. A book in which emphasis is placed on personal relationships and the interpersonal skills necessary for a successful career in teaching.

Steiner, M. (ed.) (1996) *Developing the Global Teacher.* Stoke-on-Trent: Trentham Books. 'You can only teach about justice and democracy by just and democratic means.' This book helps answer questions related to dealing with prejudice and value diversity, self-esteem and a commitment to justice and sustainable development. See Chapters 3 and 10 on teaching for justice and philosophical enquiry.

Wragg, E.C. and Brown, G. (1993) *Questioning.* London: Routledge. A book which is part of the Leverhulme Primary Project. Of particular interest is how teachers may best respond to questions.

Zins, J. E., Weissberg, R. and Wang, M. C. (eds) (2004) *Building Academic Success on Social and Emotional Learning: What does the research say?* New York: Teachers College Press. The relationships between social and emotional education and school success are discussed with a specific focus on interventions that can enhance children's learning.

Useful websites

Centre for Citizenship and Human Rights Education: **www.le.ac.uk.education/centres/citizenship**

Citizenship Foundation: **www.citfou.org.uk**

Department for Education and Skills: **www.dfes.gov.uk**

Emotional Literacy: **www.anitdote.org.uk**

Every Child Matters: **www.everychildmatters.gov.uk**

General PSHE Materials (Lucky Duck Publishing): **www.luckyduck.co.uk**

Healthy School Standard: **www.wiredforhealth.gov.uk**

Institute for Citizenship: **www.citizen.org uk**

National Curriculum: **www.nc.uk.net**

Personal and Social Education: **www.qca.org.uk/**

Primary National Strategy: **www.standards.dfes.gov.uk/primary**

9
Managing classroom interaction
Cathy Thornhill

By the end of the chapter you should have:

- **developed your understanding of the complexity of the classroom environment;**
- **understood some aspects of managing the classroom;**
- **gained some insight into the roles of other adults in the classroom;**
- **reflected upon a range of strategies in the classroom to promote effective learning including the use of others adults.**

This chapter addresses the following Professional Standard for QTS:
Q1

Introduction

Classrooms are complex working environments. As a trainee you walk into a classroom and see a number of activities going on. Usually these will be generally well ordered and it will appear that most individuals (adults and children) in the room are engaged to a greater or lesser extent with the task in hand. However, what you as the trainee need to consider is how this is achieved.

Effective working classrooms that promote children's learning do not just happen: they are complex environments that require effective management to secure effective learning for all. Your role as the teacher is to be a leader and manager of the classroom environment.

PRACTICAL TASK PRACTICAL TASK **PRACTICAL TASK** PRACTICAL TASK **PRACTICAL TASK**

Whenever you go into a classroom for the first time you need to take the opportunity to observe what is actually happening. How does the teacher manage the interactions between all those present? How is 'control' achieved? What happens with 'disruption'? How are other adults in the classroom used?

Personal presentation

As a human being, within the first few minutes of seeing and meeting anyone for the first time you start to make judgements of them; the same is true for those meeting you. First impressions are often very significant in establishing working relationships. Therefore very careful thought and attention needs to be given to the way you present yourself within the classroom; you need to make the right impression on the children and any other adults present.

There are two areas of your self-presentational behaviour that need consideration. The first is those aspects of your own behaviour over which you probably exert a considerable degree of conscious control; you make sure that work is prepared, dress appropriately and are pleasant and polite. In this you are seeking to create an explicit message of approachable, confident and organised professionalism. The second aspect of self-presentation, however, is often less conscious but just as important to the impression you create. In your body language you need to make the unspoken statement that you are the person who is 'in charge' of the classroom; the implicit message has to be of confidence. Backing up against a wall, appearing hesistant, sitting quietly in a corner, or not talking to the children and staff are all actions which give an implicit message to others that you are possibly uncomfortable or even frightened of the situation.

The manner in which you present yourself – with all its explicit and implicit messages – is very important for establishing your role as a teacher. The pupils and other adults in the class will quickly interpret your actions and words as they start to decide what kind of teacher you are going to be. Your initial self-presentation clearly sets up expectations from others about the person you are; to try to change this at a later date may appear inconsistent and can lead to resentment and conflict.

REFLECTIVE TASK

Reflect on how you present yourself to the children every time you have the opportunity to go into a classroom setting. What are you learning about yourself from these encounters? Do you need to make any changes in the impression you create?

Working in the classroom
Initial observation

Now that you are in the classroom you need to make sense of what you see around you; you need to observe clearly what the children and staff are doing, as well as what you are doing and the effects of these interactions. You need to clearly understand the expectations that are operating through the routines you see and the words and 'manner' in which the interactions take place. Then you need to consider what you are going to do when you work with a child, a group and the whole class within that context. How are you going to establish your expectations and rules?

When you are on school placement it is not always possible for you to implement your own set of rules, or sometimes expectations, as they may conflict with how the specific classroom operates. However, as you train to teach you should be developing your own set of rules and high expectations for the future.

REFLECTIVE TASK

Reflect on how you would manage a situation in which your expectations are different from those of the class within which you are working.

Managing the class

Imagine that the time has now come for you to take over the class and to teach them for a period of time when you will be 'in charge'. You have thought about your rules and expectations but the first task will be to ensure that you gain the attention of the class. This is fundamental in establishing discipline and ensuring you can teach so others can learn. Initially you will need to decide what you want from the children, usually sitting quietly, looking at you and limiting movement. Decide what you are going to say and how you are going to say it and think about whether to include gestures; do not forget the use of body language. Remember that you will need to be heard in a range of situations and that you need to take the specific context of the classroom into consideration. You will also need to consider what you will do if the class do not comply.

Once you have the attention of the class you are ready to teach the lesson. You will need to ensure that in your planning you have clearly identified the rules that apply to each activity and that you know how to make them explicit to the children. You must not assume that, just because the children behave for the teacher, you can take it for granted that they will behave for you, or that, because they always appear to know what to do when moving from the one activity to another, it will just happen. These transitions need to be managed effectively and include aspects such as entering and leaving the classroom, contributions to discussions, moving within lessons. Over time, and with consistent repetition of these patterns, a routine will develop. These routines are important in developing an effective learning environment within the classroom, providing you, as the teacher, with the chance to step back and observe what is going on and ensuring the children know what is expected of them.

PRACTICAL TASK PRACTICAL TASK **PRACTICAL TASK** PRACTICAL TASK **PRACTICAL TASK**

During your school placement examine your approach to specific aspects of classroom management. Examine your strategies for:

- **getting the class's attention;**

- **setting clear expectations and establishing rules;**

- **starting the lesson successfully.**

Try out different strategies and evaluate them to hone your skills.

Once you have established the attention of the class you are moving into a phase of 'management', where your task is to ensure that an environment is maintained where effective learning can occur.

The management of resources is a skill which needs to be developed to ensure that each child has the resources needed to promote their learning. The choice and use of the resources should have been clearly identified in your planning, but it is worthwhile just remembering that some discipline problems may arise if resources are inappropriate, e.g. too hard or difficult to use, too complex, too abundant or scarce, too unfamiliar or unusual. If you are using any ICT resources you must make sure they are working and that you know what to do if they do not work or have planned an 'alternative' activity. When working from internet sites you need to ensure you are consistent with the school policy and are clear that the sites to be accessed are suitable. You must be clear about how the resources are to be distributed, allocated and cleared away and how the children are to help with these tasks – how are you going to manage the children and other adults? Are there any rules and routines that you are going to use to ensure safe and effective use of resources for learning?

Having planned the resources and ensured beforehand they can be used effectively and conducted a successful introduction to the lesson with the children working as a whole class, where the children listened and participated in the first activity, you have to manage a transition to the next part of the lesson. The children are now working in groups on a variety of tasks which give them the opportunity to move around providing the potential for discipline issues to arise. Again your planning should have identified the most appropriate 'grouping' for the learning, e.g. pairs, small groups, ability groups, mixed ability groups, groups set by the teacher, groups chosen by the children, and also whether you will be using other adults to support the learning and what you want those adults to do. On some occasions you may sit the children in groups and yet want them to do individual work.

REFLECTIVE TASK

Reflect on how you will manage 'transitions' in your classroom context. Initially you may adopt the strategies already in use by the class teacher, but for your future as a teacher with your own class what will you do? How might these ideas be modified with different classes? How could you use other adults in these processes?

The children are now in their groups and you, as the teacher, need to monitor what is going on in the classroom as the children and adults work. This is where you need to develop the skills of working with an individual or group of children while still knowing what the rest of the class are doing. So you will need to ensure that when working with an individual or group you do not place yourself in a position where you cannot scan the rest of the class. This means that you do need to be aware of your placement within the classroom. You will then need to monitor others as they work and be prepared to intervene when the children are not getting on with the task, i.e. eye contact, a gesture, a spoken word while still offering individuals or groups specific support. Remember to use positive behaviour strategies here to ensure that the children are on task and actively engaged. For some these skills need to be constantly practised and they will develop with experience. But you also need to consider what you are going to plan for the other adult(s) and how you will manage and monitor their work.

PRACTICAL TASK PRACTICAL TASK PRACTICAL TASK PRACTICAL TASK PRACTICAL TASK

Reflect specifically on how you see experienced teachers managing the learning during your school placements. Discuss with your class teacher/mentor how you can try out different strategies to develop your skills and management repertoire.

Finally you come to the end of the lesson and this is where your detailed planning is key because you need to clear away following a specific set of instructions. The same principles apply in that you need to explicitly tell the children what you want them to do – asking them to 'Clear away please' is a recipe for disaster! You must ensure you leave time for this, especially following a very practical lesson where a number of resources may have been used, e.g. mathematics/numeracy, art, science, as this can present another part to the lesson where disruption may occur. Again you need to consider the role of other adults in this process.

Working with other adults in the classroom; the role of the Teaching Assistant and Higher Level Teaching Assistant

You will have already noted that reference has been made to 'other adults' in the classroom. Adults have been present in some classrooms for many years, depending on the school and its context. Usually this has been in the form of parents or other volunteers coming into the school to hear children read or to assist with practical lessons, preparing resourcs, running the library or giving help to children with Special Educational Needs. Increasingly, however, there has been a number of staff other than teachers working in classrooms with children.

> **PRACTICAL TASK** PRACTICAL TASK PRACTICAL TASK PRACTICAL TASK PRACTICAL TASK
>
> Identify the range of other adults to be found in the classroom during your school placements. In what ways do experienced teachers manage them in this classroom? How will it affect the way you will manage teaching and learning when you are responsible for lessons?

There are now many Teaching Assistants (TAs) in schools and an increasing number of Higher Level Teaching Assistants (HTLAs). Teaching Assistants and Higher Level Teaching Assistants work under the supervision of the teacher to develop the children's learning. This has important implications for you in the classroom and giving them appropriate direction in order to foster pupils' learning is now a central professional responsibility of a teacher.

TAs may be involved in supporting individuals or groups of pupils and HLTAs may teach the whole class (they may, for example, cover a teacher's PPA time) but the overall responsibility for determining what pupils are to learn remains with the teacher. There is a need to develop successful working relationships with the TAs and HLTAs. You need to be clear about how you are going to work with them for the benefit of the children and to work within a framework of clear, agreed expectations.

As a teacher you therefore need to:

- **ensure that TAs and HLTAs are included in all aspects of the school's processes, e.g. attending staff meetings, taking part in training, knowing, understanding and implementing school policies and procedures;**
- **agree attendance at planning meetings and so explain how you expect them to support the children's learning and your teaching;**
- **enable them to be listened to and ensure that they are able to contribute;**
- **develop clear understandings about consistency within the classroom, e.g. classroom management/behaviour strategies;**

- support the development of your TA/HLTA by encouraging them to attend training, etc.;
- develop collaborative working and team-working practices.

Conclusion

It is by constant reflection on observing experienced teachers and 'other adults' that you yourself will begin to develop as an effective teacher. You will make even more progress when you start to really reflect on your practice and begin to understand the range of strategies that are available to ensure effective classroom interactions and management.

Moving on

You will develop as an effective teacher if you really reflect on your practice and understand the full range of strategies that are available to ensure effective classroom interaction and management. It is by constant reflection on observing experienced teachers and other adults working with children that you will deepen your understanding of how classrooms function.

FURTHER READING FURTHER READING FURTHER READING

Arthur, J., Grainger, T. and Wray, D. (eds) (2006) *Learning to Teach in the Primary School.* Oxford: Routledge.

Cole, M. (2005) *Professional Values and Practice: Meeting the Standards.* London: David Fulton.

Hancock, R. and Collins, C. (eds) (2005) *Primary Teaching Assistants: Learners and Learning.* London: David Fulton.

Hayes, D. (2004) *Foundations of Primary Teaching*, 3rd edn. London: David Fulton.

Hayes, D. (2006) *Inspiring Primary Teaching: Insights into Excellent Primary Practice.* Exeter: Learning Matters.

10
Managing challenging behaviour
Kate Jacques

By the end of this chapter you should:

- **know the importance of management of emotions;**
- **understand the difference between discipline and control;**
- **recognise the difference between day-to-day behaviour maintenance and serious behavioural incidents;**
- **know how to react to challenging behaviour;**
- **understand the implications of exclusion.**

This chapter addresses the following Professional Standards for QTS: Q1, Q2, Q10, Q18

Chapters 8 and 9 gave guidance on how to create a positive classroom climate and encourage positive interactions between children. Creating the right tone in the classroom is the most effective way of keeping poor behaviour to a minimum. The purpose of this chapter is to provide you with strategies for dealing with difficult behaviour.

Even the most well-regulated classroom will experience some disruption at some times. Like most trainees you are probably more concerned about the maintenance of discipline in your classroom than almost any other aspect of teaching. You need to remember that most classrooms and schools are well-ordered, well-managed communities of people who work well together. Serious disruptions are, on the whole, rare. It is true that in some schools, in some areas, challenging behaviour is more of a problem and there are reasons for this. In general, children will behave how they have been taught to behave and where poor behaviour is tolerated or ignored, children will continue to behave in that way. So it is important from the outset that you establish the sort of behaviour you expect and that the class know and understand that you are in charge, but that you are neither a dictator nor a tyrant. The relationship you have with each child in the class is, possibly, the most powerful tool at your fingertips. If you respect children and hold them in high regard, they will do the same to you. At least that's the theory, I hear you say! Truly, it does work, but there are children for whom life is very difficult; life may have treated them badly and, as a result, they behave badly. This does not mean that you have to tolerate poor behaviour in your classroom. Simply knowing why a child behaves differently from other children helps you determine the best strategy for dealing with the child's difficulties. Many children come from quite difficult home backgrounds – even in well-heeled homes there can be emotional neglect. Some children are abused or leave home each morning without having had any breakfast; some children are victims of constant bullying, either at home or in the school playground. Part of your job is to work out strategies for reducing poor behaviour and that may mean understanding why a child is behaving in a particular way. From the start set high standards and expect them to be met. Recognise that, for some children, meeting these high standards will be difficult, but expect them anyway.

Be aware of emotions! Much has been said lately about emotional intelligence. This term is used to describe the levels of sensitivity and understanding of other people and situations. Different people have different degrees of emotional awareness. Goleman (1996) suggests that proper management of emotion can influence success more significantly than academic achievement. Whether this is true or not, our emotions play a significant role when dealing with difficult or disruptive situations. The more we are able to understand ourselves, the more we will be able to understand the effect of our emotions on others and theirs on us. Children know when the teacher arrives in the morning in a 'bad mood' or in a 'good mood'. Mood swings are not helpful when trying to manage groups of children. Therefore, know your emotional state when you arrive at school in the morning and ensure that if you are upset, angry or disappointed, this is not communicated to the children. You also need to be aware of what makes you angry and that you do not, inadvertently, overreact if a child irritates you. Children want a teacher who is largely calm and self-controlled. Similarly, you want children who are calm and self-controlled. If you can manage your own emotions and recognise feelings and sensitivities which are sometimes inappropriate, then you are in a better position to help children learn about and manage their own emotions.

REFLECTIVE TASK

Reflect on the last time you were in a classroom and write down three things which irritated you about the children's behaviour. Ask yourself if your feelings affect your performance in the classroom.

Children's emotions can be volatile and you need to be sensitive to children and how they manage their emotions. Temperament and personality do play a large part in how children behave; you need to recognise this. Some children do not know how to deal with anger and they may become violent. Encourage talk about emotions and feelings. Use circle time to allow you and your children to be open about feelings and discuss ways of dealing with anger, disappointment, hostility and discrimination.

Discipline and control

The terms 'discipline' and 'control' are frequently used as though they mean the same thing (Rogers, 1998). They are not the same. Discipline is about good order, complicity about agreed behaviour. A disciplined classroom is one which is well managed and where agreed models of conduct predominate. Classroom control, on the other hand, implies power and containment. It places the teacher in a position of authority over the children. The teacher, of course, is in a position of power and control to some extent but it is how this is employed which makes the difference to teacher/child relationships. The ideal classroom is one where the teacher is ensured of good behaviour, good interpersonal relationships and a good work ethic. This ideal classroom relies on the children subscribing to shared rules and agreeing with the teacher. The teacher does not have to tell the children what to do because they know what to do and how to do it; the explicit and implicit rules have been agreed. An authoritarian classroom, on the other hand, relies on the teacher being 'in control' and telling the children frequently what they must and must not do. In an environment where children feel 'controlled' they are more likely to engage in disruption if that control is weakened for any reason – for example, if the teacher leaves the classroom. Could you rely on the behaviour of the children if you were distracted? Think back to your own strategy in the classroom. Do you believe that you are more preoccupied with discipline or preoccupied with control? At first you need to use a combination of both but reflect on your personal style and consider how you manage behaviour.

Here are some suggestions for managing day-to-day maintenance of good behaviour.

- **Know the school behaviour policy and what it states then ensure that the children also know the school behaviour policy.**
- **Have agreed rules of behaviour displayed somewhere in the classroom. These should not be a series of 'don'ts' but a series of acceptable behaviours, for example, 'In class 4 we all agree: (i) To be careful of other people's belongings; (ii) to treat each other with respect; (iii) to help each other to learn; (iv) to listen to each other's ideas; (v) to keep our classroom tidy and safe'.**
- **Always head off trouble by being punctual and organised.**
- **Avoid scrambles at the start of the day or at the start of the lesson. Make sure what you need is to hand and cut down the excuses for chaos.**
- **Rehearse the classroom agreement at different times of the day, so that children know it is to be taken seriously.**
- **Practise strategic ignoring – don't react to noisy children on every occasion or reinforce attention seeking.**
- **Praise children at every opportunity.**
- **Deal with children calmly and quietly. Indicating your firm disapproval is sometimes quite appropriate, but losing your temper is not. Never threaten what you cannot, or should not, do.**
- **Avoid unnecessary prolonged, public confrontations. If this does happen give children the space and opportunity to back down and never, ever, humiliate a child in front of others.**
- **Don't give the children the opportunity to 'play to the gallery'. If a pupil's behaviour is getting out of hand, remove him or her from the situation. A 'slanging match' between you and a child does nothing for your image.**
- **Use your voice wisely. Remember the effectiveness of shouting is inversely proportional to its frequency. Noisy teachers help create noisy classes!**
- **Insist on basic politeness, but don't be pompous. You are entitled to be treated as a human being.**
- **Treat children fairly and with consistency.**
- **Ensure the classroom is attractive and welcoming and always tidy and organised.**
- **Ensure the classroom takes account of all children from different cultures and backgrounds and uphold a strategy for equal opportunities.**
- **Ensure that each day has pace and structure and children are not left hanging around or doing one activity for too long.**

Write a behaviour agreement which you would like to use in your own class. Make it appropriate to the age range you are likely to teach. Include recognition of the social, religious, ethnic, cultural and linguistic factors which can influence conduct and behaviour.

Challenging behaviour

Every teacher at some point in their career will deal with unexpected and outrageous behaviour and you will not be any different. The important thing to remember is that how you deal with it is what matters, not that it happened. Let us assume that two children have a disagreement over a book which leads to a serious confrontation where one child strikes another. What do you do?

1. First, stay calm and approach the scene purposefully without giving rise to alarm in the classroom.
2. Give clear instructions to the aggressor to stop and to move away from the other child.
3. Avoid confrontation and try to defuse the situation; keep your voice calm and steady and ask all the other children who have been distracted to return to their work.
4. Separate the aggressor from the rest of the class in order for him or her to regain self-control and calm down.
5. If the matter gets out of control, send another child to another teacher or the head teacher for help, especially if physical restraint is necessary.

Incidents such as these need to be followed up with the children concerned. All those involved need to talk about how it happened and the events leading up to the incident. It is important that you are seen to listen and to be fair. It is important also that you re-establish your relationship with the children involved and that if a punishment is required, it is the behaviour that is being punished, not the individual child. After any incident it is important that you quickly bring the classroom back to some normality. Be calm and firm and ensure that all children return to their activities. It is useful to give reminders of the agreed rules around the classroom, especially those about how we treat each other.

Rewards and punishments

In order to manage children's behaviour, some schools employ various systems of rewards and punishments and these can be effective. There is debate about the appropriateness of rewarding good behaviour with stickers or small treats since it could be assumed that good behaviour is the norm. Nevertheless, poor behaviour has to be seen to be punished and has to be recognised as unacceptable. It is quite difficult, however, to use punishment effectively and it can sometimes be counter-productive. It can generate hostility and resentment. Verbal reprimands can work successfully with some children, but for those for whom petty misbehaviours are part of their daily life, it is difficult to see sometimes if behaviour is improving, therefore conventional punishment may not be the answer. The aim, therefore, must be to minimise the opportunities for punishment to be the outcome. If, however, some punishment needs to be applied, and if it is threatened you must apply it and the following might be used.

- *Extra work*: This can have the unsatisfactory effect of reducing the status of the work, but it does deprive the miscreant of time.
- *Detention*: The content of detention may vary, for example, sitting in silence outside the head teacher's office or being given a task during a playtime. It can be time consuming if teachers have to supervise detention.
- *Informing parents*: A letter to parents informing them of serious incidents at school can have a powerful effect on altering the behaviour of children.
- *Conduct marks*: Some schools support the distribution of bad conduct marks for poor behaviour which are made public around the school at the end of each week and if a certain number is achieved, this may lead to detention.
- *Loss of privileges*: A child may be deprived of attending a school trip or a school function following poor behaviour.
- *Exclusion from school*: Expulsion is the most serious sanction and follows only the most serious of offences. However, schools are being discouraged from using exclusion as a punishment since this rarely helps the child and certainly doesn't help society.

Punishments do not always work and success may depend on the nature of the child and how the punishment was applied. Praise and approval from the teacher is much better and likely to have an effect and helps promote a more positive classroom environment. A phenomenon which has developed over the past few years is an increase in low level but continuous chatter in the classroom. *The most common forms of misbehaviour are incessant chatter, calling out, inattention and other forms of nuisance that irritate staff and interrupt learning* (Chief Inspector's Annual Report, 2005).

This incessant chatter irritates other children as well as class teachers. Those who want to learn and achieve should be allowed to do so and it is your job to ensure that all children in the class understand that.

We have learned that different cultural groups behave and act differently and react differently to similar situations. As the teacher we expect the whole class to behave in the same way. We need to be aware that this is a serious challenge. We need to have the highest expectations of behaviour and commitment to learning. We need also to recognise that different cultural groups react differently to our teaching strategies. Some cultures tend to be compliant, agreeable and defer to authority. Other cultures prefer to react, challenge and debate. Others neither challenge nor confront but are passive and, to be engaged, require considerable motivation. We need to realise also that we must educate ourselves to recognise that our responses and reactions influence our students.

Exclusion or inclusion?

The point at which behaviour becomes so unacceptable that the head teacher and governors decide to exclude a child is more of an issue in secondary than in primary schools.

The power of the teacher

Recent research by Morgan and Morris (1999) reveals how teachers underestimate the impact they have on children's behaviour and learning. The children in the study were very clear that they behaved differently for different teachers and that some teachers commanded, and received, more respect than others. Most trainee teachers can reflect back to their own school-days and recall the classes in which they were more likely to misbehave. Take a few minutes to look back at your own school-days and to a teacher whom you thought was ineffective in maintaining discipline. What was it about that teacher that made children, perhaps even you, want to 'play up'? Was it timidity? Was it being poorly organised? Was it being badly prepared? Was it just lack of confidence? It is true that maintaining classroom discipline comes easier to some trainee teachers than to others, but everyone can learn strategies and techniques which work. Knowing how to use one's own style and personality to best effect in creating a positive classroom climate takes time. If natural authority does not come easily to you it will also take some self-discipline and some practice to work on it. For example, respect cannot be learned if the children are not treated with respect. Trainee teachers need to ask themselves some questions.

- **'How do I come across to this class of children?'**
- **'Do the class regard me as valuing their ideas and each one as an individual?'**
- **'Am I always scrupulously fair, even to those children whom I do not like?' (And there will be some of those!).**

So what do you do if chaos breaks out and the children go berserk?

What not to do

- **Don't start screaming at the top of your voice.**
- **Don't start chasing after one or two culprits.**
- **Don't try and drag anybody to the front of the class (remember it is illegal to hit anyone).**
- **Don't tear your hair out.**
- **Don't run out of the room.**

What to do

Rehearse in your mind a scenario so that should this ever happen to you, you have thought some strategies out.

- **Keep calm and keep your dignity.**
- **Position yourself in the centre of the room and project your personality dramatically.**
- **Speak firmly and clearly and vary the volume and emphasis in your voice. Use pauses; make dominant gestures, such as hands on hips, or arms folded, or point; use an exaggerated stare at two or three people; walk slowly around the room; stop, wait, stare; repeat firmly, clearly, an earlier instruction for everyone to stop what they are doing and sit still.**
- **Write the names of two or three ringleaders on the board or in a notebook.**

This strategy may take two or three minutes but should work. Remember, you have to use the power of your personality and your charisma. However, if things are not calming down and may even be getting worse, send a child for help to the head teacher or deputy.

Such a scenario represents the worst nightmare for all trainees; fortunately it rarely happens, because you learn how to manage a large class of children over time and, after a while, managing 35 children becomes second nature – like driving a car, you forget how you are managing to do it. Experienced teachers know how to ensure that a riot does not break out. Bassey (1989) argues that children will not become disruptive if they are busy. He suggests there are two aspects to this.

1. The children should know for every minute of the time that they are in the classroom what it is you want them to do, where and when you want them to do it and what it is they are to do next.
2. The children should want to do it. You need to motivate and inspire.

He repeats the traditional advice: 'The Devil makes work for idle hands, but keep 'em busy and you'll have no bother'. This is sound advice but often hard for an inexperienced trainee when a piece of work has been set which is expected to take 40 minutes and the children have done it in four!

Conclusion

This chapter has attempted to provide some guidance and help on maintaining an orderly and well-disciplined classroom. There will be days when maintaining discipline feels like a battle, but these will be few. As you grow in experience, your competence in maintaining a purposeful, working classroom will be such that you won't know you're doing it!

Moving on

Consider how children can be taught to manage their anger effectively. Bullying is pernicious and often hidden. Make sure that it is not tolerated anywhere in school.

FURTHER READING   FURTHER READING   FURTHER READING

Birkett, V. (2006) *How to Manage and Teach Children with Challenging Behaviour*. Cambridge: LDA. This is a very practical guide, particularly relevant to teaching young children.

Commission for Racial Equality (2000) *Learning for all: Standards for Racial Equality in Schools*. London: CRE. This publication gives useful general advice and guidance on the legal position on acceptable and unacceptable behaviour.

Hopkins, D., West, M., Ainscow, M., Beresford, J. and Fielding, M. (1997) *Creating the Conditions for Classroom Improvement*. London: David Fulton. This book has lots of ideas for INSET on behaviour and discipline. It develops ideas for improving relationships in the classroom and for improving the climate of classrooms.

Morris, B. and Rae, T. (2006) *Teaching Anger Management and Problem Solving Skills*. London: Paul Chapman. This has lots of case studies to illustrate how to manage difficult situations. It tackles the emotional energy issues.

Rogers, B. (1998) *You Know the Fair Rule.* London: Pitman Publishing. This book contains lots of good advice and strategies for making management easier and also good fun. This should be recommended reading for all trainee teachers.

Rogers, B. (2004) *How to Manage Children's Challenging Behaviour.* London: Paul Chapman.

Steer, A. (chair) (2005) *Learning Behaviour: Report of the Practitioners' Group on School Behaviour and Discipline*. London: DfES.

Steer, A. (chair) (2005) *Learning Behaviour – What Works in Schools*. Section 2 of the report on School Behaviour and Discipline. London: DfES. Written with a largely secondary focus, this has nevertheless lots of excellent comments and suggestions useful for primary practitioners.

SECTION 3
CHILDREN AND INDIVIDUAL NEEDS

11
Spiritual, moral, social and cultural values in the classroom
Tony Ewens

By the end of the chapter you should have:

- reflected on and refined your understanding of the notions of children's spiritual, moral, social and cultural (SMSC) development;
- considered the relationship between children's SMSC development and the aims and purposes of *Every Child Matters: Change for Children*;
- developed ideas for promoting SMSC issues through the teaching of the subjects of the curriculum and through cross-curricular approaches, for example thinking skills;
- considered how the climate of values and relationships in the classroom helps to shape children's attitudes and behaviour;
- reviewed your vision of the aims and purposes of education with particular reference to children's personal development.

This chapter addresses the following Professional Standards for QTS: Q1, Q2, Q3, Q5, Q15, Q18

The purpose of this chapter is to help you to explore how children's education can contribute to their development as persons. It is also designed to show how, by addressing children's spiritual, moral, social and cultural development, schools can participate powerfully in the achievement of the aims and outcomes of *Every Child Matters: Change for Children* (DfES, 2004a). The chapter emphasises that you cannot fully appreciate teachers' responsibilities for children's SMSC development without reflecting deeply on what you believe about the purposes of education.

This chapter first introduces SMSC development as an educational aim, with a brief consideration of each of the four elements. It then discusses the potential contribution of SMSC issues to the fulfilment of ECM aims and outcomes. Some ideas are suggested for promoting SMSC development through the teaching of the curriculum and the teacher's role in creating and maintaining a classroom environment conducive to SMSC growth is discussed. Practical and reflective tasks will help you consider these issues, along with suggestions designed to help you to move beyond the initial QTS Standards and towards the achievement of the Standards for induction and main scale teachers.

Until recently, Ofsted inspection reports included separate sections about schools' provision for children's spiritual, moral, social and cultural development. The shorter inspections introduced in September 2005, based on a school's Self

Evaluation Form (SEF), incorporate these issues in the parts of the report dealing with ECM. Nevertheless, the definitions of spiritual, moral, social and cultural development published by Ofsted in 1995 remain a very useful starting point for grasping the concepts involved in SMSC issues.

What is SMSC and why is it a teacher's responsibility?

The Education Act of 1944 required local education authorities to promote 'the spiritual, moral, mental and physical development of the community' and that requirement has never gone away. The 1988 Education Reform Act added 'cultural' to the list of adjectives while 'social' was added in the 1992 Education Act.

You will not be surprised as a trainee teacher to be asked to foster children's mental and physical development, since the idea of a 'healthy mind in a healthy body' is a very ancient aim of education. But you may be taken aback by an expectation that you have some responsibility for children's spiritual and moral development and more recently for their social and cultural values too.

The tradition of education in England and Wales has always emphasised the importance of the development of the whole person. Some visiting trainee teachers from other European countries recently noted the following aspects of English primary schools as being significantly different from their own experience: an emphasis on good manners and a high standard of behaviour; school uniform; school assemblies, collective worship and RE; clubs and other extra-curricular activities; and what they called 'the spirit of the school'. How have these differences come about?

Part of the answer is the close relationship between the state and Christian churches in providing education. In England and Wales most church schools are also state schools, whereas in other countries religious schools are independent of the state. The intertwining of religion and politics has ensured that education in England and Wales has a strong values base. The phrase 'spiritual, moral, mental and physical' springs from a biblical verse about 'heart, soul, mind and strength', and its place in the Education Acts emphasises that people's beliefs, feelings, opinions and values cannot be divorced from their minds and bodies (Ewens, 1998, p107f).

This concern for the education of the whole person permeates the education system, particularly in the primary school sector. Whereas secondary teachers, when asked, may say that they teach mathematics or German or whatever subject, primary teachers tend to look smug and say that they teach children! This is partly a way of saying that most of them teach all the subjects, but it does also reflect a view that education is about personal formation as well as learning subjects.

The foursome of SMSC provides a useful means of categorising the broader purposes of education, and you need to think through their distinctive characteristics and contributions. However, you also need to keep in mind the 'mental and physical development' aim set out in the Education Acts, so that you keep asking the question, 'How can I promote SMSC through my teaching of the curriculum?'

What do you mean by SMSC?

This section looks briefly at each of the four elements, spiritual, moral, social and cultural and indicates how they can contribute to children's education.

> **REFLECTIVE TASK**
>
> Thinking back to your own primary education, identify some of the ways in which your school(s) contributed to your own SMSC development.

Spiritual

It is important to distinguish 'spiritual' from 'religious'. While it is true that some people associate their spirituality with a religious faith and outlook, others find great significance in their spiritual experiences without holding formal religious beliefs.

Judgements about the opportunities for spiritual development will be based on the extent to which the school provides its pupils with knowledge and insight into values and beliefs and enables them to reflect on their experiences in a way which develops their spiritual experience and self-knowledge.

(Ofsted, 1995, p82)

The key ideas here are the notions of:

- **insight (as well as knowledge);**
- **values and beliefs;**
- **reflection on experience;**
- **self-knowledge.**

Pursuing these as desirable ingredients of education is incompatible with reducing the curriculum solely to the transmission of factual information. Facts are important; however, they do not exist in a vacuum but in a value-laden context. Consider a study of Ancient Egypt in the National Curriculum for history (DfEE/QCA, 1999). The decision to include Egypt in the history curriculum is driven by value judgements. Why Egypt? Why not Finland, Paraguay, Mongolia or Papua New Guinea? Why Egypt in the second millennium BCE rather than in the 18th century or the 8th?

Primary children can certainly gather many facts about Egypt. But good history teaching also engenders a 'feel' for Egyptian civilisation and some insight into various aspects of Egyptian society. It provides opportunities for direct experience, perhaps through seeing and touching appropriate artefacts, and allows space for children to reflect on similarities and differences between 'then and there' and 'here and now'. An appreciation of a shared humanity between ourselves and the people of ancient Egypt is an important device in nurturing spiritual insight.

The importance of spiritual development is illustrated in the remark that 'education is what remains when you have forgotten everything they taught you at school'. The academic study of school subjects cannot be divorced from the formation of children as people with feelings, ideas, intuitions, emotions, opinions and beliefs.

You will need to make sure that the commendable aim of raising test scores is not achieved at the expense of the broader purpose of fostering lively, enquiring and reflective spirits in your pupils.

Moral

According to the inspectorate:

> Moral teaching 'teaches the principles which distinguish right from wrong'.

> (Ofsted, 1995, p82)

You may encounter a dilemma here. Is it your role as the teacher to tell children what is right and what is wrong? If so, whose moral code do you follow, in an era when there are sincere differences of opinion? On the other hand, is it the teacher's job to help children to make their own moral decisions and devise a personal moral code? What do you do, then, with a child who concludes that it is right to bully other children, swear at teachers or microwave the class guinea pig?

The following statements summarise my own view of a practical and principled approach to moral education:

- **Despite differences of opinion on the detail of moral behaviour, there is a considerable degree of agreement in society about underlying principles which distinguish right from wrong.**
- **The 'Golden Rule', (Don't) treat others as you would (not) want them to treat you, is applicable to many situations and is universally accepted as a basic principle.**
- **Children develop morally first by experiencing a disciplined regime in which a moral code is imposed on them, secondly by having the opportunity to test and question this code in a safe, supportive environment, and thirdly by internalising moral principles so that they can apply them to new situations.**

You have only to observe a teacher for half an hour to notice how frequently he/she imposes a moral code on the class: be quiet, don't interrupt, wait your turn, remember to say please and thank you, and so on. One piece of research noted that around 50 per cent of the interactions between teacher and children in a Key Stage 1 class were of this kind. You will undoubtedly find yourself operating in a similar way in your own classroom, if only to secure good order. As a good teacher you will also make a point of explaining the reasons for your strictures and periodically discussing moral issues with your class.

You can, however, go somewhat further in helping children to understand how moral discourse and decision-making work. A number of authors have produced classroom materials designed to help with this. These often use fictional situations in which characters are faced with moral dilemmas to enable children to explore moral decision making as an example of problem solving. Children discuss, dramatise or draw cartoon-strips to work through the issues. As the teacher, you direct the learning process by drawing attention to the consequences of alternative choices.

You may also wish to emphasise the impact on the characters' feelings of the different solutions proposed. This calls for quite sophisticated teaching skills, since your prime motive is to promote enquiry and investigation rather than teach a known 'right answer'.

Social

According to Ofsted, social development:

> *encourages pupils to relate positively to others, take responsibility, participate fully in the community and develop an understanding of citizenship.*
>
> (Ofsted, 1995, p82)

Social development is concerned with the relationship of individuals to groups. There are two main ways, which complement each other, by which you can assist this process for your pupils. One is through the content of the curriculum. For example, you may study interactions within groups through literature or in history, or when undertaking a health education project. The other is by means of your organisation of the class, which can enable children to gain experience of belonging to and working in a variety of groups. In this case your intended learning outcomes for the lesson will include some which are related to the process of learning (for example, that children will succeed in working collaboratively and that each child will make an appropriate contribution) alongside others linked to curricular content. More generally, but no less importantly, the school provides opportunities for social development by providing supervised, unstructured play-times and lunch-breaks.

Cultural

Cultural development is concerned with:

> *teaching pupils to appreciate their own cultural traditions and the diversity and richness of other cultures.*
>
> (Ofsted, 1995, p82)

The emphasis on 'own cultural traditions' is a useful counterbalance to the common view that cultural development is solely about 'other people's cultures'. But what is meant by 'culture'? Verma and Pumfrey offer the following definition: *the unique values, symbols, lifestyle, customs and other human-made components that distinguish one social group from another* (1994, p5), which makes it clear that culture is not confined to issues of ethnicity or religious faith. The Ofsted framework draws attention to the importance of developing positive attitudes towards culture, hence the word 'appreciate'. Just as with social development, you can adopt approaches based on content and process. History, geography, RE, music, art and PE provide opportunities to learn about a host of cultural issues, but you should also find occasions for children to express their own cultural traditions, share them with the class and have them affirmed by peers and teachers. This can range from telling stories and singing songs to talking about practices and customs in families, faith communities and social groups.

SMSC and ECM: an important partnership

To a significant extent, ECM can be seen as part of a long tradition in education whereby teachers regard themselves as sharing in a responsibility for children's holistic development, rather than just for their learning of the various areas of the curriculum. You can trace this trend, for example, in the legal judgement that a teacher was *in loco parentis* (in place of the parent) and should take the same care of a child as would be taken by a reasonable parent. It is reflected too, as described earlier in the chapter, in the requirement to promote children's SMSC development, since these attributes describe a broad approach to personal development rather than a narrow focus on a set of subjects.

When you consider the different possible purposes of education, you will see that there are three main types of aim:

1. **cultural transmission**: the thought that each generation should pass on to the next its accumulated store of knowledge, skill and understanding;
2. **preparation for life and work**: the view that a society's education system should equip people to play a full role in the community and the workplace;
3. **personal development**: a vision of education as enabling individuals to develop their particular talents, qualities and characteristics to the full.

In the 1980s and 1990s the emphasis in public education policy was initially on the first of these, as reflected in the production of the National Curriculum. Next came an increasing recognition in the 1990s of the importance of the second type of aim, shown, for example, in the emphasis given to fundamental competence in literacy, numeracy and ICT skills in the National Literacy and Numeracy Strategies. The Primary National Strategy (Excellence and Enjoyment) represents a bringing together of aims 1 and 2, with encouragement to teachers to be flexible in shaping the curriculum to the identified needs of their pupils and to help children to engage creatively with the curriculum.

By the middle of the first decade of the twenty-first century, stability had been achieved in the curriculum, and the policy pendulum could now move again towards children and their personal development.

It is possible to regard ECM as springing from one single event, the appalling death of Victoria Climbié, and the subsequent report (Bichard, 2004) calling for full collaboration among the public services to ensure the safety and welfare of children. It is also possible to see it more broadly as a timely stage in a cycle of policy development, focusing once again on helping children to thrive, after a phase dominated by a concern for subject knowledge and teaching methods.

PRACTICAL TASK PRACTICAL TASK PRACTICAL TASK PRACTICAL TASK PRACTICAL TASK

Visit the ECM website **www.everychildmatters.gov.uk** to gain an overview of the nature and scope of the ECM strategy.

There is an intimate connection between SMSC and the five intended outcomes of the ECM strategy, namely that children should have the support they need to:

- **be healthy;**
- **stay safe;**
- **enjoy and achieve;**
- **make a positive contribution;**
- **achieve economic well-being.**

These needs can be viewed as a hierarchy, in the sense that, unless the child's needs for a healthy, safe environment are satisfied, the other outcomes are unlikely to be achieved.

Maslow's hierarchy of needs (Maslow, 1968) is similarly based on a judgement that personal growth and fulfilment will be most likely to occur when other fundamental needs have been fulfilled. You can readily see that, once the basic life needs and the requirement for safety and security have been met, SMSC issues have a crucial role to play at the next two levels.

For example, to establish confident and secure relationships a child needs to have acquired certain social skills and to be able to operate according to a moral framework, whether this is about taking turns and sharing or avoiding hurting others' feelings. A sense of self-esteem goes along with a positive and realistic self-image, a sense of personal and spiritual identity, and perhaps of cultural identity as well.

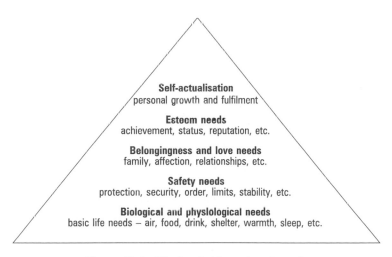

Figure 11.1 Maslow's hierarchy of needs.
Source: Maslow, 1968

The argument being advanced here is that spiritual, moral, social and cultural development are important not only for their own sake, but also because they form the core of the essential groundwork necessary if children are to make optimal progress in the rest of their learning.

There is a further point to make. By integrating the different levels and types of human need within its approach, the ECM strategy can be seen to treat children's development as holistic. This provides the rationale for its insistence on collaboration among the professions and agencies dealing with children's health, welfare and education. It also carries with it the consequence that a child's education must be viewed in its totality, rather than as the sum of different parts, and for this reason ECM is to be seen as a return to a vision of personal development as the central aim of education. Thus, the vision of the 1944 Education Act, referred to above, once again takes centre stage, reasserting the vital contribution made by spiritual, moral, social and cultural dimensions to children's learning and growth.

SMSC and the curriculum

Consider three aspects of the curriculum:

The *formal* curriculum comprises the planned, intended programmes in the various subjects taught in the school, together with the other aspects of school life such as assemblies for collective worship, the school's rules and procedures and educational outings, provided as part of the taught programmes.

The *informal* curriculum consists of the planned, but non-compulsory activities offered by the school, such as clubs and societies, and optional excursions offered as 'extras' outside school hours: everything, in short, that is often described as 'extra-curricular'.

The *hidden* curriculum refers to unplanned, unintentional consequences such as the positive or negative effects of the teacher's personality upon his/her relationship with the class.

The formal curriculum

The formal curriculum provides many opportunities to promote SMSC. The following suggestions are designed as starting points to set you thinking.

Spiritual
In addition to the history example given earlier:

- **Mathematics: the concept of infinity. Children experienced a sense of wonder and mystery as they explored the idea that you can always add one more to the largest number you can think of.**
- **Science: some six-year-olds cut through some daffodil bulbs and were mystified because they could find no yellow colouring inside.**
- **English: ten-year-olds read Libby Purves' book *The Hurricane Tree* and discussed whether there was any point in planting some acorns since every member of the class would probably be dead before an oak tree was fully grown.**

Moral
- **ICT: a group of seven-year-olds discussed how they could politely suggest that another child should not monopolise the computer.**
- **History: some eleven-year-olds argued passionately against the slave trade.**

- PE: a five-year-old group talked about how to prevent anyone being hurt by careless use of apparatus.

Social
- Design & Technology: seven-year-olds worked in groups of six to produce working models.
- Art: eleven-year-olds designed and made a large collage.
- Music: groups of children composed pieces then performed them to another class.

Cultural
- Geography: nine-year-olds spoke about the village, town or country in which they were born.
- Music: six-year-olds played rhythms on percussion instruments from Eastern Asia.
- English: ten-year-olds read poems written in England between 1850 and 1900, wrote some in a similar style and gave a presentation.

The essential point about these examples is that they are an ordinary part of every-day school life. As the teacher you will need to seek a balance in your planning to ensure that each element of SMSC is present, and that every subject of the curriculum plays some part in the development of SMSC values.

PRACTICAL TASK PRACTICAL TASK **PRACTICAL TASK** PRACTICAL TASK **PRACTICAL TASK**

Add to these lists of classroom activities with your own examples drawing upon other areas of the curriculum and/or other age groups.

The informal curriculum

The informal curriculum is the set of non-compulsory activities offered outside formal teaching time. These voluntary activities range from sports, music, drama and arts clubs to optional excursions outside school time. The social and moral value of these activities is fairly self-evident. Children have the opportunity to opt into groups, often across age groups, in which their relationships with each other, and with their teachers, are developed in less formal circumstances.

Team sports offer chances to collaborate in playing games according to rules, experience winning and losing and learn that referees are fallible people whose decisions are nevertheless accepted. The arts give access to the spiritual insights and cultural expressions of a variety of artists, composers and writers.

You would not be the first teacher to discover that your extra-curricular link with a 'difficult' child transformed the way in which you could work with him/her in the classroom.

The hidden curriculum

Apart from the taught programme derived from the subjects of the curriculum, children are strongly influenced by the quality of the relationships which they experience in school and by the values promoted, intentionally or unintentionally, by their teachers. You need to be aware of the climate of values that you are creating, and to consider the effect of your own attitudes and beliefs upon the class.

It is easy for teachers to underestimate the impact that their personal style and behaviour has on children. Parents, however, are only too aware that the teacher is a focus of great authority in their child's life, especially during the primary school phase. Parents' authority is challenged on the grounds of the teacher's observations and actions; you have a frightening degree of influence over your pupils.

Consider the following qualities.

- **Do you convey your personal enthusiasm for some subjects, or antipathy towards others, albeit unintentionally, by your approach?**
- **Do you only put the very best work on display, or do you ensure that every child has some of his/her work valued in this way?**
- **Do you distribute appropriately graded questions around the class, or do you just ask those children likely to know the answer?**
- **Do you discriminate inappropriately among children in the way in which you organise daily routines, for example lining up after break?**
- **Do you, however inadvertently, indicate some tasks as fit for girls and others for boys? If children express such judgements do you challenge and discuss them, or ignore them?**
- **Do children slow to complete tasks in English and maths have to continue with them during arts or humanities lessons or does each child experience a broad curriculum?**
- **Does your demeanour towards the class change if the lesson is being observed, for instance by the head teacher, mentor or tutor?**

This list of questions, to which I am sure you can add others, demonstrates clearly that learning to teach is far more than demonstrating competence against a list of Standards. It challenges you to clarify your own values and to check your actions against your principles. Teaching is inevitably a moral, as well as an intellectual and skilled, activity. Children are quick to spot inconsistencies between the teacher's words and deeds. While it is good for them to learn that adults can differ in mood, temperament, opinion and belief, you need to consider any significant differences between the school's proclaimed ethos and your personal views. Arguably, if you can portray to your class your own adherence to agreed policies, despite personal misgivings, you have taught them an invaluable lesson about society and contributed valuably to the SMSC programme.

REFLECTIVE TASK

Thinking of teachers who taught you when you were at school, consider ways in which they conveyed to you positive or negative messages by means of their attitudes or demeanour, and through verbal and non-verbal communication.

Personal development as an aim of education

Fashions in education come and go. A recent public concern with regard to primary education is the need to improve standards of attainment in literacy, numeracy and ICT. At other times the emphasis has been on enabling children to express themselves through a rich arts curriculum, to explore their place in the world through a diverse humanities curriculum and to analyse and order their experience through a detailed scientific and technological curriculum. The Primary National Strategy marks a move to seeing the interrelationships among the various parts of the curriculum.

The curricular pendulum will no doubt continue to swing at regular intervals. But confining educational debate to a discussion of the curriculum is to avoid the central question: 'What is the purpose of education? Is it to transmit a culture, to mould a future workforce, to help individuals to realise their personal potentials, to impose order upon the population – or some mixture of these and other aims?'

The aspiration that children should be helped to achieve higher standards in curriculum areas is incontrovertible; a counter argument would be difficult to imagine. Strictly speaking, however, such intentions are educational objectives, rather than aims. They prescribe targets to be achieved in a short to medium time-span, but say nothing about why those particular targets are important.

Those who framed the major Education Acts in 1944 and 1988 ensured that the fundamental aims of education were addressed, albeit in a broad way. The requirement to address people's spiritual, moral, social, cultural, mental and physical development indicates that a concern for the development of the whole person is central to the aims of education. The 1988 Act adds flesh to this outline by stating that the school curriculum should prepare pupils for *the opportunities, experiences and responsibilities of adult life* (DES, 1988).

Conclusion

It is important that you, the teacher, should:

- **formulate your own understanding of educational aims;**
- **consider how fostering children's spiritual, moral, social and cultural development can contribute to those aims;**
- **work out for yourself a way of thinking about the relationship between ECM and the educational aims that you espouse;**
- **develop a view of the role played by the curriculum subjects in reaching the aims;**
- **think about the part played by non-statutory, extra-curricular activities;**
- **reflect on the quality and tenor of your interpersonal relationships with children as a means to the desired ends.**

I'm sorry that you cannot just tick a box to show that you meet the standards addressed by this chapter. Generating a vision of what you want for your pupils, then striving to help them to achieve it is far too important for such a simplistic device; it's also far more satisfying.

Moving on

You could further your understanding and skills with respect to SMSC development by, for example:

- auditing your specialist subject or curriculum area to identify its potential to contribute to children's SMSC development;
- sharing your insights with non-specialist teachers and teaching assistants;
- actively seeking leadership from colleagues with specialisms other than your own so as to gain knowledge of the relationship between their subjects or curriculum areas and SMSC values;
- considering the potential of philosophical inquiry with children (Cam, 1995) as a vehicle for promoting SMSC development.

FURTHER READING   FURTHER READING   FURTHER READING

Best, R. (ed.) (2000) *Education for Spiritual, Moral, Social and Cultural Development*. London: Continuum. This edited collection of articles includes theoretical issues and practical guidance.

DfEE/QCA (1999) *Non-statutory Frameworks for Personal, Social and Health Education and Citizenship at Key Stages 1 and 2*. London: QCA. This sets out clearly the expectations for children in the primary years.

Eaude, T. (2006) *Children's Spiritual, Moral, Social and Cultural Development*. Exeter: Learning Matters.

Inman, S., Buck, M. and Burke, H. (1998) *Assessing Personal and Social Development*. London: Falmer.

Wright, A. (2000) *Spirituality and Education*. London: Falmer.

12

Promoting inclusion and equal opportunities

Rob Hyland

By the end of the chapter you should:

- understand the key requirements for inclusion and equal opportunities in school;
- be aware of some of the evidence for systematic inequalities in children's achievement;
- have considered some ways in which greater inclusiveness and opportunities for all children might be promoted in the primary school;
- recognise some of the problems inherent in notions of inclusion and equal opportunities.

This chapter addresses the following Professional Standards for QTS:
Q1, Q2, Q3(a), Q3(b), Q18, Q19, Q25(a)

This chapter discusses inclusion and equal opportunities in relation to chldren in school. It outlines the formal requirements laid upon schools – and upon you as a teacher – under equal opportunities and anti-discrimination legislation. It then discusses broader questions of inclusion and equality of opportunity in education, including some evidence for distinct patterns of achievement. Finally, it briefly considers some requirements of school policies and the individual teacher's responsibilities in the classroom.

REFLECTIVE TASK

At the outset it is useful to think about some of your own initial ideas.

- What do you understand by the terms 'inclusion' and 'equal opportunities'?
- Which opportunities should we seek to make more 'equal' in education?
- When can we say children are 'included' in the provision made by a school?

Make some notes on your immediate ideas. Reflection will probably lead you to identify some problems in defining such notions. As you work through the chapter look back at your initial ideas.

Inclusion and equal opportunities

As other chapters in this book have made clear, the notion of **inclusion** is central to education today. Inclusion has long been particularly associated with measures to

See Chapter 13 for further points on supporting children with SEN.

integrate and foster the education of children with SEN within mainstream classrooms. More recently, however, the concept has been adopted to encompass a broad range of concerns for the welfare and progress of all children:

> *Educational inclusion is more than a concern about any one group of pupils Its scope is broad. It is about equal opportunities for all pupils, whatever their age, gender, ethnicity, attainment and background.*
>
> (Ofsted, 2000, p4)

This broad definition is now reflected in key statements about inclusion in the national curriculum. Schools must provide a broad and balanced curriculum for all children and meet the specific needs of individuals and groups (QCA, 2002).

There are four broad areas in which schools and other educational institutions are challenged to be more inclusive and provide greater equality of opportunity:

1. sex/gender;
2. race/ethnicity;
3. disability and SEN;
4. socio-economic class.

These are actually four very different types of category which intersect in complex ways. The first three are quite clearly identified in legislation and other regulatory demands placed upon schools; the fourth, however, though not subject to the same kind of legislation, remains a key part of the debate over inclusion.

Equal opportunities: the legislative framework

In their treatment of children, schools and teachers are not just directed by general principles of equity and fairness, they are bound by legislation which specifically outlaws discrimination on the grounds of race, sex and disability. Anti-discrimination legislation is part of the statutory and policy frameworks within which schools operate and within which you work as a teacher. Though the legislation is complex, and changes in the statutory bodies are underway with the implementation of the Equality Act 2006, the basic principles and requirements for schools are clear.

Legislation on sex discrimination

The Sex Discrimination Act 1975 (extended and amended 1986) established the Equal Opportunities Commission (EOC) and outlawed discrimination on the grounds of sex. Anybody, including children (or those acting on their behalf), may make a complaint under the Act if they believe they are being discriminated against on the basis of sex. Discrimination need not be direct and intentional for a complaint to be made. If the indirect outcome of a policy is unfair to males or females, then a complaint of discrimination may be upheld by the courts. In education, if the outcome of a policy is that females (whether teachers or children) receive less favourable treatment than males (or vice-versa), then discrimination may be judged to have occurred. It is not illegal, for example, to separate boys and girls for certain teaching purposes, but it would be deemed discriminatory if one sex had access to curricular opportunities or advantages which were denied the other.

From 2007 the new gender equality duty puts a duty on public bodies, including schools, to promote equality. The requirements of schools include that they should gather information and assess the impact of their policies and practices, or the likely impact of proposed policies and practices, on equality between boys and girls and provide the education authority with an annual report in respect of this. The gender equality duty changes the emphasis from avoiding actual discrimination to actively promoting equality between the sexes.

Legislation on race equality

The Race Relations Act 1976 (RRA) created the Commission for Racial Equality (CRE) and outlawed discrimination on the grounds of colour, race, nationality or ethnic and national origins. Anybody, including children (or those acting on their behalf), may complain under the Act if they believe they are being discriminated against or receiving 'less favourable treatment' on these grounds. Discrimination need not be direct and intentional. If the indirect outcome of a policy is that one group receives less favourable treatment than another, then a complaint of discrimination may be upheld by the courts. The law does, however, allow for particular measures to help designated groups who have defined needs; this would cover, for example, additional support for those whose first language is not English.

The Race Relations Amendment Act 2000 broadened the responsibilities of schools and other public authorities. They are now charged with a 'general duty':

- **to eliminate unlawful racial discrimination;**
- **to promote equality of opportunity;**
- **to promote good relations between people of different racial groups.**

Again you will note this 'general duty' changes the emphasis from avoiding actual discrimination to actively promoting equality.

The CRE has produce a *Code of Practice on the Duty to Promote Race Equality for Public Authorities* (CRE 2002a), non-statutory guidance on how schools can fulfil these requirements (CRE 2002b) and *Framework for a Race Equality Policy for Schools* (CRE 2002c). The *Framework* makes it clear that all staff in school have a responsibility for:

- *dealing with racist incidents, and being able to recognise and tackle racial bias and stereotyping;*
- *promoting equal opportunities and good race relations, and avoiding discrimination against anyone for reasons of race, colour, nationality, or ethnic or national origins;*
- *keeping up to date with the law on discrimination, and taking up training and learning opportunities.*

(CRE, 2002c, p3)

Schools must also have procedures for recording and reporting racist incidents (Ethnic Minority Achievement Unit, 2006, p8).

Legislation on disability discrimination

The Disability Discrimination Act 1995 (DDA) had limited application to schools until amended by the Special Educational Needs and Disability Act 2001 (SENDA). This makes it unlawful for providers of education and related services to discriminate against disabled people. Parents who believe that discrimination has occurred can take a claim to the Special Educational Needs and Disability Tribunal (SENDIST). Schools and local authorities have a clear duty to make 'reasonable adjustment' to ensure children who are disabled are not put at a substantial disadvantage compared to their peers. SENDA introduced a planning duty which requires LAs and schools to anticipate rather than simply react to the needs of disabled children.

You should note that while there is obviously some overlap between disability and SEN, these terms are not synonymous. Children with some physical conditions (severe asthma or diabetes, for example) may have rights under the DDA but not necessarily be registered for SEN purposes. Similarly, not all SENs are conventionally classified as a disability.

The Disability Rights Commission Act 1999 created the Disability Rights Commission (DRC). The DRC produced a Code of Practice for Schools which explains the application of the DDA to schools (DRC, 2002). In 2005 the DRC published a statutory code of practice for public authorities (DRC, 2005). The new Disability Equality Duty (DED) placed a clear duty on schools to promote disability equality. Each school now has to develop a Disability Equality Scheme (DES) which sets out the measures it is taking; this will be required of primary schools from December 2007. Once again you will note the changed emphasis from avoiding discrimination to actively promoting equality.

The Equality Act 2006

The Equality Act 2006 has established a new over-arching Commission for Equality and Human Rights (CEHR). This body has been created to bring together the separate bodies (as described above) which have had responsibility for combating discrimination. With effect from October 2007, the new Commission for Equality and Human Rights takes over the work of the EOC and DRC; in 2009 it will incorporate the CRE. The CEHR will assume responsibility for the enforcement of the anti-discrimination laws already established. The Equality Act also introduces a duty on public authorities to promote gender equality and work to eliminate sex discrimination.

Inclusion and equal opportunities: the wider perspective

Though widespread use of the term inclusion in the extended sense outlined earlier is relatively recent, the idea that schools should foster greater inclusiveness in society is not. Schools have long been central to debates on how to mitigate problems associated with wider economic and social inequalities and the apparent exclusion of particular social groups. This is so for several related reasons.

- **Success or failure at school has long-term implications for the educational and occupational opportunities subsequently available to individuals in a modern society.**
- **Different groups within society have different patterns of educational achievement and occupational outcomes.**
- **Schools are widely believed to play a major role in the formation or reinforcement of social attitudes including personal aspirations and attitudes towards different groups in society.**

The principal claim is that children born into particular social groups have very different 'life chances':

> *life chance: probability of a person of a specified status achieving a specified goal or suffering a specified disadvantage.*
>
> (Reading, 1977, p120)

In the long term, this encompasses such things as employment, health care, economic well-being and less easily definable benefits like status, job satisfaction and personal autonomy. Most crucially for our purposes, 'life chances' include the greater or lesser probability of achieving educational success. It is argued that while all children have the same formal entitlement to schooling, certain background factors may influence children's opportunities – or capacity to respond to opportunities – for educational achievement. The essential argument is that an individual's educational experience (and likely outcomes) may be disproportionately constrained by factors other than their ability or potential. Educational success is not simply the result of individual ability or effort, but also relates to the rather different opportunities which might be available to particular social groups

REFLECTIVE TASK

Unequal chances?
What factors in a child's background might influence his/her educational 'life chances' or capacity to benefit from the opportunities of the compulsory years of schooling?
List the relevant factors – these can be positive or negative – and try to organise them into some pattern and rank them in significance.
Which do you think are the most significant?

Equality or equality of opportunity?

Your earlier reflections on equality and inclusion probably led you to identify some problems in defining such notions. However often 'equal opportunities' and 'inclusion' appear in official documentation, and though there are some clear legal requirements laid on schools and teachers, they are certainly not straightforward and unambiguous terms. Equality in education is a topic which has engaged philosophers for long enough and continues to be debated (Baker et al, 2004; Lynch and Baker, 2005) and equal opportunities remains a 'contestable concept' (Riley, 1994, p12). What is clear is that 'equality of opportunity' is not quite the same as 'equality of outcome' (Jencks, 1988; Richards, 1998). In education, some inequality of outcome is unavoidable: pupils do not all achieve the same level of success and it is inconceivable that this could be otherwise. Children do not have exactly the same educational potential – those interests and capacities, whether we think they are inherent or acquired, which might be relevant to academic success.

Nevertheless, while some level of educational inequality is an inescapable fact of life, we can still argue that 'equality of opportunity' is an important consideration. The objective is not equality in the absolute sense of all children achieving the same, but a concern that children reach their individual potential and that all children have the opportunity to *enjoy and succeed* and ultimately to *achieve economic well-being* as set out in *Every Child Matters*. This requires the removal of what might be identified as barriers to educational success and which may disproportionately affect particular groups of children and prevent their full inclusion in the education system.

Barriers to equality of opportunity emerge from an examination of patterns of inequalities in educational outcomes. Given that we recognise some obvious differences between children, attempts to chart educational inequalities examine populations and groups rather than individuals; claims of inequality must be demonstrated in differences in the educational performance of children which are significant, systematic and sustained.

Evidence of educational achievement

Research into educational opportunity and achievement has focused on three categories: sex/gender, race/ethnicity and social background. Disability and SEN, with its variety and gradient of divisions, is a rather different type of analytical category, though very much an equal opportunities issue (see chapters 13 and 14). The three categories have been extensively researched in terms of opportunity and achievement. Below are some broad conclusions on the basis of recent evidence (see References and Further Reading for more details).

Sex/gender

Sometimes a distinction is drawn between biological sex and sociocultural gender (e.g. Hughes, 1991, p12), but this is commonly ignored.

From the 1960s onwards, the main concern over gender was with the way the school system appeared to be more geared to the needs of boys than girls (e.g. Stanworth, 1983; Tutchell, 1990). There are certainly still concerns about sexism in schools, but in terms of academic achievement girls now equal or outperform boys on almost every formal attainment measure up to age 18. At the primary stage, the 2006 statistics for the National Curriculum assessment results at ages 7 (Key Stage 1) and 11 (Key Stage 2) indicate the pattern:

	Girls	Boys
Reading	89	80
Writing	87	76
Maths	92	89
Science	91	88

Table 12.1   Key Stage 1 test results England 2006 – percentage of children achieving level 2 or above by gender

Source: DfES SFR 48/2006

	Girls	Boys
English	84	74
Mathematics	75	76
Science	87	86

Table 12.2   Key Stage 2 test results England 2006 – percentage of children achieving level 4 or above by gender

Source: DfES SFR 04/2007

This sort of data on primary children's performance accumulated in the 1990s. Added to the customary secondary external examination results from GCSE and A level, it led to a view of boys' underachievement (Mitsos and Browne, 1998). Along with clear evidence that boys were more likely to be excluded or to exclude themselves from school, such data resulted in claims that schools needed to do more with 'disaffected boys' (Morris, 1996; Wragg, 1997a). Though these arguments provoked controversy (Wragg, 1997b; Epstein et al, 1999), this concern remains prominent in current policy debate and a number of initiatives have sought to address the underachievement of boys (Wilson, 2003; Warrington et al, 2006). It is important, however, that legitimate concerns over boys' underachievement do not blind us to the fact that girls may also underachieve and teachers may not recognise this so readily (Jones and Myhill, 2004; Jones, 2005).

REFLECTIVE TASK

Why might concern over underachievement be seen differently for boys and girls? How would you identify 'underachievement' in a child?

Race/ethnicity

You will find the word 'race' is often placed in inverted commas (e.g. Gaine and George, 1999); this is to draw attention to the fact that it is a highly debatable term and not a straightforward biological category (Klein, 1993, p4). 'Ethnic group' is a broader and more serviceable term; it can include racial, religious, national and cultural factors. These factors are often confusingly mixed, even in official classifications; there is no limit to the number of categories which can be employed and much depends on the purpose. Travellers are now usually included as an identifiable category of ethnic minority and commonly sub-divided into Traveller of Irish

Heritage and Gypsy/Roma. It is important to recognise that *everybody* has an ethnic identity; to talk of visible minorities alone as 'ethnics' is absurd as well as potentially offensive.

In 2006, 20.6 per cent of the maintained primary school population were classified as belonging to a minority ethnic group (for a detailed breakdown see DfES, 2006). Data on the performance of ethnic minority children, as measured by assessments at the Foundation Stage, National Curriculum Key Stages and GCSE, show a very complex picture of educational achievement. Some broad conclusions are as follows.

- **Many children from minority ethnic backgrounds are doing very well on formal measures of attainment and make more progress than White British children with equivalent levels of prior attainment during the primary school. Chinese, some Indian groups and those who were once termed 'East African Asians' are among the highest achieving groups of pupils by the end of compulsory schooling.**
- **Children whose families originate in Pakistan and Bangladesh still have some difficulties in the Early Years of primary school. Much of this seems related to acquiring English. Pakistani children make less progress at primary school than White British children with the same prior attainment.**
- **African-Caribbean children make less progress at primary school than White British children with the same prior attainment. African-Caribbean children are subject to a significant number of exclusions from school (DfES, 2006a) and underachieve at GCSE.**
- **Traveller of Irish Heritage and Gypsy/Roma children do least well. Although some make a reasonably promising start in primary school, they are often missing from key stage assessments; by the time they reach secondary level their attainment is generally weak.**
- **Girls from minority ethnic groups do better than boys.**

Educational opportunities and 'social exclusion'

You will recognise the explicit concern with gender, race and disability and their place in legislation but you will also be familiar with broader notions of social and economic disadvantage. There are concerns about various forms of inequality in society. The Labour Government of 1997 established a Social Exclusion Unit to pursue its concern for greater 'inclusion' of those significantly disadvantaged or on the margins of contemporary society. In a speech at Stockwell Park School, Lambeth, Prime Minister Tony Blair explained:

> *Social exclusion is about income but it is about more. It is about prospects and networks and life-chances. It's a very modern problem, and one that is more harmful to the individual, more damaging to self-esteem, more corrosive for society as a whole, more likely to be passed down from generation to generation, than material poverty.*

> (Blair, 1997)

Traditionally social and educational researchers have talked about 'social class'. We can agree that notions of social class are imprecise, yet will probably use class categories as part of our explanation of social events and people's behaviour, including our own! Several classification systems have been adopted, and though all are open to objection, researchers necessarily have to offer some sort of model and categories. Though more sophisticated scales are available, the long-established Registrar General's five-point scale remains one of the most common. This is based on occupations: classes I and II are professional/managerial; class III non manual/skilled manual; class IV semi-skilled manual; class V unskilled. Some of the official measures of the social composition of a school's intake are even cruder; often they are simply calculated on the percentage of pupils eligible for free school meals.

There has been longstanding debate in the USA and UK about the effects of social background on educational attainment and the evidence for what schools can do is contested (Davies, 1999). In crude terms, children of professional parents (classes I and II) are around four times more likely to gain five passes of C grade or above at GCSE than children of unskilled workers (class V). One conclusion is overwhelming: regardless of both ethnic origin and sex, children from more economically advantaged backgrounds outperform those who are poor (Gilborn and Gipps, 1996; Cassen and Kingdon, 2007). Patterns of inequality do change, but the great intractable issue remains of what schools can do about the most disadvantaged or 'socially excluded'. The Secretary of State for Education has recently identified one of the five 'clear priorities' as 'closing the gap in educational attainment between those from low income and disadvantaged backgrounds and their peers' (Johnson, in DfES, 2006b, p2).

Confirming or confronting disadvantage?

It is important to recognise that the evidence is shifting and that the negative and positive effects of social background, ethnicity and gender are inter-related in complex ways (DfES, 2007b). Whatever may be statistically true of 'group averages', there will always be more variation within than between groups (Gilborn and Gipps, 1996, p1). There is one simple lesson: you must never make assumptions about the potential achievement of children based on stereotypical views of group identity.

The accusation is sometimes made that some schools which have a disadvantaged intake may confirm rather than challenge low expectations of achievement. This point may be rather harsh on teachers 'at the sharp end' of social and educational inequality, but the danger of overemphasising the perceived deficiencies of children's backgrounds can be that you lose sight of what might be achieved if you concentrate on the quality of opportunities which you are providing now in your lesson. This particular twist to the opportunity debate is not one you can afford to ignore; it is an extension of arguments about the 'self-fulfilling prophecy'. It also brings the argument right back to the level of the classroom and the way you approach the curriculum and the hour-by-hour business of teaching.

School policies for fostering social inclusion and equal opportunities
Promoting access to the curriculum

Your duty as a teacher is not just to offer or even teach a curriculum: it is to do your best to ensure that the children in your care have a realistic chance of 'accessing' that curriculum. Behind this piece of jargon is an important idea: equality of opportunity has to be more than simply the formal right to be present while something is happening. As a teacher, you must *meet the full range of pupils' needs* and be aware of the requirements of equal opportunities legislation (QCA, 2002). Three principles for inclusive provision are set down:

1. setting suitable learning challenges;
2. responding to children's diverse learning needs;
3. overcoming potential barriers to learning and assessment for individuals and groups of children.

You can promote greater equality in children's capacity to access the curriculum through the specific content of your lessons and the way they are taught. This is part of what should be your general commitment to providing appropriate work for individuals. Gender, ethnicity and social background are key elements in this and the selection of appropriate materials and activities can reinforce both understanding and identity. It is particularly important to acknowledge cultural differences, religion, traditions and language as positive features while recognising that they may affect learning in specific areas. At the same time as building upon existing sociocultural knowledge you should always be seeking to broaden children's understanding of the world and give them new experiences. You should provide work to which children can relate, but provide bridges to cross from the familiar to the unfamiliar.

PRACTICAL TASK PRACTICAL TASK PRACTICAL TASK PRACTICAL TASK PRACTICAL TASK

Strategies for the classroom

In planning your work with children consider the following:

- **Choice of topic** – Whose interests does this reflect? Does it appeal to boys and girls? Does it exclude anybody? Are there any cultural or religious sensitivities to be observed? Is any child likely to be excluded from full participation on the grounds of disability?

- **Displays and visual materials** – Do they reflect different cultures? Do they show appropriate male and female role models? Do they avoid stereotypical images of different groups?

- **Language** – Is your language and that of books and other resources accessible to all? Will the vocabulary and concepts be culturally unfamiliar to some children? Is English an 'additional language' for any of your children? How can you help those who may have difficulty?

Promoting attitudes and values

A further aspect of education for greater equality is the commitment to promoting particular knowledge, skills, attitudes and behaviour which help all children take their place in a diverse society. Schools are not just concerned that children should achieve in academic terms; they are also concerned with the promotion of values for all children.

Teachers have a significant role to play in preparing children for life in a multi-cultural society. The Swann Report (1985) made it clear that 'multicultural education' was not just for minority ethnic groups. All children should be encouraged to show respect for that which is of value to others and to try to understand things which may at first appear culturally unfamiliar. Britain's multicultural society should be reflected in the curriculum. Schools can also approach diversity and equality as more explicit issues in assemblies and wherever personal and social education is carried on. This is as true for children in so-called 'all white' schools as for those in multi-ethnic areas (Knowles and Ridley, 2006).

There is also a concern that schools should explicitly combat racist attitudes and practices. Anti-racist education arose out of a sense of the limitations of multi-cultural education in the face of racism. It has long been a controversial area, but the underlying causes for the emergence of anti-racism have not gone away. In giving evidence to the Lawrence Inquiry (into the death of the black teenager Stephen Lawrence and the subsequent police investigation) on behalf of the Commission for Racial Equality, Sir Herman Ouseley, then Chairman of the CRE, said:

> *The starting point for prevention of racist crime is in the education of our children...at the present time...there is no anti-racist teaching within the National Curriculum. We are not doing anything coherently as a nation to counter racial prejudice through formal classroom activity...there will be pockets and examples of good work...but there is no coherent programme that addresses this systematically across the teaching environment.*
>
> (CRE, 1999)

The MacPherson Report (1999) made three recommendations relating to education.

1. There should be amendments to the National Curriculum to combat racism.
2. Local education authorities and school governors should implement anti-racist strategies in schools.
3. Ofsted inspectors should comment on these strategies in inspection reports.

What is very clear is that the argument which Chris Gaine characterised as *No Problem Here* remains a 'persisting myth' in some schools which see themselves as unaffected by ethnic diversity (Gaine, 1988; 1995; 2005). Racism cannot just be an issue for schools with significant visible minorities: it is an issue for all.

The same sorts of underlying principles also apply to gender. The curriculum and the way it is taught must both recognise the preferences and needs of boys and girls and prepare both for life in modern society. One of the challenges you will find in the primary classroom is to attempt the education (rather than simple coercion) of boys to allow a more equitable distribution of your attention in the classroom. This is a very definite equality of opportunity issue. It has to be more than just anti-sexism for boys, however necessary that may sometimes be; there are some very positive values to be promoted.

Heart and minds?

In what ways can a school foster tolerance, understanding and opposition to discrimination and prejudice among its children concerning:

- **socially disadvantaged groups;**
- **ethnic diversity;**
- **disability;**
- **gender?**

Promoting (e)quality in your classroom

The objective of equal opportunities policies is to reduce any disproportionate educational disadvantages experienced by members of particular groups. It may sound trite, but there is little point in simply promoting *equality* of opportunity within the school without promoting *quality* of opportunity. The most fundamental aspect of both quality and equality in your classroom is that all children must have the opportunity to learn, to make progress in academic and personal terms. However 'equal' the experience you provide for children may be, unless they make solid educational progress your achievement as a teacher is rather hollow.

Think about your policy for inclusion and equal opportunities. What can you as an individual teacher do to promote greater inclusion and more equal opportunities in your classroom?

Conclusion

There is no escaping that the issues which come under the heading of 'equal opportunities and inclusion' are some of the most controversial in education: they are obviously political and often deeply personal. How teachers, individually and collectively, may enhance or diminish the opportunities available to children is always an awkward question: it is nonetheless a question which reflective teachers ask repeatedly of themselves.

Moving on

Though all teachers need a broad awareness of equality and inclusion matters, you will need to add to your knowledge about specific issues which relate to the context in which you work. Many of these issues relate to the local communities served by your school. It will be increasingly important to be aware of the work of other professionals who may work with children and families. If your school receives refugee children or has children from particular ethnic groups, there are things you might do to enhance your appreciation of their situation and cultural background. There are likely to be local sources of information and perhaps courses or activities which can help you with this. You might consider, for example, just learning some basic phrases in a relevant language so that you can show you welcome newcomers.

FURTHER READING   FURTHER READING   FURTHER READING

There are many books and articles on these issues. Below are just some available sources:

Claire, H. (ed.) (2005) *Gender in Education 3–19: A Fresh Approach*. London: Association of Teachers and Lecturers. Available online via ATL website: **www.atl.org.uk/**

Cole, M. (ed.) (2006) *Education, Equality and Human Rights: Issues of Gender, 'Race', Sexuality, Disability and Social Class,* 2nd edn. London: Routledge. Offers a comprehensive review of the underlying issues.

Cole, M., Hill, D. and Shan, S. (eds) (1997) *Promoting Equality in Primary Schools.* London: Cassell. This includes both theoretical background on equality issues and practical guidance geared to primary teachers.

Gaine, C. and George, R. (1999) *Gender, 'Race' and Class in Schooling: A New Introduction.* London: Falmer. This is a good introduction to research across the three areas; it discusses some of the complexity of concepts such as race and class.

Gaine, C. (2005) *We're All White Thanks. The Persisting Myth About 'White' Schools*. Stoke-on-Trent: Trentham.

Knowles, E. and Ridley, W. (2006) *Another Spanner in the Works: Challenging Prejudice and Racism in Mainly White Schools*. Stoke-on-Trent: Trentham.

Lane, J. (2006) *Right from the Start: A Commissioned Study of Antiracism, Learning and the Early Years*. London: Focus Institute on Rights and Social Transformation (FIRST). **www.focus-first.co.uk**

Lewis, A., Parsons, S. and Robertson, C. (2007) *My School, My Family, My Life: Telling it Like it is.* London: Disability Rights Commission. This reports on the experiences of disabled children, young people and their families in Great Britain in 2006. It includes material on their experience of primary schools.

Ofsted (2005) *Race Equality in Education: Good Practice in Schools and Local Education Authorities*. London: Ofsted. Online: **www.ofsted.gov.uk/assets/1006.pdf**

Rees, B. (2003) *Promoting Racial Equality and Cultural Diversity.* Harlow: Pearson. This includes both background on racial equality legislation and practical guidance on implementing policy in schools.

Richardson, R. (2005) *Race Equality and Education A Practical Resource for the School Workforce*. London: Association of Teachers and Lecturers. Online: **www.askatl.org.uk**

Runnymede Trust (2003) *Complementing Teachers. A Practical Guide to Promoting Race Equality in Schools*. London: Granada Learning. This book and its accompanying CD provide guidance on the promotion of race equality and cultural diversity in the classroom including lesson ideas, background material and sources of further information.

Skelton, C. and Francis, B. (eds) (2003) *Boys and Girls in the Primary Classroom*. Maidenhead: Open University Press.

Warrington, M., Younger, M. and Bearne, E. (2006) *Raising Boys' Achievements in Primary Schools*. Maidenhead: Open University Press.

Race Equality Teaching: this journal (published by Trentham Books) is a good source of informed but relatively brief and accessible articles.

Useful websites

Commission for Racial Equality: **www.cre.gov.uk/gdpract/cj_sli_2-oral.html**. CRE site includes links, lists of publications and online material such as the *Code of Practice* and the *Race Equality Duty.*

DCSF: **www.dcsf.gov.uk** and Teachernet: **http://www.teachernet.gov.uk/**. These sites include or provide links to information, legislation, guidance and statistics on many issues related to equal opportunities and social exclusion. The DfES has just produced a guide to legislation:

DfES (2007) *Legislation on Equality and Diversity: A Guide for Schools*. London: DfES. Available online: **www.teachernet.gov.uk/docbank/index.cfm?id=11059**

Disability Rights Commission: **www.drc-gb.org**. The DRC has produced guidance for schools in England and Wales on the application of the DDA and their responsibilities to promote equality.

Equal Opportunities Commission: **www.eoc.org.uk**. Site includes links, lists of publications and some on-line material.

Insted Consultancy: **www.insted.co.uk**. Links to articles about race equality in education, multiculturalism and guidance on dealing with racist incidents.

Multiverse: **www.multiverse.ac.uk/**. Teacher education site with resources on the educational achievement of children from diverse backgrounds.

National Association of Teachers of Travellers: **www.natt.org.uk**. Includes links to information and resources on travellers and their education.

The Guardian: **education.guardian.co.uk/**. This includes access to a series of special reports in 1999 and 2000 by Nick Davies and ensuing correspondence; several of these discuss evidence of inequalities in educational provision, poverty and achievement.

See also:

Joseph Rowntree Foundation: **www.jrf.org.uk**. Information on social equality issues including education. See, for example, the report on *Tackling Low Educational Achievement* (Cassen and Kingdon, 2007).

www.nc.uk.net/inclusion.html. QCA National Curriculum statement on inclusion.

Home Office National Refugee Integration Forum: **www.nrif.org.uk/Education/index.asp**. Information on education and refugee children.

www.standards.dfes.gov.uk/ethnicminorities/

www.standards.dfes.gov.uk/genderandachievement/

13
Recognising special educational needs
Lisa Genesis

By the end of this chapter you should:

- **understand the importance of recognising children with SEN;**
- **be aware of a range of needs which children are likely to present in the mainstream classroom;**
- **understand your responsibilities under the SEN Code of Practice;**
- **be aware of the implications of the ECM agenda.**

This chapter addresses the following Professional Standards for QTS:

Q1, Q2, Q3, Q5 , Q7, Q8, Q9

When faced with the title 'Recognising special educational needs', you might well question your ability to do so. You may have a number of concerns.

- **How will I know if a child has a SEN?**
- **How will I ever have time to learn about all the varied learning difficulties and disabilities that exist?**
- **What do all the abbreviations teachers use in school mean?**
- **What will I do if parents do not agree that their child has a SEN?**
- **Who will support me in identifying the best strategies to support the child?**
- **How will I cope if I am in a class without any teaching support?**

Be reassured at the outset: recognising and supporting a child identified as having a SEN is not a task for one individual alone; it is achieved through partnership with colleagues in school, as well as external agencies. You do not have to be the holder of all knowledge and you are not expected to be.

This chapter will provide you with an overview of the legislation that informs SEN provision in schools, as well as providing suggestions for the effective support of children with SEN.

It is important at this point to stress that we should not refer to a child as 'the SEN child' rather as 'the child who has SEN'. To use the former description is to imply that their need is fixed with no room for improvement or deterioration. Every child is an individual who is more than their need and should not be so labelled. It is also important to remember that just because a particular strategy works for one child with a given SEN, this does not mean it will necessarily always work with another child who has been identified as having the same type of SEN.

All children have needs concerning their well-being. The term 'well-being' covers the five key outcomes of ECM as expressed in the Children Act 2004. The aim is for every child, whatever their background or circumstances, to have the support they need to:

- be healthy;
- stay safe;
- enjoy and achieve;
- make a positive contribution;
- achieve economic well-being.

Removing Barriers to Achievement: The Government's Strategy for SEN makes clear that meeting children's special educational needs is an integral part of ensuring that the ECM objectives are realised (DfES, 2004b).

However, a child with SEN has specific needs relating to their learning. The *Special Educational Needs: Code of Practice* (DfES, 2001) provides a definition derived from the Education Act 1996:

> *A child has special educational needs if he or she has a learning difficulty which calls for special education provision to be made for him or her.*
>
> *Children have a learning difficulty if they:*
>
> a. *have a significantly greater difficulty in learning than the majority of children of the same age;*
> b. *have a disability which either prevents or hinders the child from making use of educational facilities of a kind provided for children of the same age in schools within the area of the Local Education Authority;*
> c. *are under five and fall within the definition at a) or b) above or would do so if special educational provision were not made for the child.*
>
> *A child must not be regarded as having a learning difficulty solely because the language or form of language of the home is different from the language in which they are, or will be taught.*
>
> (DfES, 2001, 1:3).

The core principles are clear, but as will be quite apparent, the legal definition still involves a degree of interpretation and judgement.

During your placements you will encounter a wide range of abbreviations that teachers may use when discussing SEN. Here are a few of them:

ADHD	Attention Deficit Hyperactivity Disorder
ASD	Autistic Spectrum Disorder
COP	Code of Practice
EBD	Emotional and Behavioural Difficulties
ECM	Every Child Matters
EBSD	Emotional, Behavioural and Social Difficulties
EP	Educational Psychologist
IEP	Individual Education Plan
MLD	Moderate Learning Difficulties
PLD	Profound Learning Difficulties

PRU	Pupil Referral Unit
SENCO	Special Educational Needs Co-ordinator
SENDA	Special Educational Needs and Disability Act
SLD	Severe Learning Difficulties
SpLD	Specific Learning Difficulties

PRACTICAL TASK PRACTICAL TASK **PRACTICAL TASK** PRACTICAL TASK **PRACTICAL TASK**

Establish your own glossary of abbreviations and other SEN terms you encounter in school or in your reading. Do this in a notebook or as a computer file. You can keep adding to this as you go through your school experiences.

The policy background to SEN

The 1978 Warnock Report (DES, 1978) had a major impact on SEN policy in the United Kingdom. Among many findings and recommendations, two related points have been central to subsequent practice and debate. Firstly, it established a much broader concept of SEN than had previously been recognised; as many as one in five children might at some point be deemed to have a SEN. Secondly, it advanced the principle that children with a wide range of special needs who had hitherto been educated separately should, as much as possible, be integrated into mainstream schools. No longer should only a small percentage of children in specially designated schools be regarded as requiring particular provision; there would now be a range of levels of intervention and support. All schools would be involved in identifying and meeting the varied SEN of a wide range of children.

These principles became enshrined in the Education Act 1981 and have been carried forward and elaborated in subsequent legislation and policy. The Special Educational Needs and Disability Act 2001 (SENDA) linked disability discrimination legislation to SEN. It imposed a clear duty on schools and local authorities not to discriminate and to make 'reasonable adjustment' to ensure children with disabilities are not disadvantaged. It also established a Special Educational Needs and Disability Tribunal (SENDIST) to which parents may appeal.

Initially the model of integration within schools for children with more extensive special needs was limited, in that systems remained largely unchanged and the focus was not on reducing the barriers to the child's learning. Over time, however, there have been moves towards a firmer model of inclusion. This can be seen as part of a wider concern that schools meet the needs of all learners. The three principles needed to ensure a more inclusive curriculum were set out in the National Curriculum Inclusion Statement (1999) as:

- *setting suitable learning challenges;*
- *responding to pupils' diverse learning needs;*
- *overcoming potential barriers to learning and assessment for individuals and groups of pupils.*

These have a clear application to all children and provide a useful, concise checklist of principles for evaluating lesson by lesson provision for children with SEN.

In the broader context, the Children Act 2004 established the ECM agenda; this calls for a multi-agency approach to meeting the needs of children and young people. Again this reinforces many of the principles for meeting the SEN of children.

The Code of Practice on the Identification and Assessment of SEN

In 1994 a *Code of Practice on the Identification and Assessment of SEN* was established. This set out how all schools and local authorities should assess and make provision for children with SEN. This statutory code was revised in 2001 and provides an outline of principles for schools. The new *SEN Code of Practice* (DfES, 2001) signalled a subtle but significant shift in approach to the classification of needs. Whereas previously much of the attention seemed to focus on identifying conditions, the focus was now rather on meeting needs:

> *This guidance does not assume that there are hard and fast categories of special educational need. ... Children will have needs and requirements which may fall into at least one of four areas, many children will have inter-related needs. The impact of these combinations on the child's ability to function, learn and succeed should be taken into account.*
>
> (DfES, 2001, para 7.52)

The four identified areas are:

1. *cognition and learning;*
2. *behaviour, emotional and social development;*
3. *communication and interaction;*
4. *sensory and/or physical needs.*

(DfES, 2001, para 7.52)

The revised Code of Practice established a graduated approach to meeting the needs of a child with SEN:

- **initial monitoring**
- **Early Years/School Action**
  – set IEP
- **Early Years/School Action Plus**
- **statutory assessment**
  may lead to formal statement of SEN.

Monitoring and assessing progress in school

On your placement, you may encounter children with a wide range of SEN. You may, for example, be teaching children who have been identified as having behavioural difficulties or ADHD, or they may be dyslexic, or dyspraxic; you will also teach children who have the particular needs of the gifted and talented. Schools have to identify and support many different needs.

To be able to recognise and support children with SEN, a school has to have a system in place that monitors a child's progress. Records need to be kept and there need to be clear communication channels between all involved in the child's learning, including the use of specific forms to document observations. Schools often have their own formats that correspond to the levels of graduated response to meet a child's SEN which are highlighted in the Code of Practice (DfES, 2001).

The code suggests a number of ways to evaluate the progress of children if there are concerns. It suggests children may be identified by referring to:

- *their performance monitored by the teacher as part of ongoing observation and assessment;*
- *the outcomes from baseline assessment results;*
- *their progress against the objectives specified in the National Literacy and Numeracy Strategy Frameworks;*
- *their performance against the level descriptions within the National Curriculum at the end of a key stage;*
- *standardised screening or assessment tools.*

(DfES, 2001, para 5.13)

The assessment process outlined in the SEN Code of Practice (DfES, 2001, para 5:6) advises a four-fold approach, examining the relationship between the child's learning characteristics, the environment, tasks and style of teaching. Once monitoring has taken place (and some schools create initial monitoring forms) it may be necessary, because the child is making inadequate progress, to take School Action. Early Years Action/School Action provides interventions from within the school (DfES, 2001, para 5:43). However, should performance continue to be at a level of concern that requires the involvement of external agencies, then Early Years Action Plus/School Action Plus is set in place. If, after a period of monitoring and reviews, there are still concerns, it may be necessary to request that a statutory assessment takes place (DfES, 2001, para 5:62). This is where the local authority conducts an assessment to decide whether or not to issue a statement of SEN. This statement is a legal document; it details the provision the child requires from the school and the local authority. It is also directly transferable across schools and it may state which school the child should attend.

PRACTICAL TASK PRACTICAL TASK PRACTICAL TASK PRACTICAL TASK PRACTICAL TASK

On placement, find out what the range of SEN is across your school. What level of action are the children on? Choose two children from different age phases and produce a map of provision. Liaise with the class teacher about your observations and assessments of the children in your class so that you are able to assist in the process of reviewing and setting targets.

The Code of Practice (DfES, 2001b) clearly states that, once a child's needs have been recognised, your role as teacher is to:

- **monitor the child's progress;**
- **reduce barriers to their learning;**
- **differentiate the curriculum to allow maximum access;**
- **set and review IEP targets;**
- **work in partnership with others.**

An IEP is a working document that outlines the intervention for children with SEN. Its purpose is to specify targets that a child needs to achieve over a period of time. It needs to be devised in collaboration with the child and their parent. It should identify the targets, the strategies to be adopted and achievable success criteria. A child's IEP must be referred to when planning, monitoring and assessing.

During your different placements, you will see that there is no one standardised format for an IEP. However, they should all share the following information:

- **specific area of difficulty;**
- **targets to be achieved with success criteria;**
- **resources available;**
- **teaching support;**
- **strategies to be utilised;**
- **contributions from parent and child;**
- **review date.**

An example of an IEP is provided in Figure 13.1

PRACTICAL TASK PRACTICAL TASK **PRACTICAL TASK** PRACTICAL TASK **PRACTICAL TASK**

In your various placements ask for a copy of an IEP, so that you might build up a bank for reference. Find out when full review meetings of IEPs are taking place and see if you can attend these.

When planning a lesson, or part of a lesson, that you are going to teach, consider how you will make it inclusive of all children. Once you have delivered the lesson, evaluate its success in terms of the targets set on the IEP of any child with SEN.

The role of the SENCO and other agencies

On your placement, your first point of call, besides your class teacher and mentor is the SENCO. They are your contact in the school for highlighting concerns about a child's development, and for gaining support and guidance on issues relating to SEN.

Every school has a SEN policy and SENCOs ensure the day-to-day operation of that policy. They are responsible for co-ordinating the provision for children with SEN. They ensure that teachers in the school follow the procedures as laid out in the SEN Code of Practice and they liaise with other agencies who support children's learning.

A multi-agency approach is required in order to meet the needs of children identified as having SEN. This includes educational psychologists, speech therapists,

INDIVIDUAL EDUCATION PLAN
Child's name: Simon Griffiths Year group: 5 Area of concern: Social and communication difficulties Stage of action: School Action Review date: Class teacher(s): Mrs R. Jackson
Targets (T) and **Achievement Criteria** (AC) T: To follow simple and complex instructions given by the class teacher AC: To follow 3 simple and 3 complex instructions on 4 out of 5 occasions T: To be able to communicate a message accurately to another teacher AC: To deliver messages accurately on 4 out of 5 occasions T: To be able to speak and write in complete sentences AC: To be able to respond to adults in a complete sentence on 4 out of 5 occasions T: To take part in a small group discussion AC: To make a significant contribution in 2 out of 5 group discussions
Strategies (includes teacher support and differentiated resources) 1. Teacher and other adults model correct language structure. 2. Provide a buddy who is a good role model. 3. Use visual prompts. 4. Use open question cards and games.
Child and parent/carer contribution Child: Think about what needs to be said before saying sentence. Repeat instructions to ensure understanding. Talk on a one-to-one with buddy. Make small contributions in group discussions. Parent/carer: Ask child to repeat simple then complex instructions. Model correct language structure. Provide lots of encouragement and praise.
Class teacher's signature: Child's signature: Parent's signature: SENCO's signature: Date:

Figure 13.1 Example of an IEP

occupational therapists and other specialist services. It can extend to any agency or organisation that may have a direct input in the well-being of the child. With the implementation of the ECM agenda, this wider involvement of other professionals will increase.

Increasingly, SENCOs are expected to be skilled in the management of provision of SEN services across the school and are seen as being able to influence the development of policies for whole school improvement. *SENCOs play a pivotal role, coordinating provision across the school and linking class and subject teachers with SEN specialists to improve the quality of teaching and learning* (DfES, 2004b, 3:14).

As Cheminais observes, the role of the SENCO is becoming more specialised:

> They are more likely to be at the forefront of innovative inclusive classroom practice in terms of facilitating and enhancing pupils' learning and well being.

(2005, p3)

PRACTICAL TASK PRACTICAL TASK PRACTICAL TASK PRACTICAL TASK PRACTICAL TASK

- **Find out about the role of the SENCO and the SEN Governor in your placement school.**
- **Familiarise yourself with the SEN policy. Discuss the contents with the SENCO or the SEN Governor.**
- **Find out whether any of the children have a statement of SEN and how this is met. What agencies does your school work with in order to meet the child's needs?**

Parents

In order to recognise and meet the needs of children, it is critical to have a working partnership with parents. They contribute to the picture you are building of the child by providing information relating to the child's behaviour at home. For example, if the child has been diagnosed as being on the autistic spectrum, it is essential that you know their routines at home and what they particularly like or dislike.

You must be prepared to have to work hard at forming and maintaining a positive relationship with parents. This may not always be easy to do. For instance, the parent who is told that their child has been identified as having SEN may respond with disbelief or denial. They will need to be supported through the process so they understand what it means to have an IEP and how this details the support available to their child and detailed in the IEP. The Code of Practice is very clear on outlining the importance of involving parents: *It is essential that all professionals actively seek to work with parents and value the contribution they make* (DfES, 2001, 2:2).

Remember that parents need to know that you intend to ensure that their child becomes an independent learner, not someone who is reliant on the support of a teacher or teaching assistant in order to achieve success. However, their child needs additional support at this stage in their education; this may or may not need to continue. They will need to be reassured that monitoring is in place and reviews will be held and this involves meeting with them.

ICT and SEN

This can be approached from two angles.

1. There are a number of ICT packages being used to assist in the identification of SEN.
2. ICT is being used to support teaching and learning. *ICT should be used to give children with special educational needs maximum access to the curriculum and to help them reach their learning potential* (DfEE, 1997b, 1:30).

PRACTICAL TASK PRACTICAL TASK **PRACTICAL TASK** PRACTICAL TASK **PRACTICAL TASK**

What ICT packages are used in your placement to assist in the identification of a SEN?

REFLECTIVE TASK

What do you consider to be the challenges to providing an inclusive education which caters for a wide range of SEN? What further knowledge and experience do you think you require?

Conclusion

Recognising SEN is the responsibility of all in the school. There have been major changes in the way in which children with SEN are supported, from the initial focus in 1978 to date. The culture is now one of inclusion, where the child is given as broad an access to the curriculum as possible. The multi-agency approach to supporting children with SEN means that there can be early intervention and greater support for teachers in terms of their increased knowledge about specific needs and implementation of appropriate strategies to support the child.

Moving on

With time and experience, you will become more familiar with various forms of SEN as you encounter a wider range of children with different special educational needs. This will sometimes lead you to research further how to deal with particular needs. There are national organisations that provide information and resources relating to SEN. A few of these are listed at the end of the chapter along with further reading and useful website addresses. As well as published materials, schools, local authorities and other organisations may offer training sessions. To further your knowledge, you may want to attend SEN conferences that are taking place. Many of these are advertised in the *Times Educational Supplement* or other publications. It is critical to keep your knowledge up to date so that you can ensure equality of opportunity for all children.

FURTHER READING   FURTHER READING   **FURTHER READING**

ATL (2002) *Achievement for All: Working with Children with Special Educational Needs in Mainstream Schools and Colleges.* London: Association of Teachers and Lecturers. Available online via ATL website **www.atl.org.uk/**

Birkett, V. (2003) *How to Support and Teach Children with Special Educational Needs.* Cambridge: LDA. LDA publish a range of short books dealing with Special Educational Needs including several on specific needs which you may encounter in your classroom.

DfES (2001) *Special Educational Needs: Code of Practice.* London: DfES. **www.teacher-net.gov.uk/_doc/3724/SENCodeOfPractice.pdf**

DfES (2001) *SEN Toolkit.* London: Department for Education and Skills. **www.teachernet.-gov.uk/wholeschool/sen/sentoolkit/** This *Code of Practice* and the related *SEN Tool Kit* (2001) are critical references for anyone working with children with SEN. The Toolkit is an excellent resource, providing examples of how schools can implement the statutory guidance set out in the Code.

DfES (2004) *Removing Barriers to Achievement. The Government's Strategy for SEN.* London: Department for Education and Skills.

Gross, J. (2002) *Special Educational Needs in the Primary School: A Practical Guide*, 3rd edn. Buckingham: Open University Press.

Soan, S. (2005) *Primary Special Educational Needs Reflective Reader*. Exeter: Learning Matters.

USEFUL ADDRESSES   USEFUL ADDRESSES   **USEFUL ADDRESSES**   USEFUL ADDRESSES

ADD/ADHD Family Support Group, 1a High Street, Dilton Marsh, Westbury, Wilts BA13 4DL

British Dyslexia Association, 98 London Road, Reading, Berkshire RG1 5AU

Dyslexia Action, Park House, Wick Road, Egham, Surrey TW20 0HH

National Association for Gifted Children, Suite 14, Challenge House, Sherwood Drive, Bletchley, Milton Keynes HK3 6DP

National Autistic Society, 393 City Road, London EC1V 1NG

Useful websites

www.bdadyslexia.org.uk
www.becta.org.uk/teachers
www.dcsf.gov.uk
www.dyspraxiaireland.com
www.everychildmatters.gov.uk
www.inclusion.org.uk
www.nas.org.uk
www.ofsted.gov.uk
www.standards.dfes.gov.uk
www.teachernet.gov.uk/wholeschool/sen

14

Every Child Matters in your classroom: approaches to personalised learning
Kath Langley-Hamel

By the end of this chapter you should:

- have considered ways in which principles relating to equality, diversity and inclusion can be translated into practice in the classroom;
- have considered the holistic needs of all children;
- be aware of the importance of a common assessment framework to identify needs;
- be aware of the importance of identifying and responding to individual needs in helping children to enjoy learning and to achieve;
- have positive and confident approaches to diversity;
- be aware of the role of the teacher in creating a climate in which children can feel safe, secure and valued;
- be aware of the role of the teacher in fostering creativity in all children;
- be aware of relevant legal frameworks promoting the well-being of children.

This chapter addresses the following Professional Standards for QTS:

Q1, Q2, Q3, Q4, Q5, Q7

This chapter considers the holistic needs of children as they enter and progress through school and reflects issues at government, whole-school and classroom level. Consideration will be given to the ways in which the principles of government policies such as *Every Child Matters: Change for Children* (DfES, 2004a), *Excellence and Enjoyment* (DfES, 2003), the National Curriculum (1999) and the Curriculum Guidance for the Foundation Stage (2000) can be translated into practice. The chapter reflects on ways in which these principles influence the ethos, interaction and communication between all members of the school community. Emphasis will be placed on the importance of a rigorous approach to pedagogy and connections will be made between effective, motivating, creative teaching and the reduction of frustration, anxiety and potential bullying. Detailed consideration will be given to the role of the class teacher in creating a safe, supportive environment in which all children can thrive socially and academically. The chapter will include a range of practical and positive ways to promote effective observation and intervention.

Needs of all children

All of us have basic needs, regardless of our age. We need to feel that we belong, that we are safe and secure, that our differences are accepted and others value our contributions. When these needs are met, children are able to thrive and develop, emotionally, physically and creatively. They are able to explore, take risks and discover; secure in the knowledge that they will be taken seriously and valued. In school, when children are away from the support of their families, this need to feel comfortable is an essential aspect of successful learning. Learning is maximised when self-esteem is high and children feel confident. This philosophy underpins many school policies and influences most teachers' interaction with children.

It is realistic to acknowledge that for a minority of children early childhood may have been a troubled experience; sadly, for some of these children it may have been traumatic. The policy document *Every Child Matters: Change for Children* (DfES, 2004a) aims to ensure all organisations involved in supporting and protecting young children collaborate to share information, adopt a common approach to the assessment of needs and provide maximum support for vulnerable children. The Common Assessment Framework, reflecting the principles of ECM, will be implemented in all local authorities by 2008. The framework outlines straightforward, collaborative procedures reflecting a holistic approach to the identification of the strengths and needs of children in order to provide effective support for children and their families. This collaboration should provide protection, and promote the five outcomes identified by the document, helping children: to be healthy, to stay safe, to enjoy and achieve, to achieve economic well-being and make a positive contribution to the life of the school and community. It is important to consider the ways in which these significant outcomes can be reflected at whole-school and classroom level.

Social and emotional support

It is important to acknowledge that for some children the emotionally stable learning environment of school may be the most secure and constant aspect of their lives. Such children who are disturbed as a result of their life experiences, may have difficulty in engaging with school and the process of learning, Poor self-esteem may inhibit their willingness to learn and to interact socially. Emotions based on fear and anger may spill over into the classroom, resulting in distracted thinking and disturbing behaviour.

There has been increasing awareness, in recent years, of the significance of the concept of emotional intelligence in helping children to understand their feelings and their behaviour. Goleman (1996) emphasises the importance of supporting children to become emotionally self aware, to learn to manage their emotions and to read the emotions of others and to empathise with them. He considers that school-based support in this area can have lifelong benefits, helping *children to turn moments of personal crisis into personal competence*. Corrie (2003) identifies a strong connection between emotional intelligence, raised self-esteem and success. She advocates the use of a three-part model to promote the development of interpersonal and intrapersonal intelligence. This encourages children to know themselves and understand their own feelings, to make choices about their responses, to shape their thinking and to make a positive difference to the world around them. This model is compatible with the aims of *Every Child Matters: Change for Children* (DfES, 2004a) working towards the outcomes relating to enjoyment and achievement and making a positive contribution.

The teacher's contribution to the emotional and social development of children is pivotal. Goleman (1996) warns that it is not possible to teach emotional intelligence as an isolated set of skills unrelated to the teacher's behaviour. Corrie notes that the *creation of the emotionally intelligent classroom must begin with the teacher* (2003, p7). Children are perceptive; they learn a great deal from watching the ways in which the teacher interacts with others in the classroom. This behaviour is often internalised by the children and is subsequently reflected in their own interaction.

The class teacher: attitude, communication and empathy

The attitude of the teacher is crucial in establishing a climate of respect within the classroom. An inconsistent and negative teacher can diminish the curiosity and attention of the children, promoting an uncertain ethos and resulting in negative social interaction. An atmosphere of fear is created, where risk taking is minimised, individuality depressed and creativity stagnates. This can have long-term consequences. All too often, adults can recall the feeling of being undervalued and confused in the classroom. Conversely, a teacher who acts as a positive role model can have far-reaching effects on life within and beyond the classroom. 'When teachers are empathetically understanding, their students tend to like each other better. In an understanding classroom every student tends to feel liked by all the others, has a more positive attitude towards self, and a positive attitude towards school'. (Schmuck in Rogers, 1983, p128)

The manner in which teachers communicate provides evidence of how the children are perceived. Interaction, which is consistent, measured and respectful, gives a sense of calm, organisation and purpose. Taking time to talk and understand children as individuals, to know their family connections and their current interests is important in establishing a learning community. This will allow children to approach new learning opportunities with confidence, an expectation of success and a sense of being valued. Positive interaction between teacher and child must be modelled by all members of staff in a school community, to ensure that the environment is safe and comfortable, promoting a sense of belonging and well-being.

Teaching for creativity by responding to individual needs: the role of the teacher

There has been a growing recognition of the importance of creativity in the primary curriculum in recent years. A range of initiatives has been launched to encourage teachers to identify and foster creativity in all children. In 1999 the National Advisory Committee on Creative and Cultural Education published a report for the DfES *All Our Futures: Creativity, Culture and Education*. This advocated the implementation of a national strategy to raise the status of creativity in school. The report stressed the importance of teachers establishing a balance between teaching skills, the development of understanding and the encouragement of risk taking and innovation. Creativity is a key aspect of *Excellence and Enjoyment: A Strategy for Primary Schools* (DfES, 2003). This document recognises the importance of creativity in raising self-esteem and achievement, promoting lifelong learning and developing individual talents. The importance of creativity was further emphasised in the report *Expecting the Unexpected: developing creativity in primary and secondary schools* (Ofsted, 2003c).

All these initiatives emphasise the fact that creativity cannot be taught in isolation as a bolt-on extra. It is an integral element of the curriculum, embedded in the teacher's approach and reflected in the classroom ethos. Creativity is unlikely to thrive unless conditions in the school and the classroom are favourable. Risk-taking and innovative thinking are unlikely to happen in an uncertain and confrontational atmosphere. Joubert (2005) emphasises the link between creativity and the role of the teacher. She notes that teachers who create a supportive ethos, in which children feel confident, are able to teach creatively themselves and to develop the creative abilities of their pupils. In such a culture the concept of creativity is not elitist; it is not only restricted to the arts, or directed exclusively towards the gifted and talented, but is an important aspect of inclusive education as teachers recognise and respond to the creative potential in individual children.

Whole-school responses to meet the needs of all children

Support from the start: induction into school

The first encounter with school is a vital time for the young child and his or her family. The quality of support during induction can have long-term consequences. Research findings by Tizard et al (1988) revealed that children who made a confident and positive start to school made the greatest progress throughout the primary school. Underpinning the Curriculum Guidance for the Foundation Stage (2000) are the central principles that all children have the right to feel included, secure and valued and that no child should feel excluded or be disadvantaged. It is vital that the induction process is inclusive and effective, valuing parents and preparing children thoughtfully and sensitively for the transition ahead.

Starting school may prove to be a daunting and bewildering experience for many children. Fabian notes that an essential feature of managing the home/school transition lies in children's understanding of the contrasts between the two worlds. She observes *children must make sense of the differences between home and school and overcome these obstacles if they are to succeed* (Fabian, 2002, p3). Early Years practitioners recognise the challenges and respond to the diverse needs of the children. Young children have to come to terms with and make sense of the following.

The physical demands of the school

A young child may feel alienated by the size of the buildings, the layout of the rooms, the unfamiliarity of resources and furniture, the strangeness of communal toilets and the vastness of the playground.

The social demands of the school

Entering the classroom presents many social challenges for children who may be leaving the secure and informal world of home for the first time. Children have to come to terms with the numbers of unfamiliar children; the noise level may prove overwhelming for some. They have to accept new adults, come to terms with a very different adult/child ratio and begin to understand the concept of turn taking.

Cultural differences

Every child begins school with a set of unique experiences, interests and expectations. For some children the contrast between the worlds of home and school will be very great. Early Years practitioners must respond positively to this diversity: recognising what children already know, building on this, accepting that there will be many different starting points to meet individual needs.

The language of school: the role of the teacher

The language of school is a critical factor in successful transition for many children; it may also have long-term effects on their learning. Some children may speak another language at home. Others may take time to become accustomed to Standard English. Many children may be confused by the language structures and the style of interaction in the classroom. Tizard and Hughes (1984, p210) produced powerful evidence to show that the verbal behaviour of young children can be very different at home and at school. Some children are puzzled by teachers' use of language, in particular 'teacherly questions' to assess understanding. These children all too quickly become the passive recipients of language, the answerers of organisational and procedural questions and not the questions rooted in curiosity.

Unwillingness to ask questions based on curiosity may have long-term effects on children's ability to enjoy life in the classroom and achieve their potential throughout the primary school and beyond. It will certainly restrict confident and creative thinking. Craft (2000) emphasises the importance of children being able to question in fostering imagination and creativity, and developing *possibility thinking*. She notes that children may not simply respond to questions, but may answer questions with further questions, in order to discover more about the world and to make sense of it. Research studies have shown that teacher talk tends to dominate classroom interaction (Mercer, 1996; Smith et al, 2004). Teachers need to be aware of the impact of their language on the ethos and interaction in the classroom and on children's ability to learn, to question and discover.

REFLECTIVE TASK

Reflect on your own use of language.

- **Do you give children experiences and opportunities that encourage them to question?**
- **Do you build on their responses?**
- **Do you encourage children to question each other to clarify their thinking?**

Personalised learning

The DfES have placed emphasis on the educational philosophy of personalised learning in tailoring education to reflect children's individual needs, interests and aptitudes (DfES, 2004c). In order for all children to feel secure, valued and settled, teachers need to be able to identify and respond to individual needs and talents, providing appropriate learning opportunities to reflect diversity. To achieve this, it is important to understand the requirements of legislation relating to equality of opportunity, in particular the Sex Discrimination Act 1975, The Race Relations Act 1976, The Disability Discrimination Act 2005 and the Special Educational Needs and Disability Act 2001. The implications of legislation are discussed in greater depth in the Chapter 15.

The National Curriculum (DfEE/QCA, 1999, pp30–37) outlines principles relating to inclusion to ensure that all children have a legal right to access to a broad and balanced curriculum and to effective learning opportunities. The three main principles of inclusion relate to:

- **setting suitable learning challenges;**
- **providing an effective response to diversity;**
- **overcoming barriers to learning for individuals and groups.**

From principles to practice: a positive response to diversity.

In order to ensure that personalised learning in an inclusive classroom becomes a reality and not a distant goal, it may be useful to reflect on your teaching experience and consider the following points.

REFLECTIVE TASK

- **Does the learning environment reflect the diverse backgrounds of the children?**
- **Does the learning environment reflect the ways you value children?**
- **Does the classroom ethos ensure that children feel safe from harassment and bullying?**
- **Does the classroom ethos encourage children to take risks and feel confident enough to make mistakes?**
- **Do you plan learning opportunities to develop self-esteem, promote enjoyment and motivation?**
- **Does your planning reflect creativity?**
- **Do teaching strategies support different learning styles to reflect diverse needs?**
- **Do you help children to reflect on the ways in which they learn?**
- **Do assessment strategies provide an insight into the ways children think?**

Responding to individual needs: providing additional support

Some children may require additional support in an inclusive setting to meet their needs. They may find it difficult to meet the social and academic demands of the classroom, even in a positive and supportive climate. This can challenge, frustrate and confuse the child and the teacher. Both are aware that progress is not being made, as it becomes increasingly clear that these children may require provision additional to, or different from, that generally available for all children. In the past this might have resulted in the child being excluded from the curriculum, or even from the mainstream school. The current inclusive climate is underpinned by several significant pieces of legislation. It has been noted that the revised National Curriculum (1999) was amended to include a section on inclusion. The Special Needs Disability Act 2001 strengthened the right of children with SEN to a mainstream education.

The revised Code of Practice for children with Special Educational Needs (DfES, 2001) provides clear guidelines on the ways schools should identify, assess and support children with SEN. The emphasis in this document is on meeting the needs of these children within mainstream schools wherever possible. The code sets out a graduated response to the meeting of needs.

Supporting individual needs

Meeting children's pastoral needs is dependent on effective teaching. Providing appropriate support plays a major role in diminishing anxiety and frustration for many children. A great deal of disruptive behaviour is rooted in fear of failure. Many children would rather opt out, refuse to participate or become aggressive, rather than admit inability to understand the demands of a task. Appropriate support usually promotes a more positive learning environment for the whole class. Effective support for children with SEN is likely to lead to effective provision for all children.

Observation: the first step towards effective support

Observing children in the process of learning provides the opportunity to assess aspects of learning and behaviour for all children and identify those who may need extra help and support. Observation is a significant aspect of the process of identifying and responding to individual needs. Base your conclusions on evidence, not assumption.

Unstructured approaches may result in an oversimplification of the process and an inaccurate and unhelpful picture of the child's needs. It is dangerously easy to adopt a deficit-based approach, in which the focus of the observation is restricted to all aspects of the classroom life which the child finds difficult or threatening. This provides limited information and a negative starting point for intervention resulting in finding out what the child can't do and giving the child lots more of it. It is obviously important to identify the precise nature of areas of difficulty, but these should be counterbalanced by the assessment of the child's strengths and interests.

The difficulties that children experience are not static; they are context-specific. The interaction between the child, the teacher and the learning environment should be the focus of the observation. The child may struggle in one aspect of the curriculum, or tend to be more disruptive in certain situations. It is important to adopt this holistic approach in order to obtain realistic and useful information.

Suggested areas for observation

- **What do you consider to be the strengths of the child?**
- **What does the child perceive to be his/her strengths?**
- **How does the child respond to other children/adults?**
- **How do other children respond to the child?**
- **Which social aspects of the classroom present difficulties for the child and for those with whom he/she works?**
- **What aspects of the curriculum present the child with difficulties?**
- **What learning styles does the child prefer?**
- **Which aspects of learning, teaching and classroom management may result in difficulties for the child (and the teacher!), e.g. timing, whole-class work, group work, and communication?**
- **What physical aspects of the classroom present difficulties?**

It may be useful to focus on children at times when they struggle with the learning environment. This should help you to identify the overt response and the underlying trigger for the problem.

How does the child respond when experiencing problems?

The following prompts might provide insight into the nature of the child's difficulties. Is the child:

- **making demands on the teacher according to rules agreed in the class;**
- **making demands on the teacher, not according to a rule;**
- **showing attention seeking behaviour;**
- **seeking assistance from other children;**
- **refusing to work;**
- **adopting a range of work avoidance strategies?**

The strategies children use to avoid work are varied. They may choose to be openly confrontational. They may seek to distract all the children in a group so that no one succeeds and no child is seen to fail. The uncertainty which this engenders creates a lack of security which can be felt by all the children. In extreme cases some children may respond to this by seeking to take control themselves and intimidate successful learners. This amounts to bullying which may begin in the classroom, but can spill out into other aspects of school life. It is also likely that you will encounter children who avoid work by adopting a helpful and supportive role in the classroom; these children are constantly ready to volunteer to help. The teacher may view this positively, but the children may use this strategy, consciously or unconsciously, to avoid situations which they may consider to be difficult or worrying. Children are frequently more comfortable opting out than putting themselves at risk of failure. Assessing this effectively and positively is an essential step towards meeting the pastoral needs of all children and ensuring that they achieve their potential and enjoy learning.

Observe the child in a range of contexts

Effective observation must be manageable and useful, providing a picture of a child in a range of situations. It should reflect all aspects of development – social, intellectual and physical. It should also reflect enjoyment and creativity. It is important to assess the child in a range of groupings, including whole-class, small group, in pairs and in individual work.

Involve the child

Children may feel excluded from the process of assessment and identification of needs. In fact, they have a great deal to contribute; they have first-hand experience of the situation and their own interpretation of events in the classroom. It is important that you encourage the child to enter into discussion with you to set targets, to recognise strengths, to express anxieties and, where appropriate, to realise the impact of their behaviour on other children.

Involve the parents

It is essential to ensure parental support, encouraging them to reflect on the child's strengths and difficulties, both at home and at school. This rapport with parents establishes a positive working relationship, maintaining a dialogue while needs are identified and interventions planned. A collaborative approach, wherever possible, is much more likely to promote successful learning and a happy child.

PRACTICAL TASK PRACTICAL TASK PRACTICAL TASK PRACTICAL TASK PRACTICAL TASK

Carry out a structured observation using some of the areas above as a focus. Have you observed and recorded an equal number of strengths and weaknesses? What is your evidence for your observations?

What form might the support take?

Children might require support in the following areas if they are to gain access to the curriculum and the wider aspects of classroom life:

- **responding to spoken language;**
- **responding to written language;**
- **gaining and retaining knowledge and skills;**
- **meeting the organisational and social demands of the classroom.**

Responding to spoken language

The most obvious response to differentiation may be considered to relate to the modification of activities, the type of resources and the adaptation of written work. However, often the most relevant starting point is the need for teachers to be aware of the complexity of the demands of their communication and to adapt their communication accordingly. Children who have difficulty in processing spoken language may be bewildered by the length of sentences, the complexity of the syntax used and the number of commands given in rapid sequence. They may well be confused by the use of technical vocabulary in the classroom. Children experiencing hearing loss may find communication in the classroom demanding, tiring and sometimes isolating. It is important that you are aware of the significance of spoken language in promoting (or restricting) success for many children.

The following suggestions do not provide an exhaustive list, but they may be a useful starting point for effective interaction in the classroom. You should be aware of:

- **the length of your utterances: could these be reduced at times?**
- **the complexity of your syntax, e.g. the use of the passive tense can be very confusing;**
- **the demands of vocabulary and the need for explanation;**
- **the difference that making eye contact can have in facilitating communication for some children;**
- **the pace of your spoken language – it is easy to 'fire' questions at children without allowing thinking time or time for children to talk together;**
- **the need to evaluate your use of language.**

It is equally important to present children with good models of language.

Responding to written language

Differentiation has been discussed in Chapter 3. However, the following brief points may prove useful in approaching personalised learning.

- **Some children need strategies to help the written word to become more accessible. Using visual cues such as colour coding words or common spelling patterns can reinforce visual patterns.**
- **Some children may be daunted by the volume of writing. Attention to layout and avoiding dense passages of print can prompt a much more positive response.**
- **Help children to identify key words to make the text more accessible.**
- **Think creatively about recording. While it is clearly necessary to develop skills in writing, are there times when children could present information in other ways, e.g. graphs, diagrams, pictures?**
- **Consider the self-esteem of the learner – must the differentiated resources look markedly different from other resources?**

The factors outlined above are only a small part of successful differentiation. However, attention to these aspects might reduce fear of failure, decrease tension and promote a more positive approach to learning for everyone in the classroom.

Gaining and retaining knowledge and skills

It has been emphasised throughout this chapter that uncertainty about the likelihood of success can result in tension and possible aggression. This has an obvious adverse effect on all those in the classroom. Some children are acutely aware of the fact that they have difficulty in gaining and retaining knowledge. A girl who experienced difficulty in writing exemplified this when she picked up her pencil at the start of a task, looked it at accusingly and remarked, 'This pencil makes it come out wrong every time'. This anxiety can prompt a downward spiral in which the child does not expect to succeed, senses failure, fails, and brings a sense of resignation of failure to any new task. If we are not careful we, as teachers, can contribute to this by low expectations.

PRACTICAL TASK PRACTICAL TASK PRACTICAL TASK PRACTICAL TASK PRACTICAL TASK

When planning lessons, focus on two instructions that you plan to give verbally or in written form. Analyse your use of language in terms of complexity of syntax, vocabulary and the volume of information. Will this prevent some children from engaging in the activity?

Meeting the social demands of the classroom

This can be the most challenging aspect of the inclusive classroom for you, the child, his/her peers and other adults in the room. Social interaction is complex, dynamic and situation specific. It is not my intention to provide simplistic solutions to every occasion and every context. However, an awareness of some of the underlying tensions and consideration of possible strategies may be a useful starting point.

Acknowledge the complexity of classroom life

A range of factors, many of which are beyond your immediate control, influences interaction in the classroom:

- the requirements of the curriculum;
- the organisational demands of the school;
- whole-school ethos and expectations;
- the previous experience of the children;
- the experiences of the children outside the school.

Watkins and Wagner (1988) observe that classrooms are busy, public places and that classroom events are multidimensional. It is important to acknowledge the influence of these factors if you are to analyse events in the classroom and respond effectively and consistently. As teachers we wish to create a positive and supportive learning environment promoting a sense of well-being, enjoyment and achievement (DfES, 2004a).

Carry out an audit

Despite our best efforts to create a supportive learning environment it may feel at times as if this is under attack from all sides. Carrying out an audit on the demands that children make on your time and your response to these may reveal issues related to organisation, use of time, effectiveness of liaison with teaching assistants and other adults, communication and expectations, which could be addressed to enhance the learning environment.

Support social interaction between children

Positive social interaction between children is fostered by the supportive class-room climate that has been promoted in this chapter. Teachers can model respectful dialogue and ensure inappropriate talk is discouraged through recog-nising the effect on others, and how it may result in bullying which is insidious and needs to be eliminated. It is easy to adopt a heavy-handed approach to bullying which can exacerbate the problem. You need to be able to observe and analyse the triggers of bullying behaviour, and be able to listen to the bully, the victim and their parents. It is important to remember that no happy or confident child engages in bullying tactics, nor falls foul of a bully. Clearly, bullying must not be tolerated; therefore teachers must recognise the complexity of the situation in order to make an informed and effective response. Schools adopt a whole-school approach to minimise bullying. It is important that indivi-dual teachers reflect on elements of their own teaching which could contribute to a climate of insecurity and promote bullying.

Exploring serious issues which may concern children

The Children Act 1989, implemented in 1991, gave legal recognition to *the ascer-tainable wishes and feelings of the child* (section1(3)). This Act brought together all aspects of child health, welfare and protection and set out the legal framework for a multi-agency approach to these issues. Teachers in daily contact with children need to be aware of the legal position. The Education Act 2002, implemented in June 2004, implemented duties of child protection on governing bodies. *Every Child Matters: Change for Children*, underlines the need for an integrated multi agency approach to child protection.

The Children Act 1989 identified four categories of abuse:

- **neglect resulting in failure to thrive;**
- **physical abuse including non-accidental injury;**
- **sexual abuse;**
- **emotional abuse, severe or persistent emotional ill treatment or rejection resulting in adverse effects on behaviour and emotional development.**

Every school has a policy setting out the school's approach to child protection issues. When you go into school, it is essential that you become familiar with this policy and identify the designated member of staff to whom you would refer any serious concerns.

Although the majority of children are well cared for and protected, it is equally important to maintain vigilance through careful observation. Teachers must estab-lish a rapport with children that encourages them to express their wishes and feelings. Individual children should feel able to disclose more sensitive information about their lives, which may include abuse. This may be taking place in school in the form of bullying. If it is used effectively, circle time promotes communication in an atmosphere that fosters trust and builds up a climate of trust in which sensitive issues could be explored. Circle time may be used to:

- **build up self-esteem, encouraging children to recognise their own strengths and those of their peers;**
- **celebrate success in the classroom;**
- **discuss such issues as work avoidance and identify possible causes and solutions;**
- **discuss individual likes, dislikes and interests.**

Conclusion

This chapter has explored ways in which the holistic needs of children can be met, to ensure that the learning outcomes at the heart of ECM are realised. Emphasis has been given to the importance of a whole-school approach, ensuring children's legal rights are protected. The concept of partnership and collaboration between all those involved in the school has been stressed throughout. Consideration has been given to the importance of translating policies into principles that are then reflected in the daily life of the classroom. Finally a central theme has been the role of the teacher in promoting a safe, welcoming environment in which all children are valued, safe and secure. It has been emphasised throughout the chapter that the teacher's attitude is crucial in establishing a learning community in which children can enjoy learning, respond positively to diversity, take risks confidently, discover more about the world and develop their creative potential. The DfES recognises that the consequences of responding effectively to individual needs, interests and aspirations of all children, will extend beyond the classroom making a strong contribution to equity and social justice (DfES, 2004c)

Moving on

To promote the learning outcomes, 'stay safe' and 'enjoy and achieve' at the heart of *Every Child Matters: Change for Children*, you could explore the Primary National Strategy Materials, *Excellence and Enjoyment: Social and Emotional Aspects of Learning* (DfES, 2005a). These materials address significant themes relating to social and emotional development in a systematic framework for each year group from the Foundation Stage to Year 6. They provide practical examples of the ways in which you can respond positively to diversity and will help you to develop a supportive and collaborative ethos in the classroom. They will help the children to recognise their own strengths and those of their peers, to develop confidence and self-esteem and promote self-awareness, supporting children in understanding and managing their own emotions and feelings and empathising with others.

Carry out further reading on emotional intelligence in order to understand more about the children in your class, to help them to develop self-awareness and to promote your own self-knowledge.

FURTHER READING   FURTHER READING   FURTHER READING

Corrie, C. (2003) *Becoming Emotionally Intelligent*. London: Network Educational Press Ltd.

Craft, A. (2000) *Creativity Across The Primary Curriculum*: *Framing and Developing Practice*. London: Routledge.

DfES (2005) *Excellence and Enjoyment*: *Social and Emotional Aspects of Learning*. DfES Publications.

DfES (2004) *A National Conversation About Personalised Learning.* DfES Publications.

Fabian, H. (2002) *Children Starting School: A Guide To Successful Transitions and Transfers for Teachers and Assistants*. London: David Fulton.

Farrell, M. (2003) *Understanding Special Educational Needs*: *A Guide for Student Teachers*. London: RoutledgeFalmer.

15
Teachers' professional duties and statutory responsibilities
Rob Hyland

> **By the end of the chapter you should:**
>
> - **understand the framework of professional regulation within which teachers work;**
> - **have considered some of the legal implications of becoming a teacher;**
> - **be aware of a teacher's contractual rights and obligations as an employee;**
> - **be aware of a teacher's statutory responsibilities in relation to children within and without the classroom;**
> - **be familiar with the regulations which govern a teacher's actions in disciplining children.**
>
> This chapter addresses the following Professional Standards for QTS:
>
> **Q3(a), Q3(b), Q21(a), Q21(b), Q30, Q31**

The professional standards for QTS require that you be aware of the statutory framework within which teachers work, their professional duties and the nature of the policies and practices which apply in the workplace. This chapter considers the statutory responsibilities, legal liabilities and professional duties which apply to teachers, particularly when working within state-maintained schools in England and Wales. These include:

- the requirements for professional registration for teachers;
- their general contractual commitments and conditions of service;
- their common law duty to ensure that children are healthy and safe;
- their responsibility for promoting children's welfare;
- their obligations with regard to race relations and gender discrimination;
- the rules which govern discipline and the physical restraint of children;
- and the requirement to develop their own practice.

Joining a regulated profession

Though some of this may seem rather remote at the beginning of your training, it is important that from the outset you understand some of the requirements and expectations of teachers. Once you accept appointment as a teacher, signing your contract implies acceptance of those roles, responsibilities and conditions which are framed by law. Not being familiar with laws and regulations will not excuse you from observing them: while you cannot hope to master *all* the intricacies of the rules and regulations which apply to schools, it is important to know in broad terms just what you will be taking on in terms of responsibilities and obligations when you become a NQT.

In qualifying as a teacher you will be joining what is quite properly a regulated profession. There are laws and regulations which determine who may be a teacher – particularly in a school maintained by the state – and what such teachers must, may and may not do. Also – as will become of increasing interest to you – there are regulations which determine just how much teachers are paid for their labours.

The way that the teaching profession is regulated and teachers' rights and responsibilities are structured is, however, quite complex. Some of the obligations and entitlements which will apply to you are rooted in general legislation (e.g. employment and anti-discrimination laws) which applies to all employers and employees in the United Kingdom. Other obligations and entitlements are based on education law and regulations which relate specifically to teachers and their employers. You should note that some regulations apply to independent (private) schools as well as to state-maintained schools, but many do not; most obviously, independent schools set their own pay and conditions of service. Education legislation and policy is often specific to the constituent countries of the United Kingdom. Though much of the legislation which applies to education in England also applies, with some minor variations, in Wales, the systems are diverging under the influence of devolution; Scotland's and Northern Ireland's education systems are administered separately.

Certain key powers to bar or restrict the employment of teachers lie with the Secretary of State. The DCSF keeps the infamous 'List 99' which identifies teachers who are deemed unsuitable to work in schools, either for particular reasons of misconduct or on certain medical grounds. Certain criminal convictions and being on the Sex Offenders' Register mean being debarred from teaching. A check through the Criminal Records Bureau requiring 'enhanced enclosure' will be requested when you take up a new appointment or have a break in service of three months or more, or if the school or LA has any concerns about your suitability to work with children. Teachers are exempted from the 'spent convictions' provisions of the Rehabilitation of Offenders Act 1974. Failure to disclose convictions or any other significant misrepresentation (e.g. of qualifications) in applying for posts is regarded very seriously.

When you take a post as a teacher in a UK state school you are required to be registered as a member of the relevant General Teaching Council – for England (GTCE), Wales (GTCW), Scotland (GTCS) or Northern Ireland (GTNI). These GTCs play an important role in the upholding of professional standards. Through the Disciplinary Function Regulations, the GTCs of England and Wales have been given powers to investigate professional conduct and competence and also have a particular role in hearing NQT appeals over induction. They hold hearings into allegations of misconduct or incompetence and, subject to certain rights of appeal, can suspend a teacher's registration in ways similar to other regulated professions; their judgements are also published.

As with any employment, in addition to serious criminal or professional misde-meanours, proven professional incompetence or incapacity to fulfil your contractual obligations can also result in your dismissal. Governing bodies are required to have 'capability procedures' and attendance monitoring policies for such cases. Teachers dismissed on capability grounds are reported to the relevant General Teaching Council and may have their registrations withdrawn. In all such matters there are procedures and rights of appeal to protect the interests of teachers who – rightly or wrongly – believe themselves to be the victims of unfair judgements. As a job applicant, employee or GTC registrant you are, of course, protected by the Race Relations Act 1976, the Sex Discrimination Act 1975, the Disability Discrimination Act 1995, the Human Rights Act 1998 and general employment legislation including the Employment Equality (Sexual Orientation) Regulations 2003, the Employment Equality (Religion or Belief) Regulations 2003 and the Employment Equality (Age) Regulations 2006.

Teachers' conditions of employment

Teachers' contracts

As a teacher in a state-maintained school in England and Wales, your professional duties and the financial structure which governs the rewards you can expect for your work are set out in the *School Teachers' Pay and Conditions Document* (STPCD), sometimes referred to as the Blue Book. This document changes annually, following the government's response to the report of the School Teachers' Review Body (STRB). Explanatory guidance accompanies the formal document to explain its appli-cation. Your contract of employment relates to the version then current; it implies acceptance of subsequent versions as pay scales are adjusted and new contractual requirements are introduced. In the STPCD and guidance there are references to 'relevant bodies' rather than 'employers'. This terminology is necessary because of some of the variation in teachers' employment arrangements. If you work in a nursery or very small school without a 'delegated budget', or as an 'unattached teacher' for a central service, then the LA is the 'relevant body' as well as your employer. However, in almost all maintained schools the governors will be the 'relevant body' for appoint-ing you and determining your exact salary; they are required to have a policy which explains how particular judgements are made within the national framework. Whether the governing body or the LA is your contractual employer depends upon the formal legal status of the school.

There are four major categories of maintained schools in England which may have some influence upon your contractual conditions:

- **Community schools (formerly known as 'county schools'): the LA is the employer.**
- **Voluntary Controlled (usually Church of England, though there are some Methodist VC schools and some without religious affiliation): the LA is the employer, but the governing body determines worship; it may make some conditions of appointment related to the school's religious ethos.**
- **Voluntary Aided (particularly Roman Catholic schools, but also some Anglican, Jewish and Muslim schools): the governing body is the employer; it determines religious instruction and may make some associated conditions of employment including religious commitment.**

- **Foundation: the governing body is the contractual employer. This category would include the new Trust schools, which are foundation schools that have acquired a charitable trust.**

Contracts of employment may be permanent, fixed term, or temporary. The contract of employment is a formal document but the contract to which you work also includes your job description and school policy documents. As a teacher you should expect a clear job description which can subsequently be changed through negotiation.

What do the 'conditions of service' demand of teachers?

Teachers' formal 'conditions of employment' are set out in the *School Teachers' Pay and Conditions Document*. There are some very particular conditions which apply only to head teachers, some conditions which apply to all teachers other than heads, and a few specific conditions which apply to deputy and assistant head teachers or to advanced skills teachers, excellent teachers (this is a formal category, not just an evaluation) and fast track teachers.

The introduction to the 'conditions of employment' section makes clear that a teacher *shall carry out the professional duties of a teacher as circumstances may require* (para 74.1) *under the reasonable direction of the head teacher of that school* (para 74.1.1) and *such particular duties as may reasonably be assigned to him [sic]* (para 75.1). Though the document goes on to itemise duties *deemed to be included*, the language is very broad and inclusive: teachers have wide-ranging responsibilities.

The professional duties under 'teaching' include (para 76.1):

- *planning and preparing courses and lessons;*
- *teaching, according to their educational needs, the pupils assigned to him, including the setting and marking of work to be carried out by the pupil in school and elsewhere;*
- *assessing, recording and reporting on the development, progress and attainment of pupils.*

The document outlines a long list of further responsibilities associated with teaching. It makes clear your obligation to:

- **promote the general progress and well-being of children;**
- **participate in public examination and assessment procedures;**
- **keep records;**
- **write reports;**
- **communicate with parents and attend meetings;**
- **attend staff meetings;**
- **contribute to your own and others' appraisal;**
- **review your methods of teaching;**
- **undertake further professional development;**
- **cover for absent colleagues (though for no more than 38 hours in any school year);**

- **carry out administrative and organisational tasks such as registering and supervising children.**

If you consult this section of the document and the accompanying guidance, you should be under no illusions on one point: the duties of a teacher extend some way beyond simply teaching children in the classroom.

The teacher's 'working time' requires you to be available up to 195 days in the school year and you can be required to teach on 190 of these (para 78.2). Five days are normally reserved as training days. In addition to the normal school day, you have to *be available to perform such duties at such times and such places as may be specified by the head teacher... for 1265 hours in any school year* (para 88.5) though these have to be 'allocated reasonably' within the 195 days. In other words, head teachers have the authority to make your attendance at certain activities such as staff meetings and parents' evenings a contractual obligation within the 1265 hours, or what is commonly referred to as 'directed time'. These 1265 hours include teaching itself, and designated planning and preparation time, but they do not cover all of a teacher's routine preparation, marking and general burning of midnight oil. The document makes clear that a teacher must *work such reasonable additional hours as may be needed to enable him to discharge effectively his professional duties* and that the *amount of time required for this purpose beyond the 1265 hours... shall not be defined by the employer* (para 78.7). Most of the voluntary extra-curricular activities to which you might contribute out of school hours are not usually reckoned within 'directed time'.

The conditions of service and related guidance do grant you some rights and place some limitations on the demands made of you as a teacher. You are entitled to a break in the middle of the day. Lunch-time supervision is not part of your normal contract. Attendance at 'assemblies' for administrative purposes is part of your contract in all schools, but outside of religiously affiliated schools attendance at school worship can be declared a matter of conscience. As a result of 'workforce remodelling' more non-teaching tasks are gradually being carried out by other staff in school; the conditions of service include an explicit list of administrative and clerical tasks which should not be the responsibility of the teacher (Annex 5). The introduction of protected time for planning and preparation (PPA time) of *not less than 10% of the teacher's time-tabled teaching time* has been a significant change in primary schools. As a NQT you will also be entitled to a reduction in teaching load; this should be not more than 90 per cent of the normal teaching commitment and PPA time should then be subtracted from this.

Further details of non-statutory agreements between the National Employers' Organisation for School Teachers (NEOST), which represents the LAs, and the teacher unions are set out in what is traditionally referred to as the *Burgundy Book,* more formally the *Conditions of Service for Schoolteachers in England and Wales* (NEOST/LGA/ATL/NASUWT/NUT/PAT/SHA, 2000). This is periodically revised as details are renegotiated. It sets out many of your entitlements as a teacher and includes important information of many matters from maternity/paternity leave to the recognition of teacher unions.

Legislation and regulations which apply to schools and teachers

Education law is both extensive and complex so this cannot be anything like a full list. Below are some of the key areas of which you should be aware. In all of these areas schools will have their own policies and procedures. The obvious point is that school policies and practices must not contravene statutory requirements.

> **PRACTICAL TASK** PRACTICAL TASK PRACTICAL TASK PRACTICAL TASK PRACTICAL TASK
>
> Look at the staff handbook (or equivalent) for a school. Match the instructions and advice given to the key areas below.

Acts concerning rights and discrimination

Teachers, schools and education authorities are bound by many of the provisions of national legislation on rights and discrimination: the Sex Discrimination Act 1975; the Race Relations Act 1976; the Disability Discrimination Act 1995; and the Human Rights Act (HRA) 1998. These acts, identified above as applying to your own rights as an employee, apply to the school and to the work you do with children. Some indications of their application to children are given in Chapter 12.

School policies on discipline

The framework for school discipline is set out in *School Discipline and Pupil Behaviour Policies: Guidance for Schools* (DfES, 2007a). This guidance explains the requirements of the Education and Inspections Act 2006, Part 7, Discipline, Behaviour and Exclusion (HM Government, 2006). This Act established (arguably for the first time) a clear legal basis for the authority of teachers in enforcing school discipline. It makes clear what schools must or may do in the promotion and indeed the enforcement of discipline.

The governing body is responsible for setting the general principles of behaviour policy and producing a written statement to guide the head teacher. The head teacher is charged with establishing *the more detailed measures (rules, rewards, sanctions and behaviour management strategies) on behaviour and discipline that form the school's behaviour policy* (DfES, 2007a, para 3.1.1) and securing the policy's implementation. Parents must be clearly informed about the policy.

The guidance is clear on the aim and principle concerns of such policies:

> *School behaviour policies should aim to establish a positive school ethos and promote effective learning by establishing:*
> - *clearly stated expectations of what constitutes acceptable behaviour;*
> - *effective behaviour management strategies;*
> - *processes which recognise, teach, reward and celebrate positive behaviour;*
> - *processes, rules and sanctions to deal with poor conduct.*
>
> (DfES, 2007a, para 3.1.6)

Schools must have a policy on bullying. Bullying has been defined as: *deliberately hurtful behaviour, usually repeated over a period of time, where it is difficult for those bullied to defend themselves* (HM Government, 2006, p. 201). The three main types of bullying are identified as:

See Chapter 12 for further points on legislation on racial equality.

- **physical (e.g. hitting, kicking, theft);**
- **verbal (e.g. racist or homophobic remarks, threats, name-calling);**
- **emotional (e.g. isolating an individual from the activities and social acceptance of their peer group).**
- **Schools must also have procedures for recording and reporting racist incidents (Ethnic Minority Achievement Unit 2006: 8).**

Bullying is to be treated seriously: as a teacher you cannot simply ignore it as commonplace.

Schools develop their own polices on discipline and bullying. These policies will set out the procedures which staff should follow. These will commonly be placed in a staff handbook and you should be familiar with and comply with the procedures established.

Physical restraint and sanctions

You will not be surprised to find that this is a controversial and fraught area in law as well as in routine practice. It is important to be clear on certain basic principles. The Education (no 2) Act 1986 prohibited physical ('corporal') punishment in state schools; this was reaffirmed in the Education Act 1996. It is thus classed as a form of common assault and such a charge is a serious one. More difficult for teachers is that instant and informal actions taken to control a child could also be construed as assault.

The School Discipline chapter of the Education and Inspections Act 2006 clarifies when teachers may use physical force to restrain a child. It allows you to use *such force as is reasonable* to prevent a child from:

(a) *committing any offence;*
(b) *causing personal injury to, or damage to the property of, any person (including the pupil himself); or*
(c) *prejudicing the maintenance of good order and discipline at the school or among any pupils receiving education at the school, whether during a teaching session or otherwise.*

(para 93)

The provisions of the Act do not just apply in school, but whenever you have *lawful control or charge of the pupil concerned*.

Circular 10/98 (para 21) attempted to exemplify reasonable physical interventions:

- *physically interposing between pupils;*
- *blocking a pupil's path;*
- *holding;*

- *pushing;*
- *pulling;*
- *leading a pupil by the hand or arm;*
- *shepherding a pupil away by placing a hand in the centre of the back; or,*
- *(in extreme circumstances) using more restrictive holds.*

You must seek to avoid doing anything which *might reasonably be expected to cause injury* (para 23) or *touching or holding a pupil in a way that might be considered indecent* (para 24) and s*hould always try to deal with a situation through other strategies before using force* (para 25). The guidance circular makes it clear that records should also be kept of any incidents where force is used. These should give details of what has occurred, why it was necessary, and any consequences (paras 28–9). It is good practice to inform parents and to discuss any such incident with them.

The law does not prevent you from taking action in self-defence or in some other form of emergency, when it might be reasonable to use force. However, in all cases of physical contact with children it may ultimately be for a court to decide whether you have acted 'reasonably'. The consequences of an error of judgement can be serious and you should always seek to avoid any possible grounds for complaint.

The Education Act 1996 established rules concerning detention; these have been reaffirmed in the Education and Inspections Act 2006. The clearest principles are that parents must be informed of the school's policy and in each instance given 24 hours' notice of any disciplinary detention unless it is simply during a break between school sessions on the same day. Schools have to take into account difficulties which detained children might have in returning home safely. Informal 'keeping behind' is a dangerous practice.

The Children Act 2004

See Chapters 11 and 13 for further references to ECM.

The Children Act 2004 provides the legal underpinning for ECM and its five key principles. The Act lays a responsibility on public agencies to co-operate in providing services and protection for vulnerable children. This Act is likely to have long-term implications for you as a teacher as policies in key areas are reworked in the light of its basic principles. There are, however, some long-standing aspects of your responsibilities as a teacher of which you should be aware.

Child protection

Safeguarding Children in Education (DfES, 2004d) sets out the responsibilities of LAs and schools in protecting children from abuse and neglect. This may include physical, sexual and emotional abuse and neglect which exposes the child to danger or seriously compromises their development. Schools are required to have a child protection policy and a designated person to liaise with statutory agencies; this policy must include procedures for handling suspected cases of abuse of children, including those to be followed if a member of staff is accused of abuse.

The key points which relate to you as an individual teacher are that:

- you should be given a written copy of the school policy and be familiar with the procedures;
- you should be alert to any signs of potential abuse and report such to the designated person;
- you must not attempt to investigate cases of alleged or suspected abuse but are bound to pass the concerns on to the designated person;
- you must never guarantee confidentiality to a child – if a child seeks to confide in you then you must explain that you may need to pass information to other professionals to help keep the child or other children safe.

A detailed list of behaviours which might lead to charges of abuse against a teacher or other staff member is set out in *Safeguarding Children in Education: Dealing with Allegations of Abuse against Teachers and Other Staff* (DfES, 2005b).

Physical contact with children

Note that the legislation on discipline and child protection does not make it illegal for you simply to touch a child. As Circular 10/98 makes clear: *There are occasions when physical contact with a pupil may be proper or necessary...*, for example to assist in PE or CDT or reassure a child in distress (para 33). Nevertheless, as a teacher you must bear in mind that some children may find any physical contact distressing and *even innocent and well-intentioned physical contact can sometimes be misconstrued* (para 34).

Health and safety

The Health and Safety at Work Act 1974 applies to schools as well as other places of work and its provisions are wide. As employers, the LA (in Community and Voluntary Controlled schools) or the governing body (in Foundation and Voluntary Aided schools) is formally responsible for the overall written safety policy; the head teacher is normally charged with its implementation but schools have a designated Health and Safety Officer.

As a teacher, like other employees, you have a responsibility to be aware of safety procedures and to draw attention to any shortcomings in safety arrangements or facilities. You should, for example, be clear about the school's policy on such matters as:

- the identity of the safety officer;
- fire drill and other emergency procedures;
- medical facilities;
- reporting and recording accidents;
- school security;
- intruders;
- abusive and threatening visitors;
- PE equipment;
- school visits.

Section 8 of the Act also states that you must not *intentionally or recklessly interfere with or misuse anything which is provided in the interests of health, safety or welfare in pursuance of any of the relevant statutory provisions*. Obstructing access to a fire door or fire extinguisher with an elaborate display or large sports equipment, for example, might be considered as reckless interference with safety provisions.

Teachers' 'Common Law' duty of care to children

While the LA or governing body have formal legal responsibility as employers for health and safety, head teachers and teachers have a general duty of care towards children. The notion of acting as a 'reasonable parent' has long been upheld in English courts as the duty of teachers deemed to be acting *in loco parentis*. Case law has created precedents for most commonly imaginable circumstances.

This advice may seem rather alarmist, but if something does go wrong you might have to explain in court that the risk was reasonable or entirely unforeseeable and that you were not negligent. You should always assess the risks of an activity for children in view of such factors as their age, known health problems, skills and the level of supervision available. Accidents, including serious ones, can always happen but the duty of care demands that you take steps to prevent what might reasonably be foreseen. For many activities which carry some obvious risk, such as swimming, outdoor activities or the use of sharp tools, schools and local authorities should have explicit guidelines. You should adhere to these both for the safety of children and your own protection. Off-site visits, for example, require a more formal 'risk assessment' and all those responsible for supervising children should be made aware of the outcomes. If you are in *any* doubt as to the safety of an activity, you should err on the side of caution and seek appropriate advice.

A note on liability

Schools must have employer public liability insurance. This means that for most purposes you are covered against third party claims arising from your actions on school-related business. Provided you have not deliberately behaved illegally or dishonestly, you would normally be covered by this. If you are negligent in some way, however, you can expect that your employer might take some disciplinary action. You can also expect to feature in the media – this is not the 15 minutes of fame you want!

There is, however, one aspect of insured liability which you are responsible for arranging. If you take chidlren in your own car or otherwise use your vehicle on school business you must ensure – and insure – that you are covered by your policy to do so. You must not assume that your motor insurance necessarily covers this.

REFLECTIVE TASK

How might the five key principles of ECM be related to the professional duties and statutory responsibilities of teachers?

Conclusion

As a teacher and a responsible professional you should be personally aware of your rights and responsibilities. You need to be very clear about your legal and contractual obligations: in law, ignorance is not a good defence. You should never lose sight of the fact that your right to practise as a teacher is a conditional one: it can be withdrawn. Equally, as an employee you also need to understand your rights and entitlements. This can be particularly important as an NQT, but applies throughout your career.

It is crucial you understand the basic principles and also that you appreciate these are complex matters. In the course of training or on joining a school staff you will be approached by teacher unions inviting you to become a member. The most honestly expressed and sensible advice given by a union representative to a group of would-be teachers was: 'I want to persuade you to join my union, but the most important thing is that you join one.' This is sound advice: you never know just what difficulties you may be faced with and when you might require support and representation. Nevertheless, you should not lose sight of the fact that most teachers pass their working life without legal drama or major contractual conflicts with their head teacher, governors or local authority. It is easy to forget that in most schools and for most of the time, most teachers are peacefully – and even more or less contentedly – going about their business of teaching children.

Moving on

As a trainee your first task is clearly to meet the Standards for attaining QTS. In becoming a teacher you are, however, joining a profession which demands an ongoing commitment to personal professional development. It is part of your professional responsibility to review your practice; it must also be part of your development to keep up-to-date on your contractual and statutory responsibilities.

FURTHER READING FURTHER READING **FURTHER READING**

A number of books are available which deal with education law and the teacher's rights and responsibilities. See, for example:

Hyams, O. (2007) *Employment in Schools: A Legal Guide*, 2nd edition. Bristol: Jordans.

A useful summary of legislation is provided in:

University of Bristol Graduate School of Education (2005) *Teachers' Legal Liabilities and Responsibilities: The Bristol Guide.* Documentary Summary Service, University of Bristol.

Books quickly become out of date. Many schools pay for a subscription service to *The Head's Legal Guide,* or *The Teacher's Legal Guide*. Kingston upon Thames: Croner. These guides have regular updates.

The best sources of current information and links to official documents are the DCSF website **www.dcsf.gov.uk/** and TeacherNet: **www.teachernet.gov.uk/**. These give access to much useful information: and links to legislation, guidance and press releases on many topics. Key documents are now normally available online. It is particularly worth consulting:

Circular 10/98, *Section 550A of the Education Act 1996: The Use of Force to Control or Restrain Pupils*. London: DfEE.

DfEE (1998) *Health and Safety of Pupils on Educational Visits*. London: DfEE. See also the supplementary guidance on Group Safety at Water Margins and Standards for Adventure (DfES, 2002).

DfES (2007) *School Discipline and Pupil Behaviour Policies: Guidance for Schools*. **www.teachernet.gov.uk/_doc/11321/SCHOOL%20DISCIPLINE%20AND%20PU-PIL%20BEHAVIOUR%20POLICIES%20GUIDANCE1.pdf**. This explains the main provisions of the School Discipline chapter of the Education and Inspections Act 2006

Ethnic Minority Achievement Unit (2006) *Recording and Reporting Racist Incidents Guidance*. London: DfES.

On pay and conditions see the documents on the DCSF website **www.dcsf.gov.uk/**. For the Burgundy Book see: NEOST/LGA/ATL/NASUWT/NUT/PAT/SHA (2000) *Conditions of Service for Schoolteachers in England and Wales*. London: Employers' Organisation for Local Government. This can be accessed online via the ATL website (see below). A copy of these must also be made available in schools for teachers to consult.

Useful websites

The various professional associations all produce guidance for members. Union representatives in schools will have much of this published material. Some guidance is freely available on the websites of the various professional associations:

ATL Association of Teachers and Lecturers: **www.atl.org.uk/**

NASUWT National Association of Schoolmasters Union of Women Teachers: **www.nasuwt.org.uk/**

NUT National Union of Teachers: **www.nut.org.uk/**

PAT Professional Association of Teachers: **www.pat.org.uk/**

Section 4
Becoming a Professional

16
Emerging as a professional
Kate Jacques

By the end of the chapter you should:

- be aware of the importance of effective working relationships with children and all colleagues in the educational community;
- have an overview of the many different responsibilities teachers have outside the classroom;
- know that teachers have to take responsibility for their own professional development and career profile;
- have an understanding of the term 'professional' and what is meant by professionalism.

This chapter addresses the following Professional Standards for QTS: Q7, Q8, Q9, Q32, Q33

Why become a teacher?

To be a real professional you need to be:

Professionally autonomous
Responsible
Organised
Fair
Educated
Skilled
Self-regulatory
Independent
Open
Neutral
Accountable
Learned

Above are listed some of the essential characteristics of a professional. How many of them apply to you? There are, of course, many other features of being a professional but the key ingredients are your attitude to your work and your ability to achieve the characteristics above and be effective. Moreover you need to be able to evaluate your own performance.

Elsewhere in this book there have been frequent references to the fact that teachers do much more than simply teach children in a classroom. Almost every school and classroom activity signals the need for you as a class teacher to have additional skills in dealing with parents, colleagues and support staff as well as children. It is the rich diversity of knowledge, skills, attitudes and understandings which makes teaching a unique profession and one which demands much more of the person than almost any other job.

This chapter is intended to clarify what teaching as a profession means and how we recognise and judge professionalism. Most importantly, it will give guidance on how to achieve and sustain the professional values and practice encapsulated in the QTS Standards. In many ways, Section 1 is the most significant part of the document because for many trainee teachers it encompasses the main reason teaching was selected as their preferred career. Teaching provides opportunities for highly professional behaviour in many areas and frequently attracts people who are conscientious, hardworking and committed to caring for and improving the lives of those with whom they work. These days teaching is demanding and only those determined to strive to achieve the highest standards feel comfortable in the job. Achieving high standards is determined in part by the quality of your relationships with children, colleagues, parents and support staff and also the relationship you have with yourself and your career. Relationships have to be positive, optimistic and trusting. Most of all they must transcend divisions of race, culture, class, religion, and ability and disability.

Talking to trainee teachers and newly qualified teachers shows there is little doubt that many want to be teachers no matter what the pay, no matter what the rewards. They feel they have a contribution to make in extending and developing the careers and lives of young people. You may be one of those who chose teaching because you wanted to create an environment where improvement is allowed to happen. Most trainee teachers want to make a difference to young people's lives and provide better opportunities. They want to have a strong, trusting relationship with children, parents and colleagues. Largely they subscribe to a principle that states that children and teachers should want to come to school, enjoy it when they are there and leave it each day better informed and more enriched than the previous day. Inevitably there will be factors that mean that some people have a more difficult job than others. But even in difficult schools, some heroic work is being done by excellent teachers, who have spirit, integrity and enjoy the demands of the job, remaining optimistic and enthusiastic. It is important, therefore, that you know why you want to be a teacher and the sort of teacher you want to be, as it will affect your approach to the job.

Many teachers enter the profession knowing that it is going to be hard, knowing that it is not well paid, knowing that it is not glamorous, but knowing that the rewards can be great. In a developed world where the workplace has been taken over largely by profit margins, image and ruthless competition, teaching still attracts many people who care about humanity.

In Chapter 8 four reasons were suggested why people pursue teaching. Here are some more:

- **a desire to work with children;**
- **a desire to create a better school experience;**
- **a desire to work as a member of a team;**
- **a desire to be creative and imaginative;**
- **a desire to be stimulated intellectually;**

- a desire to have a job that is varied, challenging and worthwhile;
- a desire to influence the community and society.

REFLECTIVE TASK
REFLECTIVE TASK

Write down the three main reasons which decided you to choose teaching as a career. Now identify three concerns you have about joining the profession and explain why they bother you.

Is teaching a profession?

It would be useful at this stage to consider what the term 'profession' means and how it is applied to teaching. The *Longman Dictionary of Contemporary English* (1975) defines the term 'profession' in the following way: *a form of employment, especially one that is respected in society, is honourable and is possible only for an educated person, and after training in some special branch of knowledge.* Other definitions include the notion of being client-centred and the need for special expertise to support the interest of the client. In medicine it is clear the client is the patient, in law it is clear that the client is the victim or the accused, in commerce the client is the customer. Who is the client in education? Is it the child, is it the parent or is it the state? The answer to this question could be quite important in how you view your job as a professional. My view is that the best interests of children must come first and then the interests of other stakeholders.

Teachers are educated certainly and undergo very rigorous training in a special branch of knowledge. When the long anticipated point arrives and you assume the responsibilities of a qualified teacher you will define yourself as a member of the teaching profession. Later you will almost certainly complain about the public standing of the profession, its status and its rewards and you will wonder why schools and teachers attract criticism from the media. You will also begin to describe work-related behaviours as 'professional' or 'unprofessional' in a variety of contexts.

Children are very clear about their perceptions of professionalism in teachers. They observe very closely and have high expectations of their teachers' performance; to children it is important for teachers to be on time, to be well prepared, to be a competent class manager, to be honest and fair. They want their teacher to be a good role model, to be someone they can look up to. This does not mean to say mistakes cannot be made; it means that they are acknowledged. Being professional does not mean you have to be perfect, but it does mean you have to know how to handle yourself and present a professional image.

It is worth giving a couple of minutes to the traditional understanding of what it meant to be a professional or part of a profession. In 1970 the Monopolies and Mergers Commission identified seven characteristics of professions. These seven characteristics concur with the original notion of professions, which were considered to be medicine, law and the church. The characteristics are as follows.

To be a true professional you must:

- **possess specialised skill to enable you to offer a specialised service;**
- **undergo intellectual and practical training in a well-defined area of study;**
- **maintain detachment and integrity in exercising personal judgement on behalf of a client;**
- **establish direct personal relations with clients based on confidence, faith and trust;**
- **collectively have a particular sense of responsibility for maintaining the competence and integrity of the profession as a whole;**
- **belong to an organised body which, with or without state intervention, is concerned to provide machinery for testing competence and regulating standards of competence and conduct.**

The teaching profession has some, but not all, of these characteristics. It is not autonomous, for example, but all professions and not just teaching are now subject to influence by government agencies and professional bodies which regulate conduct.

Since September 2002 all teachers have been expected to be a member of the General Teaching Council (GTC). While the establishment of a Teaching Council may have helped to promote the status of teaching, the GTC cannot provide the professional autonomy some teachers desire. It is argued that teachers and schools are paid for out of public funds and, like all publicly funded services, must therefore be held accountable and rigorously scrutinised. Put this way it does not seem unreasonable that pressure should be exerted to ensure high quality provision and high quality performance from all teachers.

Eric Hoyle (1980) identified two kinds of teachers. He described one group as the 'extended professional' and the other as the 'restricted professional'. The contrast between the two reflects an attitude to work and quality of performance. Restricted professionals work hard but have a limited view of their role. They see their job as doing what is necessary to get the tasks done but remain rigid in their interpretation of the employment contract. In contrast the 'extended professional' takes the full range of duties and tasks very seriously and does more than is expected. The extended professional seizes initiatives, works extended hours without complaint, and is committed, conscientious and diligent.

The restricted professional:

- **has a high level of classroom competence;**
- **has a degree of skill in understanding and handling children;**
- **derives much satisfaction from personal relationships with pupils;**
- **evaluates performance in terms of his/her own perceptions of changes;**
- **attends short courses of a practical nature.**

The extended professional has all of these qualities, but additionally:

- **views work in the wider context of school, community and society;**
- **participates in a wide range of professional activities – for example, subject panels, governors, conferences and so on;**

- **tries to link theory and practice;**
- **has a commitment to some form of curriculum development and mode of evaluation.**

(Hoyle, 1980)

In addition the extended professional will know and implement the legislation on disability and race relations and ensure that individual pupil learning plans take account of ethnicity, cultural diversity, language acquisition and special needs, be they physical or emotional.

The Hay/McBer report (2000) commissioned by the DfEE identified three measurable factors as influencing teachers' effectiveness. Some of what this report says chimes with Hoyle's observations. The factors are teaching skills, professional characteristics and classroom climate. The most effective teachers have a knack of employing just the right teaching strategies while using their very wide professional knowledge to promote a positive classroom climate where children are enthusiastic and want to learn. Much of what the report says about effectiveness is identified elsewhere (see Hayes, 1997; Kyriacou, 1998; Stephens and Crawley, 1994 and in Further Reading, page 214) but it is the emphasis on professional characteristics and how they are used which is illuminating. *The professional characteristics are deep seated patterns of behaviour which outstanding teachers display more often, in more circumstances and to a greater degree of intensity than effective colleagues.*

From now on it is the 'extended professional' who has a serious future in teaching. Appraisals and threshold reviews will ensure that every teacher is fully aware of their targets for that year and the process by which they are going to achieve them. Most importantly, underperformance will not be tolerated. Continuous and rigorous staff development will be an expectation for all, not just a few.

The purpose of the performance review is to establish a shared commitment to high performance, improved learning for children and improved support and recognition for teachers. It is seen as a way of attracting the high regard and recognition of the public. This is being introduced alongside the arrangements for performance-related pay and the expectation that any teacher worth their salt will have high ambition for themselves and high expectations of their pupils. The agenda for your career is therefore now set. It will be monitored, tracked and reported to you throughout your work. This is something that happens regularly in other professions and in industry. It is intended to be welcomed as a motivator and an incentive to promote aspirations. It is intended to help emphasise the value of each individual teacher and the value of classroom teaching. Not surprisingly some experienced teachers unaccustomed to this level of scrutiny find it intrusive. They interpret the process as one which shows distrust of their professionalism rather than affirmation of it.

Let us look now at what you have to do to be recognised as a professional operating in a demanding, challenging world which, in your case, is the world of schools, standards and educational achievement.

REFLECTIVE TASK

REFLECTIVE TASK

Would you describe yourself as a professional?

What in your view should be done to enhance the professionalism of teachers and the standing of teaching as a profession?

Read the GTCE (2002) *Professional Code for Teachers* (London: GTCE) and assess your commitment against the code.

A professional environment

Staff-rooms reveal a lot about a school. At first, listen! Among the factors affecting how you will feel about your first school placement will be where the school sits in the league tables, the approach to and the management of Ofsted inspections, National Curriculum test results, pupil disaffection, even teacher dissatisfaction. Schools face different challenges in trying to achieve the best for the children they teach. It is not always the case that schools located in the most disadvantaged and deprived areas are the most difficult. A united staff that shares the same values and high aspirations and which takes collective responsibility for the welfare and well-being of everybody can create a positive environment in which to work and learn. In a school in a leafy suburb where staff are not united and find the pressure from parents stressful the atmosphere can be difficult. The problem can be aggravated if staff resent these pressures and are not working in harmony with each other, with their pupils, with the governors or even the community. The tone in the staff-room can say a lot about the staff team. Already you will have noticed the variation that exists in the climate of school staff-rooms. In some schools there is a positive attitude and approach which recognises the pressure the education system is under but responds in such a way as to take the school, children and each other forward.

Collective negativity is depressing and counter-productive. It is possible that you may find yourself in such a staff-room. If there is constant grumbling about Ofsted, the National Curriculum, National Curriculum tests, the children, the parents, the LA, the neighbourhood, the buildings and everything else in life you will have to think of strategies to cope. You may in the end decide to move to a different school. You must, however, rise above it while you are there and not allow unprofessional attitudes to contaminate your own professional ones. There is everything to be said for thoughtful, informed, critical dialogue but there is little to be said for relentless grumbling. You need to recognise the difference between the two and participate in genuine discussion about professional issues.

Fortunately, few schools are full of moaning minnies, although some schools have one or two. If you can, avoid them.

Whether a trainee or a newly qualified teacher, you are new and you must enter the staff-room with sensitivity and courtesy. You should nevertheless be able to make some observations about the physical conditions and the social construction of the staff-room and consider how either of these might affect the professionalism of the staff.

How can you tell the difference between professional debate and grumbling?
How will you try to deal with staff-room discontent?

A professional staff-room should be:

- brightly decorated and well furnished;
- clean, tidy and well ordered;
- equipped with appropriate catering facilities;
- equipped with an area for staff study and/or preparation;
- equipped with a computer to provide access to the internet and e-mail;
- equipped with an area for books, journals and other literature relevant to the profession;
- an area for serious discussion and meetings;
- an area where all support staff are welcomed.

It should have:

- well organised and differentiated noticeboards or plasma screens which indicate:
  - messages from the head teacher and others with leadership roles;
  - messages from the support staff and catering staff to teachers about matters that affect them;
  - messages and information from outside agencies including the LA, education welfare officer (EWO), educational psychologists (EPs), child support, etc.;
  - messages and information about trainee teacher placements and mentor training;
  - information about courses and conferences and other professional development opportunities including national initiatives;
  - information from governors;
  - information about parents and parents' evenings, etc.;
- access to the internet.

A professional staff-room should:

- promote a positive image of teaching;
- encourage engagement in professional advancement;
- encourage debate and discussion about educational issues;
- welcome into it all members of staff including assistants, trainees and technicians;
- provide an impression of which all staff would be pleased and proud;
- present an image of professionalism that would impress visitors to the school;
- promote the achievements of children;
- recognise disability and ethnic and cultural diversity.

Professional relationships

Relationships with children

Building good relationships with all children is essential to effective teaching. It is the one area in which good NQTs start out with the best of possible intentions but most frequently misjudge. The secret is to keep the relationship professional. You do not want fans; you want achievers. If they achieve they are likely to be your fans too.

Remember, remember, and remember what it is like to be a child and speak to each one with respect! Ask yourself from time to time: 'What would it be like if I were spoken to in such a way? Would I be happy to be addressed in such a manner?' At times you will encounter difficult children and you will be under pressure. Keep your cool. The respect you get from children will depend on the respect you give them.

You will encounter children in contexts other than in the classroom. You will have to settle disputes in the playground, manage a whole-school assembly and help manage the movement of children around the school. There will be children to manage other than those in your class. The image you portray to all children in the school is critical. You need to consider how children might talk about you when you are not there!

A number of studies have now been completed on children's judgements of their trainee teachers and teachers. The overwhelming demand is that the teachers are strict, fair, kind and humorous. The Hay/McBer Report (2000) offers the following from pupils in describing a good teacher:

is kind
is generous
listens to you
encourages you
has faith in you
keeps confidences
likes teaching children
likes teaching their subject
takes time to explain things
helps you when you're stuck
tells you how you are doing
allows you to have your say
doesn't give up on you
cares for your opinion
makes you feel clever
treats people equally
stands up for you
makes allowances
tells the truth
is forgiving

Other responses from children about the characteristics they rate in teachers are as follows.

- **The relationship you have with them as individuals is as important as subject knowledge.**
- **Children appreciate teachers who are well organised, are predictable and have routines and whose expectations of behaviour are high and well understood.**
- **Children say they want their teachers to be fair, kind and funny. Children are very clear**

they do not want their teachers to be over friendly; they want them to demand high standards of behaviour and performance from them and also from teachers. They want them to be fair. Nothing infuriates either individual children or whole classes as much as injustice and an intemperate reaction to incidents from the teachers. More than anything they dislike intensely the notion that it is possible to punish the whole class for the misdemeanours of one or two.

- Children claim they want to see their teachers as people in authority, with authority, but sympathetic to the needs of all children. The high fliers in the class appreciate evidence of understanding of the low fliers in the class. High fliers in the class who are unsympathetic to other children and their particular needs look to the teacher to instruct and improve the attitude of those children.
- Children appreciate their accomplishments being recognised and commented on. All children want to be treated with respect and regard and all teachers want to be treated with respect and regard.

Relationships with colleagues

In Chapter 8 the importance of classroom climate was emphasised and earlier in this chapter we considered staff-room climate. Equally important is the notion of school climate and a positive school climate which comes over to all who enter the school. It should be one of trust, co-operation, collaboration and achievement. In a school where teachers work together, share the same goals and aspirations for themselves and for the children, and where the mission is understood there is likely to be a positive climate.

In the past teachers guarded jealously what went on in their classrooms and were frequently unwilling to share their practice or what the children were learning with anyone else and indeed resented interference, even from the head teacher. Nowadays good teachers want to collaborate and share good practice and engage in the discussion which good teachers have about the quality of children's progress and the quality of children's learning. Most schools these days have their staff grouped into teams, and teachers may belong to more than one team – for example, a year team in a large school or curriculum team. Teamwork is essential if sound planning is to be shared by all colleagues and a whole-school strategy developed around good practice and professional development.

See Chapter 8 for further points on classroom climate.

As a new entrant to the profession, it is important to understand and be sensitive to the feelings of experienced members of staff. Some will welcome you as:

- a breath of fresh air!
- the new expert!
- the one with all the new ideas!
- the fount of all knowledge about personalised learning!

Others will regard you as:

- a threat!
- an upstart!
- a novice!
- a probationer who needs to 'forget all that stuff from college and learn the real job'!

- **one to be ignored!**
- **one who needs to be told what to do very often.**

Most, however, will treat you:

- **with respect;**
- **with good humour and understanding;**
- **as a new colleague in need of support and guidance;**
- **as a human resource with additional skills and knowledge which will enhance the school;**
- **as a newly qualified teacher with entitlement for time each week from a mentor for support, for professional development, for regular feedback on performance.**

It is easy to feel indignant and angry if you are made to feel small and undervalued by more experienced colleagues. If it does happen, keep cool, keep the matter in perspective and always be willing to reflect on your own inexperience. Humility can work wonders with the arrogant. Even when you feel done down, react carefully and remember that colleagues who react against trainees and newly qualified teachers tend to feel threatened and insecure.

If you are a good communicator you are likely to be an effective teacher, an effective colleague and an effective team leader.

As a trainee or newly qualified teacher, you will have a mentor who will be responsible for guiding and assessing your progress in school. The relationship you have with your mentor is critical. Again mutual respect is important if you are both to succeed. Your mentor will want you to succeed So remember that as part of your professional behaviour, you should be able to:

- **take criticism without taking offence;**
- **respond to criticism without giving offence;**
- **avoid blaming others when things go wrong;**
- **seek help and support when you need it – you are entitled to it;**
- **learn from mistakes.**

If you are a trainee you will be expected to complete a Career Entry and Development Profile (CEDP) at the end of your training, which will identify your strengths, weaknesses and areas for further professional development.

If you are a newly qualified teacher, arrangements should be made for you to:

- **teach only 90 per cent of contact time;**
- **have opportunities for contact with experienced, good teachers;**
- **be mentored, observed and counselled regarding progress;**
- **receive appropriate professional development and training;**
- **receive help with special educational needs provision;**
- **be allowed to network with other NQTs.**

Most mentors take their professional responsibility seriously and are anxious to ensure that you are well supported. In a minority of schools, mentors find they have not been allocated sufficient time to give you regular feedback. If this happens, you must employ your negotiating skills to let the head teacher know that you need more support.

Relationships with other support staff in school

Sound working relationships with the staff who support teachers and their work is essential. But there is another group of staff in the school who are very important too. They include classroom assistants, secretaries, caretakers, catering staff and welfare assistants and then a whole range of trainees of one sort or another who may be in the school; for example trainee nursery nurses, trainee teachers and trainee child development students. There are many other people in schools beside teachers and it matters how you treat them.

First, keep in mind that, no matter to whom you are speaking, for whatever reason, everyone has a right to expect a high level of respect and regard and to get as much of your attention as is possible. The strength of a school can be affected enormously by the quality of the relationships between all the people in it. Many schools these days provide training and support for groups such as catering staff, secretaries, classroom assistants, nursery nurse support staff, to ensure that they too feel that they are as important to the welfare of the school as are the teachers. Without them the school cannot function. That is something the children need to understand.

Classroom assistants will be of particular importance to you if you have them in your classroom. If you have a classroom assistant, it is part of your role to manage them effectively so that they support your teaching and children's learning. They tend to be poorly paid but enjoy what they do, so it is important that you demonstrate how much you value their contributions. Ensure that they are included in the planning so that they are prepared for the week ahead. Each morning indicate to them what you would like them to do and be very clear about the instructions. It is important to be clear about:

- **how you employ them;**
- **what you ask them to do with particular children;**
- **how you feed back to them on their performance on what you have asked them to do;**
- **how they become involved in the planning and development of the classroom activities you wish them to support;**
- **how you use your authority and expertise.**

PRACTICAL TASK PRACTICAL TASK PRACTICAL TASK PRACTICAL TASK PRACTICAL TASK

Suggest three advantages of having a positive working relationship with all the support staff in your school.

Write a sentence about how you think the relationship between you and the head teacher should develop in your first year as an NQT, indicating what sort of professional development activity you would like to receive and making your career intentions clear to the head and to your mentor.

What should you do if your mentor is not finding time to give you feedback and support?

Let's look at how you talk to classroom assistants and all other support staff:

- **Do you treat them with the same regard and respect as other staff in the school?**
- **Do you consult them about the behaviour of children and respect and regard the comments they give back to you?**
- **Do you include them in regular meetings about the job they do and how it affects work in the classroom? Suggest a way this might happen.**

Classroom assistants are probably the most high profile group in schools and you may or may not have a formal classroom assistant. This group are often striving towards a qualification and towards becoming a highly competent classroom support person, even if they are not intending to become teachers in the distant future. Find out what their career intentions are so that you can support their staff development and ensure that they have the appropriate kinds of experiences with children. Nothing is more frustrating than lack of clarity about what it is you have been asked to do, so make sure that your classroom assistant understands what it is you want them to do and what outcomes you expect. Used appropriately classroom assistants and other support staff will help you teach more effectively. They can relieve you of the many important non-teaching tasks, which you would normally have to do. In particular, they can help keep your classroom and resources organised.

Classroom assistants tend to be highly motivated, well-intentioned, able and intelligent people. Thus they are an enormously valuable asset in the classroom and they can, if directed well by the class teacher, make a 100 per cent difference in children's learning simply because they are able to support the work of a good class teacher. You must try to assess the abilities of your classroom assistant and then determine how best they can assist the learning of the children in the classroom and compensate for the work that you are unable to do. Most important, however, is to recognise and utilise the skill and the knowledge they have. You have responsibility to guide and direct them clearly.

Working with support staff

Good support staff play a significant role in enhancing the quality of school life. The numbers of support staff in schools have grown significantly over recent years and look set to increase even further in the future, with far more classroom assistants being employed to support class teachers. Other support staff in the school, including secretaries, bursars, catering staff, etc., all can make your job easier if they have a good relationship with you. Ensure that all support staff are treated with courtesy and respect and always thank them for their assistance. It is important, too, that if they ask for your help in dealing with challenging children, you give them that help.

Playground supervisors frequently encounter supervision difficulties with children. You are trained to deal with children who need to be disciplined and they are not, so even if it is your lunch period, do intervene and help support staff either if you can see they need it or if they ask for it.

Relationships with parents and significant others

Cementing good working relationships with other teachers in the school, your head teacher and other line managers, and with all other support staff is important. Once you have learned how to do that effectively you will understand just what a bonus that is. Parents of the children you teach are the other group to whom you must relate well. In the past a number of schools made misjudgements about working relationships with parents, but in the recent past this has improved. There was a time when schools discouraged parents from meeting teachers frequently or from coming in to see classrooms and work that children are doing in school. That is not the case now and parents are encouraged to visit the school as often as they wish and talk to classroom teachers as often as they need to as well as talking to the head teacher.

If you think back to the early part of this chapter when we were asking whether or not teachers were professionals, the issue arose as to whether teachers were able to respond to their client group. It is an interesting question about teaching, 'To whom are teachers accountable?' Is it to children? Is it to government? Or is it to parents? The answer is that teachers are accountable to a number of different groups but parents, of course, are a particular and significant group. Parents deserve and need to know how well their children are doing in school and they need to be informed about any learning difficulties their child may have. They are entitled, also, to learn if their children have strengths and exceptional talents. Keeping records of the profile of children's attainments, as described earlier in this book, is an essential part of the teacher's job but in talking and working with parents it is important that the class teacher is able to discuss with them from an informed position the strengths and weaknesses of their child's learning profile.

See Chapter 4 on page 46 for further points on recording attainments.

It is often hard to give parents difficult messages if their child is not performing well. This is an important part of your job, to communicate to parents the precise position in which their child lies in relation to other children in the class and indeed, then, in relation to other children nationally. It is not always easy to talk to parents but you have to learn how to give feedback honestly and you need to do that early. Many newly qualified teachers feel they have not had the opportunity to undertake this role in their training. This is not surprising given that many parents are not willing to accept comments from trainee teachers but they will from qualified teachers. Therefore, this is something you have to learn, and learn the hard way, early in your career.

Negotiations with parents need to be learned but they can be a rewarding and profitable experience. Just like children, parents feel flattered when you take interest in them and, particularly, if you take interest in their children. We all know that there are some youngsters who have behavioural problems, but we all know too that they are in a minority and that there is another minority who are withdrawn. Knowing the background of children helps you understand behaviour. Make an effort to get to know families and when you see parents outside the school gate, talk to them. You need to recognise that the school is a world in which some parents have failed and they fear that their children may fail also. School is a world where some parents have not felt welcome in the past. It is a world where some parents do not have the self-esteem to feel able to talk to teachers.

Some parents do carry a sense of guilt and feel they are responsible for the misdemeanours of their children and most parents want the opportunity to discuss, frankly and fully, the problems they perceive in their children.

Parents are as different as the children in your class and it is a mistake to think that all parents are the same. Spend time talking to them whenever possible and encourage them to trust you and know that you will tell them the truth while being fair. Some newly qualified teachers have felt ill-prepared to deal with aggressive and abusive parents and, true, it is difficult to train anyone to be ready for rudeness and discourtesy. Never lose your temper with parents and never, ever respond in an aggressive or discourteous manner. If you encounter parents who shout and won't listen, keep your cool and wait until they calm down. If remarks become seriously abusive, then you will need to summon the help of the head teacher. Do not ever say anything to a parent which you may later regret or which may get you into trouble.

Here are some of the encounters you may have to deal with.

- **A parent bursting in to school at the end of the day clearly high on something, insisting that their child has been misjudged over an incident.**
- **A parent insistent that their child has been overlooked in selection for a competition in, say, music, sport or community work.**
- **A parent of a high-achiever who learns that their son or daughter is not, currently, literate or numerate to their expected level.**

What will you do? How will you respond?

Parents' meetings

If parents' evenings are to be profitable both for the parent and for you, they need to be fully prepared for. Plan in advance what you are going to say about each child and make sure that you can begin with something positive and, hopefully, conclude with a small anecdote that places the child in a good light. This helps reassure parents that you do know their child very well. If you have negative things to say about a child, make sure that they are presented in a way that indicates to parents that you want them to help you overcome the problem. For example, in the case of repeated non-completion of work because a child is very easily distracted, emphasise that better progress will be made if work is completed and you want some assistance from the parents in ensuring that work is completed, and reward the completion of all work without concentrating on punishing performance. Talk to parents about setting targets and rewarding successful achievement.

Writing reports for parents, every teacher knows, can be daunting. Nevertheless, these are important documents for parents as well as for children. All of us can remember reports from school that told us very little because the style was too general and ambiguous. Make sure your reports are not like this. Identify very clearly what has been achieved and at what level and ensure that you have evidence to support what you are saying. Identify clearly also areas of weakness and how these must be improved to reach the desired level. Set targets that are achievable and indicate how you intend to involve the child in assessing his/her own progress. Indicate how parents might help the child improve on areas of concern, emphasising how parents can help motivate children by giving praise where appropriate. It is important that your report is businesslike and free from phrases that parents will not understand or are too 'airy-fairy'. Parents are also interested in where their child stands in relation to the rest of the class and they are entitled to have this information. Remember always that parents are, in a sense, your professional clients. You are accountable to them for the performance of their child and they are entitled to know what you are doing to support their child's learning.

The final point here is to treat with professionalism all staff and children and parents with whom you come into contact.

Your own professional development

In this final section you are asked to consider your future and where you expect to be in five years' time for example. At the beginning we identified specialist knowledge as a characteristic of a profession. As in other professions, knowledge and expertise about education is growing and changing all the time. It is up to you to keep up to date both with your subject and with new developments in primary education. It is impossible to judge and analyse new initiatives effectively if you don't fully understand them. Make sure that you are up to date with educational literature, that you frequently read educational journals and newspapers such as the *Times Educational Supplement* and/or *Primary Education*. Once you have completed your induction year that's not it! You will be a better teacher and a more self-fulfilled individual if you feel that you are constantly growing and developing as a teacher and as an educator. Teachers, quite justifiably, feel short of time and frequently hard-pressed. It is important that you manage your time efficiently and ensure that there is a balance in your working day and in your life outside school. You cannot do everything to perfection all the time, nor should you wish to. Appreciate that if you visit the doctor or solicitor, or a dentist, or the bank manager, your time with them is limited and an appointment has to be made which will finish on time. Too many teachers are over-generous with their time and feel unprofessional if they do not deal instantly with every request.

If you are planning on promotion within the next five years, think about it and think about how to organise your time so that you have space for further study and opportunities to attend courses and conferences.

The future is advanced technology. You must be able to develop your teaching so that both you and your pupils are familiar with e-mail and the internet and can capitalise on the technology to improve your effectiveness.

As you emerge as a professional and begin the task of becoming a fully qualified teacher, do remember to raise your head above the level of the classroom and school to look at the big picture and remind yourself why you are a teacher and why you are so proud to be one.

FURTHER READING   FURTHER READING   FURTHER READING

Browne, A. and Haylock, D. (2004) *Professional Issues for Primary Teachers*. London: Paul Chapman.

Davies, R., and Ferguson, J. (1997) 'Teachers' views of the role of Initial Teacher Education in developing their professionalism.' *Journal of Education for Teaching*. 23 (1) pp. 40-55. Provides authentic feedback from teachers about the ways in which they see working with trainees as helping develop reflection on their own practice and improving levels of personal behaviour.

GTCE (2001) *Professional Learning Framework*. London: GTCE.

GTCE (2002) *Professional Code for Teachers*. London: GTCE.

Hayes, D. (1997) *Success on your Teaching Experience*. London: Hodder & Stoughton. This book targets the trainee teacher and is full of useful and valuable advice about beginning teaching in school. In terms of professionalism, Chapter 1 'The student teacher in school' and Chapter 8 'Achieving Competence' give reliable guidance on orientation in school and professional behaviour and conduct.

Hoyle, E. (1980) 'Professionalism and de-professionalism in education', in Hoyle, E. and Hegarty, J. (eds) *World Yearbook of Education: Professional Development of Teachers*. London: Kogan Page.

Kyriacou, C. (1998) *Essential Teaching Skills*. Cheltenham: Stanley Thornes. This book is a classic and will assist you in a full range of the chapters dealt with in the book. In terms of professionalism, Chapter 8 on reflection and evaluation addresses the importance of managing your professional conduct and gives lots of useful tips.

Lawton, D. (1996) *Beyond the National Curriculum: Teacher Professionalism and Empowerment*. London: Hodder & Stoughton. This book has a more theoretical base and offers a sound analysis of teacher professionalism and empowerment for those who wish to consider the subject in more depth. Professor Lawton examines the tensions between the status of teachers as a profession and the problems such a professional group has in maintaining a positive public image. It contains a very useful appendix, which charts the growth of teacher professionalism across the twentieth century.

Hay/McBer (2000) *Research into Teacher Effectiveness, Phase 11 Report: A Model of Teacher Effectiveness*, DfEE Report. This report is a comprehensive consolidation of the characteristics and behaviours which go into making an effective teacher. While many teachers may argue there is nothing new in this report, the findings are of interest certainly to any new teacher entering the profession, if not to experienced teachers. Many references are made between professional characteristics of teachers and children's progress. On page 114 there is an interesting section on continuing professional development, career planning and performance management, which will be of interest to those with long-term career plans.

Stephens, P. and Crawley, T. (1994) *Becoming an Effective Teacher*. Cheltenham: Stanley Thornes. An easy to read book about the challenges of entering teaching and classrooms for the first time. Chapter 6 is particularly useful in providing guidance on relationships with colleagues and parents and on considering professional development issues.

Thody, A., Gray, D. and Bowden, D. (2000) *The Teacher's Survival Guide*. London: Continuum. This book contains lots of tips in a very easy to read volume focusing on success. It gives guidance on success with children, colleagues and yourself. It addresses a number of professional matters about achieving professional standing, working successfully and still finding time for yourself. For example, on page 103 it gives advice on managing time to ensure that you have time for leisure. The final recommendation suggests marking Friday with a deep bubble bath, gin and tonic, aerobics class and a meal with friends! It contains many other very practical ways of maintaining professionalism, which sometimes means having to say no.

Appendix: Professional Standards for Teachers in England

1. Professional attributes

Those recommended for the award of QTS (Q) should:

Q1 Have high expectations of children and young people including a commitment to ensuring that they can achieve their full educational potential and to establishing fair, respectful, trusting, supportive and constructive relationships with them.

Q2 Demonstrate the positive values, attitudes and behaviour they expect from children and young people.

Q3 (a) Be aware of the professional duties of teachers and the statutory framework within which they work.
   (b) Be aware of the policies and practices of the workplace and share in collective responsibility for their implementation.

Q4 Communicate effectively with children, young people, colleagues, parents and carers.

Q5 Recognise and respect the contribution that colleagues, parents and carers can make to the development and well-being of children and young people and to raising their levels of attainment.

Q6 Have a commitment to collaboration and co-operative working.

Q7 (a) Reflect on and improve their practice, and take responsibility for identifying and meeting their developing professional needs.
   (b) Identify priorities for their early professional development in the context of induction.

Q8 Have a creative and constructively critical approach towards innovation, being prepared to adapt their practice where benefits and improvements are identified.

Q9 Act upon advice and feedback and be open to coaching and mentoring.

2. Professional knowledge and understanding

Those recommended for the award of QTS (Q) should:

Q10 Have a knowledge and understanding of a range of teaching, learning and behaviour management strategies and know how to use and adapt them, including how to personalise learning and provide opportunities for all learners to achieve their potential.

Q11 Know the assessment requirements and arrangements for the subjects/curriculum areas they are trained to teach, including those relating to public examinations and qualifications.

Q12 Know a range of approaches to assessment, including the importance of formative assessment.

Q13 Know how to use local and national statistical information to evaluate the effectiveness of their teaching, to monitor the progress of those they teach and to raise levels of attainment.

Q14 Have a secure knowledge and understanding of their subjects/curriculum areas and related pedagogy to enable them to teach effectively across the age and ability range for which they are trained.

Q15 Know and understand the relevant statutory and non-statutory curricula and frameworks, including those provided through the National Strategies, for their subjects/curriculum areas, and other relevant initiatives applicable to the age and ability range for which they are trained.

Q16 Have passed the professional skills tests in numeracy, literacy and information and communications technology (ICT).

Q17 Know how to use skills in literacy, numeracy and ICT to support their teaching and wider professional activities.

Q18 Understand how children and young people develop and that the progress and well-being of learners are affected by a range of developmental, social, religious, ethnic, cultural and linguistic influences.

Q19 Know how to make effective personalised provision for those they teach, including those for whom English is an additional language or who have special educational needs or disabilities, and how to take practical account of diversity and promote equality and inclusion in their teaching.

Q20 Know and understand the roles of colleagues with specific responsibilities, including those with responsibility for learners with special educational needs and disabilities and other individual learning needs.

Q21 (a) Be aware of the current legal requirements, national policies and guidance on the safeguarding and promotion of the well-being of children and young people.

(b) Know how to identify and support children and young people whose progress, development or well-being is affected by changes or difficulties in their personal circumstances, and when to refer them to colleagues for specialist support.

3. Professional skills

Those recommended for the award of QTS (Q) should:

Q22 Plan for progression across the age and ability range for which they are trained, designing effective learning sequences within lessons and across series of lessons and demonstrating secure subject/curriculum knowledge.

Q23 Design opportunities for learners to develop their literacy, numeracy and ICT skills.

Q24 Plan homework or other out-of-class work to sustain learners' progress and to extend and consolidate their learning.

Q25 Teach lessons and sequences of lessons across the age and ability range for which they are trained in which they:

(a) use a range of teaching strategies and resources, including e-learning, taking practical account of diversity and promoting equality and inclusion.

(b) build on prior knowledge, develop concepts and processes, enable learners to apply new knowledge, understanding and skills and meet learning objectives.

     (c) adapt their language to suit the learners they teach, introducing new ideas and concepts clearly, and using explanations, questions, discussions and plenaries effectively.

26 (a) Make effective use of a range of assessment, monitoring and recording strategies.

     (b) Assess the learning needs of those they teach in order to set challenging learning objectives.

Q27 Provide timely, accurate and constructive feedback on learners' attainment, progress and areas for development.

Q28 Support and guide learners to reflect on their learning, identify the progress they have made and identify their emerging learning needs.

Q29 Evaluate the impact of their teaching on the progress of all learners, and modify their planning and classroom practice where necessary.

Q30 Establish a purposeful and safe learning environment conducive to learning and identify opportunities for learners to learn in out-of-school contexts.

Q31 Establish a clear framework for classroom discipline to manage learners' behaviour constructively and promote their self-control and independence.

Q32 Work as a team member and identify opportunities for working with colleagues, sharing the development of effective practice with them.

Q33 Ensure that colleagues working with them are appropriately involved in supporting learning and understand the roles they are expected to fulfil.

References

Ager, R. (2003) *Information and Communications Technology in Primary Schools.* London: David Fulton.

Amabile, T.M. (1983) *The Social Psychology of Creativity*. New York: Springer Verlag.

Assessment Reform Group (2002) *Assessment for Learning: 10 Principles. Research-based principles to guide classroom practice.* **www.qca.org.uk/ libraryAssets/media/4031_afl_principles.pdf.**

Ausubel, D.P. (1968) *Educational Psychology: A Cognitive View*. New York: Holt, Rinehart and Winston.

Ausubel, D.P. (1968) *The Psychology of Meaningful Learning: An Introduction to School Learning*. New York: Grune and Stratton.

Baker, J., Lynch, K., Cantillon, S. and Walsh, J. (2004) *Equality: From Theory to Action*. Basingstoke: Palgrave Macmillan.

Bassey, M. (1989) *Teaching Practice in the Primary School*. East Grinstead: Ward Lock Educational.

Bearne, E. (ed) (1996) *Differentiation and Diversity in the Primary School*. London: Routledge.

Becta (2006) *Becta's view: E-assessment and e-portfolios*. Coventry: British Educational Communications and Technology Agency.

Bennett, N. and Dunne, E. (1992) *Managing Classroom Groups.* London: Simon and Schuster Education.

Bichard, M. (2004) *The Bichard Inquiry Report*. London: The Stationery Office.

Blair, T. (1997) Bringing Britain together. Speech, Stockwell Park School, London, 8 December 1997.

Bliss, T. and Tetley, J. (2006) *Circle Time*. London: Sage Publications.

Braddy, S. (1988) Personal, social and moral education in the infant school: a practical approach, in Lang, P.C. (ed) *Thinking about Personal and Social Education in the Primary School.* Oxford: Blackwell.

Bruce, T. (2004) *Developing Learning in Early Childhood Education*. London: Paul Chapman.

Bryant, P.E. (1974) *Perception and Understanding in Young Children*. London: Methuen.

Cam, P. (1995) *Thinking Together: Philosophical Inquiry for the Classroom.* Alexandria, VA: Hale and Iremonger.

Cassen, R. and Kingdon, G. (2007) *Tackling Low Educational Achievement*. York: Joseph Rowntree Foundation. **www.jrf.org.uk/bookshop/eBooks/2063-education-schools-achievement.pdf**

Cheminais, R. (2005) *Every Child Matters: A New Role for SENCOs. A Practical Guide.* London: David Fulton.

Cheminais, R. (2006) *Every Child Matters: A Practical Guide for Teachers*. London: David Fulton.

Child, D. (2007) *Psychology and the Teacher*, 6th edn. London: Cassell.

Clarke, S., McCallum, B. and Lopez-Charles, G. (2001) Gillingham Partnership formative assessment project: interim report on the first term of the project – communicating learning intentions, developing success criteria and pupil self-evaluation. **www.aaia.org.uk/pdf/Gillingham1.pdf.**

Clarke, S. and McCallum, B. (2001a) Gillingham Partnership formative assessment project: interim report on the second term of the project – oral feedback and marking against learning intentions. **www.aaia.org.uk/pdf/Gillingham2.pdf.**

Clarke, S. and McCallum, B. (2001b) *Gillingham Partnership formative assessment project: final report on the third term of the project and final conclusions – third term focus: target setting.* **www.aaia.org.uk/pdf/Gillingham3.pdf.**

Clarke, S. (1998) *Targeting Assessment in the Primary Classroom.* London: Hodder & Stoughton.

Clarke, S. (2001) *Unlocking Formative Assessment.* London: Hodder & Stoughton.

Clarke, S. (2003) *Enriching Feedback in the Primary Classroom.* London: Hodder & Stoughton.

Clarke, S. (2005) *Formative Assessment in Action: Weaving the Elements Together.* London: Hodder Murray.

Clegg, D. and Billington, S. (1994) *The Effective Classroom: Management and organisation of teaching and Learning.* London: David Fulton.

Colloby, J. (2005) Providing learning support in a mathematics lesson, in Hancock, R. and Collins, J. (eds) *Primary Teaching Assistants: Learners and Learning.* London: David Fulton.

Condie, R., Munro, B., Seagraves, L. and Kenesson, S. (2007) *The Impact of ICT in Schools: A Landscape Review.* Coventry: Becta.

Convery, A. and Coyle, D. (1993) *Differentiation: Taking the Initiative.* London: Centre for Information for Language Teaching and Research.

Corrie, C. (2003) *Becoming Emotionally Intelligent.* Stafford: Network Educational Press Ltd.

Craft, A. (2000) *Creativity Across The Primary Curriculum: Framing and Developing Practice.* London: Routledge.

Craft, A. (2001) Little c. creativity in Craft, A., Jeffrey, B. and Leibling, M. (eds) *Creativity in Education.* London: Continuum.

CRE (1999) CRE's oral evidence to the Lawrence Inquiry, CRE Website.

CRE (2002a) *Code of Practice on the Duty to Promote Race Equality.* London: CRE.

CRE (2002b) *The Duty to Promote Race Equality: A Guide for Schools.* London: CRE.

CRE (2002c) *Framework for a Race Equality Policy for Schools.* London: CRE.

Davies, N. (1999) Poverty is the key, *The Guardian*, 23 September. **www.educationunlimited.co.uk/specialreports/educationincrisis/story/0,5500,84129,00.html**].

Dawes, L. Mercer, N. and Wegerif, R. (2000) *Thinking Together – a programme of activities for developing speaking, listening and learning skills for children aged 8–11.* Birmingham: Imaginative minds. **www.thinkingtogether.org.uk** July 2006.

DES (1978) *Special Educational Needs: Report of the Committee of Enquiry into the Education of Handicapped and Young People* (The Warnock Report). London: HMSO.

DES (1988) *Education Reform Act, 1988.* London: HMSO.

DfEE (1997) *Policies for Excellence.* London: DfEE.

DfEE/QCA (1999) *The National Curriculum Handbook for primary teachers in England Key Stages 1 and 2.* London: DfEE.

DfES (2001) *Special Educational Needs: Code of Practice.* DfES.

DfES (2002) *Birth to Three Matters: A Framework to Support Children in their Earliest Years.* London: DfES.

DfES (2003) *Excellence and Enjoyment: A Strategy for Primary Schools.* London: DfES.

DfES (2004a) *Every Child Matters: Change for Children*. London: DfES.

DfES (2004b) *Removing Barriers to Achievement: The Government's Strategy for SEN*. London: DfES.

DfES (2004c) *A National Conversation About Personalised Learning.* London: DfES.

DfES (2004d) *Safeguarding Children in Education.* London: DfES.

DfES (2005a) *Excellence and Enjoyment*: *Social and Emotional Aspects of Learning.* London: DfES Publications.

DfES (2005b) *Safeguarding Children in Education: Dealing with Allegations of Abuse against Teachers and Other Staff*. London: DfES.

DfES (2006a) *Ethnicity and Education: The Evidence on Minority Ethnic Pupils, 2006 Edition*. London: DfES.

DfES (2006b) *The Five Year Strategy for Children and Learners: Maintaining the Excellent Progress*. London: DfES.

DfES (2007a) *School Discipline and Pupil Behaviour Policies: Guidance for Schools*. London: DfES.

DfES (2007b) *Gender and Education: The Evidence on Pupils in England*. London: DfES. **www.dfes.gov.uk/research/data/uploadfiles/RTP01-07pdf**

Dickinson, C. and Wright, J. (1993) *Differentiation: A Practical Handbook of Classroom Strategies*. Coventry: National Council for Educational Technology.

Donaldson, M. (1978) *Children's Minds*. London: Fontana.

DRC (2002) *Code of Practice for Schools*. London: TSO.

DRC (2005) *The Duty to Promote Disability Equality: Statutory Code of Practice*. London: TSO.

Dunne, E. and Bennett, N. (1990) *Talking and Learning in Groups*. Basingstoke: Macmillan.

Edgington, M. (2004) *The Foundation Stage Teacher in Action: Teaching 3, 4 and 5 year olds.* London: Paul Chapman.

Epstein, D., Elwood, J., Hey, V. and Maw, J. (eds) (1999) *Failing Boys? Issues in Gender and Achievement.* Buckingham: Open University Press.

Ethnic Minority Achievement Unit (2006) *Recording and Reporting Racist Incidents Guidance*. London: DfES.

Ewens, A. (1998) Teacher education and PSMSC: Implications of the new requirements, in Richards, C., Simco, N. and Twiselton, S. (eds) *Primary Teacher Education: High Status? High Standards?* London: Falmer.

Fabian, H. (2002) *Children Starting School: A Guide To Successful Transitions and Transfers for Teachers and Assistants*. London: David Fulton.

Flavell, J.H. (1985) *Cognitive Development*, 2nd edn. Englewood Cliffs, N.J.: Prentice Hall.

Fontana, D. (1995) *Psychology for Teachers*, 3rd edn. Basingstoke: Macmillan.

Furlong, J. and Maynard, T. (1995) *Mentoring Student Teachers.* London: Routledge.

Gaine, C. (1988) *No Problem Here,* revised edn. London: Hutchinson.

Gaine, C. (1995) *Still No Problem Here*, Stoke on Trent: Trentham Books.

Gaine, C. (2005) *We're All White Thanks. The Persisting Myth About 'White' Schools*. Stoke-on-Trent: Trentham.

Gaine, C. and George, R. (1999) *Gender, 'Race' and Class in Schooling: A New Introduction.* London: Falmer.

Gilborn, D. and Gipps, C. (1996) *Recent Research on the Achievements of Ethnic Minority Pupils.* London: Ofsted/HMSO.

Goleman, D. (1996) *Emotional Intelligence.* London: Bloomsbury.

Hay/McBer (2000) *Research into Teacher Effectiveness: A Model of Teacher Effectiveness*. Report to DfEE.

Hayes, D. (1997) *Success on Your Teaching Experience*. London: Hodder & Stoughton.

HM Government (2006) *Working Together to Safeguard Children: A Guide to Inter-agency Working to Safeguard and Promote the Welfare of Children*. London: The Stationery Office.

HMI (1989) *Personal and Social Education from 5–16: Curriculum Matters 14.* London: DES.

Hoyle, E. (1980) Professionalization and deprofessionalization in education, in Hoyle, E. and Hegarty, J. (eds) *World Yearbook of Education: Professional Development of Teachers*. London: Kogan Page.

Hughes, P. (1991) *Gender Issues in the Primary Classroom.* Leamington Spa: Scholastic.

Huitt, W. (2003). The information processing approach to cognition. *Educational Psychology Interactive*. Valdosta, GA: Valdosta State University. **chiron.valdosta.edu/whuitt/col/cogsys/infoproc.html**

Jencks, C. (1988) Whom must we treat equally for educational opportunity to be equal? *Ethics*, 98(3): 518–33.

Jones, S. (2005) The invisibility of the underachieving girl. *International Journal of Inclusive Education*, 9(3): 269–86.

Jones, S. and Myhill, D. (2004) Seeing things differently: teachers' constructions of underachievement. *Gender and Education*, 16(4): 531–46.

Joubert, M. M. (2005) *Creativity in education*. A guide to the creativity workshops presented at the DfES Regional Teaching Awards by Mathilda Joubert, Rosemary Hill, Andy Jukes and Christine Warwood, supported by the DfES Innovation Unit. Online: **www.softnotes.com/files/DfES%20Innovation%20 Unit%20Creativity%20booklet.doc.**

Kerry, T. and Kerry, C. (1997) Differentiation: teachers' views of the usefulness of recommended strategies in helping the more able pupils in primary and secondary classrooms. *Educational Studies*, 23(3): 439–57.

Kershner, R. and Miles, S. (1996) Thinking and talking about differentiation, in Bearne, E. (ed) *Differentiation and Diversity in the Primary School*. London: Routledge.

Kessler, R. (2000) *The Souls of Education: Helping Students find Connection, Compassion and Character at School.* Alexandria, VA: Association for Supervision and Curriculum Development.

Klein, G. (1993) *Education Towards Race Equality*. London: Cassell.

Knowles, E. and Ridley, W. (2006) *Another Spanner in the Works: Challenging Prejudice and Racism in Mainly White Schools*. Stoke on Trent: Trentham.

Kyriacou, C . (1998) *Essential Teaching Skills.* Cheltenham: Stanley Thornes.

Laslett, R. and Smith, C. (2002) Four rules of class management, in Pollard, A. (ed) *Readings for Reflective Teaching*. London: Continuum.

Lefrançois, G.R. (1999) *Psychology for Teaching*, 2nd edn. Cheltenham: Stanley Thornes.

Lepper, M.R. and Hodell, M. (1989) Intrinsic motivation in the classroom, in Ames, C. and Ames, R. (eds) *Research on Motivation in the Classroom*, vol 3, pp73–

105. San Diego, CA: Academic Press.

Lewis, A. (1991) *Primary Special Needs and the National Curriculum*. London: Routledge.

Lynch, K. and Baker, J. (2005) Equality in education: an equality of condition perspective. *Theory and Research in Education*, 3(2): 131–64.

MacPherson, W. (1999) *The Stephen Lawrence Inquiry.* London: The Stationery Office.

Maslow, A. (1968) *Toward a Psychology of Being,* 2nd edn. New York: Van Nostrand Reinhold.

McGarvey, B., Morgan, V., Marriott, S. and Abbot, L. (1996) Differentiation and its problems: the view of primary teachers and curriculum support staff in Northern Ireland. *Educational Studies*, 22(1): 69–82.

McNamara, D. (1994) To group or not to group, in Pollard, A .(ed) (1996) *Readings for Reflective Teaching in the Primary School.* London: Cassell Education.

Mercer, N. (1996) English as a classroom language, in Mercer, N. and Swan, J. (eds) *Learning English: Development and Diversity*. London: Routledge.

Miller, G.A. (1956) The magical number seven, plus or minus two: some limits on our capacity for processing information. *Psychological Reviews*, 73: 81–97.

Mitsos, E. and Browne, K. (1998) Gender differences in education: the under-achievement of boys. *Sociology Review*, 8(1): 27–31.

Morgan, G. and Morris, C. (1999) *Good Teaching and Learning*. Buckingham: Open University Press.

Morris, E. (1996) Labour's plans to give boys new hope. *The Times*, 1 November.

Moss, G. (1996) *A Strategy for Differentiation*. Birmingham: Questions Publishing Ltd.

Moyles, J. (ed) (2005) *The Excellence of Play,* 2nd edn. Buckingham: Open University Press.

Moyles, J. and Robinson, G. (eds) (2002) *Beginning Teaching: Beginning Learning in Primary Education.* Buckingham: Open University Press.

NEOST/LGA/ATL/NASUWT/NUT/PAT/SHA (2000) *Conditions of Service for Schoolteachers in England and Wales*. London: Employers' Organisation for Local Government.

OFSTED (1995) *Guidance on the Inspection of Nursery and Primary Schools.* London: Stationery Office.

Ofsted (2000) Evaluating Educational Inclusion. London: Ofsted.

Ofsted (2003a) *Handbook for Inspecting Primary and Nursery Schools.* London: Ofsted.

Ofsted (2003b) *Inspecting Schools: Framework for Inspecting Schools.* London: Ofsted.

Ofsted (2003c) *Expecting the Unexpected: developing creativity in primary and secondary schools*. London: Ofsted.

Ofsted (2003d) *The National Literacy and Numeracy Strategies and the Primary Curriculum*. London: Ofsted.

Ofsted (2005a) *Every Child Matters: Framework for the inspection of schools in England from September 2005.* London: HMI.

Pollard, A. (1997) *Reflective Teaching in the Primary School,* 3rd edn. London: Cassell Education.

Proctor, A., Entwistle, M., Judge, B. and McKenzie-Murdoch, S. (1995) *Learning to teach in the primary classroom.* London: Routledge.

QCA (2000a) *Curriculum Guidance for the Foundation Stage.* London: QCA.

QCA (2000b) *Personal, Social and Health Education and Citizenship at Key Stages 1 and 2*. London: QCA.

QCA (2001) *Planning for Learning in the Foundation Stage.* London: QCA.

QCA (2002) *National Curriculum*. London: QCA.

QCA (2003) *Using assessment to raise achievement in mathematics*. London: QCA.

QCA (2005) *Seeing steps in children's learning*. London: QCA.

Raiker, A. (2002) Spoken language and mathematics. *Cambridge Journal of Education*, 32(1): 45–60.

Reading, H.F. (1977) *A Dictionary of the Social Sciences.* London: Routledge & Kegan Paul.

Reason, R. (1993) Group Practice in Group Work, in Pollard, A. (ed) (1996) *Readings for Reflective Teaching in the Primary School*. London: Cassell.

Richards, J.R. (1998) Equality of opportunity, in Mason, A. (ed) *Ideals of Equality*. Oxford: Blackwell.

Riley, K.A. (1994) *Quality and Equality: Promoting Opportunities in Schools.* London: Cassell.

Rogers, C. (1983) *Freedom to Learn for the 80's*. Columbus, OH: Merril.

Rogers, B. (1998) *You Know the Fair Rule*. London: Pitman.

Skinner, B.F. (1968) *The Technology of Teaching*. New York: Appleton.

Smith, F., Harman, F., Wall, K. and Mroz, M. (2004) Interactive whole class teaching in the National Literacy and Numeracy Strategies. *British Educational Research Journal*, 30(3): 395–411.

Stanworth, M. (1983) *Gender and Schooling: A Study of Sexual Divisions in the Classroom.* London: Hutchinson.

Stephens, P. and Crawley, T. (1994) *Becoming an Effective Teacher*. Cheltenham: Stanley Thornes.

Stradling, R., Saunders, L. and Weston, P. (1991) *Differentiation in Action.* Slough: NFER.

Swann, M. (chair) (1985) *Education for All* (Swann Report). London: HMSO.

Tattum, D.P. (1988) Social education in interaction, in Lang, P.C. (ed) *Thinking about Personal and Social Education in the Primary School*. Oxford: Blackwell.

Tizard, B., Blatchford, P., Burke, J., Farquhar, C. and Plewis, I. (1988) *Young Children at School in the Inner City.* Hove: Lawrence Erlbaum.

Tizard, B. and Hughes, M. (1984) *Young Children Learning*. London: Fontana.

Tutchell, E. (1990) *Dolls and Dungarees: Gender Issues in the Primary School.* Buckingham: Open University Press.

Tyler, K. (1992a) *Enhancing Children's Self-concepts in the Primary School*. Loughborough: Loughborough University Department of Education.

Tyler, K. (1992b) *Personal and Social Education in Primary Schools.* Loughborough: Loughborough University Department of Education.

Visser, J. (1993) *Differentiation: Making it Work*. Tamworth: National Association for Special Educational Needs.

Vygotsky, L.S. (1978) *Mind in Society: The Development of Higher Psychological Processes.* London: Harvard University Press.

Warrington, M., Younger, M. and Bearne, E. (2006) *Raising Boys' Achievements in Primary Schools*. Maidenhead: Open University Press.

Waterson, A. (1998) Managing the classroom for learning, in Jacques, K. and Hyland, R. (eds) (2003) *Professional Studies Primary Phase.* Exeter: Learning Matters.

Watkins, C. and Wagner, P. (1988) *School Discipline: A Whole School Approach*. Oxford: Blackwell.

Webster, A. (1995) Differentiation, in Moss, G. (ed) *The Basics of Special Needs: A Routledge Special Children Survival Guide for the Classroom Teacher*. London: Routledge.

Whitebread, D. (ed) (2003) *Teaching and Learning in the Early Years,* 2nd edn. London: Routledge.

Wilson, G. (2003) *Using the National Healthy School Standard to Raise Boys' Achievement*. London: DfES.

Woods, P. (1990) *Teacher Skills and Strategies.* Lewes: Falmer Press.

Woods, P. (1993) *Critical Events in Teaching and Learning.* Lewes: Falmer Press.

Woods, P. (1996) Teachers and classroom relationships, in Pollard, A. (ed) (1996) *Readings for Reflective Teaching in the Primary School*. London: Cassell Education.

Wragg, T. (1997a) Oh boy!, *Times Educational Supplement,* 16 May.

Wragg, T. (1997b) Support for boys need not hurt girls. *Times Educational Supplement,* 30 May.

Index